BIOGRAPHICAL OBJECTS

BIOGRAPHICAL OBJECTS

How Things Tell the Stories of People's Lives

JANET HOSKINS

ROUTLEDGE

New York and London

Published in 1998 by
Routledge
29 West 35th Street
New York, NY 10001

Published in Great Britain in 1998 by
Routledge
11 New Fetter Lane
London EC4P 4EE

Copyright © 1998 by Routledge

Printed in the United States of America on acid-free paper
Design and Typography: Jack Donner

Library of Congress Cataloging-in-Publication Data

Hoskins, Janet.
    Biographical objects : how things tell the stories of people's lives / Janet Hoskins.
       p.   cm.
    Includes bibliographical references (p. 199) and index.
    ISBN 0–415–92011–6 (hardcover : acid-free paper). — ISBN 0–415–92012–4 (pbk.)
    1. Ethnology—Indonesia—Kodi.   2. Ethnology—Biographical methods.
3. Material culture—Indonesia—Kodi.   4. Kodi (Indonesia)—Biography.
5. Kodi (Indonesia)—Social life and customs.   I. Title.
    GN635. I65H68   1998
    306'.09598'6—dc21   97–40989
                                                      CIP

For Valerio, In Memoriam

Ndara ole ura	The horse companion of my spirit
Bangga ole ndewa	The dog companion of my soul
A ando koti lighya nggu	The post that my ginger vine creeps up
A nggallu mbaku haghu nggu	The enclosure of my tobacco patch
Bu otungguka henene	If you leave me now
Ku kapepe nja pa todi	I will be the basket left without a lid
Ku halidi nja hamera	I will be a container without its counterpart

CONTENTS

ACKNOWLEDGMENTS

This book will appear almost twenty years after I first came to the Kodi district of Sumba. Doctoral dissertation research, from 1979 to 1981, was supported by the Fulbright Commission, the Social Science Research Council, and the National Science Foundation, under the auspices of the Indonesian Academy of Sciences (LIPI) and Universitas Nusa Cendana, Kupang. Six months of additional fieldwork in 1984 and a three-month trip in 1985 were funded by the anthropology department of the Research School of Pacific Studies, Australian National University. In 1986 I returned to Kodi with filmmaker Laura Whitney, supported by the Faculty Research and Innovation Fund of the University of Southern California. In 1988 we continued our research project for six more months with funding from NSF grant no. BMS 8704498 and the Fulbright Consortium for Collaborative Research Abroad. In 1996 I received a University Teacher's Fellowship from the National Endowment for the Humanities, which provided relief from coursework and some additional travel funds. I am grateful to all of these agencies for having made this form of long-term fieldwork possible.

My research began as a graduate student at Harvard University, under the guidance of Marie Jeanne Adams, David Maybury-Lewis, and Stanley Tambiah. In the period 1984–85, I was a postdoctoral fellow at the Research School of Pacific Studies in the anthropology department, then headed by Roger Keesing and James J. Fox. Many of the ideas I have finally developed here germinated in lively discussions with members of a research group on gender, power, and production—Marilyn Strathern, Nicholas Thomas, Deborah Gewertz, Frederick Errington, James F. Weiner, Jill Nash, Christine Jourdain, Michael Young, and Greg Acciaioli. I began work on women's narratives in 1990–91, when I was a member of the Institute for Advanced Study, Princeton, and part of an interdisciplinary group focusing on the historical turn in the social sciences, led by Joan Scott and Clifford Geertz. I tried to work out early versions of these chapters in lectures given in 1992 at the Institute for Social Anthropology in Oslo, Norway, headed by Signe Howell. In 1995–96, I was a scholar associate at the Getty Research Institute for the History of Art and the Humanities, headed by Salvatore Settis. I am grateful to people at each of these institutions for their companionship and assistance.

This manuscript was read, in many disjointed and incomplete versions, by Gillian Goslinga, Lene Pedersen, Marilyn McCabe, Joel Kuipers, William Germano, and Gelya Frank, as well as three anonymous readers selected by the publisher. I am especially grateful to Gelya for hours of inspiring conversation, many additional references, and insights culled from a long engagement with the study of life histories. Others who have contributed to the development of these ideas are Nancy Lutkehaus (who, like Gelya, has taught courses with me at USC where some of these problems were addressed), Ariane Gaetano, Marie Jeanne Adams, Signe Howell, Olaf Smedal, Penelope Graham, Webb Keane, and Jane Atkinson. I owe a much longer and deeper debt to Valerio Valeri, who has been much more than a reader and a critic, but was not able to be as involved as he might have been in the final stages of this book because of his illness.

This book reconsiders various arguments that I have advanced earlier, often with somewhat different interpretations. For permission to reprint sections of earlier published articles, I thank the *Journal of Anthropological Research* ("A Life History from Both Sides: The Changing Poetics of Personal Experience" [1985] 41, 2: 147–69), Cambridge University Press ("Complementarity in This World and the Next," in *Dealing with Inequality: Analysing Gender Relations in Melanesia and Beyond*, ed. M. Strathern, 1987), *Social Science and Medicine* ("The Drum is the Shaman, the Spear Guides His Voice" [1988] 27, 2: 819–29), Stanford University Press ("Doubling Descent, Deities and Personhood," in *Power and Difference: Gender in Island Southeast Asia*, ed. J. Atkinson and S. Errington, 1990), and Center of Non-Western Studies, Leiden ("Sacrifice and Sexuality," in *For the Sake of Our Future: Sacrificing in Eastern Indonesia*, ed. S. Howell, 1996).

As always, I remain immensely grateful to the people of Kodi, both those I have named in these pages and those who remain unnamed, for sharing their lives and stories with me. I hope they will recognize themselves in this book.

1.

INTRODUCTION

Ordinary objects which have long been used by one master take on a
sort of personality, their own face, I could almost say a soul, and the
folklore of all nations is full of these beings more human than humans,
because they owe their existence to people and, awakened by their
contact, take on their own life and autonymous activities, a sort of
latent and fantastic willfulness.

—Paul Claudel, *Meditation on a pair of shoes,*
Prose works, Bibliotheque de la Pleiade, 1965, p. 1243

There are no ideas but in things.

—William Carlos Williams, *Paterson,* 1947

Recent theoretical interest in the study of personal narrative has highlighted
the extent to which storytelling is a formative process: Through "telling
their lives," people not only provide information about themselves but also
fashion their identities in a particular way, constructing a "self" for public
consumption. Anthropologists have long had an interest in personal narratives, but earlier accounts of "life histories" have operated as if they existed
"out there," already formed, and needed only to be "collected," recorded,
and transcribed.

More recent ethnographic writing has recognized that neither narratives
nor selves are so easily "discovered."[An ethnographic interview, whether
conducted at one time or over many years, is a complex dialogue, a co-
creation of a narrative that is in part structured by the listener's questions
and expectations] The context of the story told has come back to center
stage, as well as the hidden relationship between the storyteller and the
person to whom the story is told—the "biography in the shadow" (Frank
1979, 1985). A number of recent experiments in ethnographic writing (Abu-
Lughod 1993, Behar 1993, Kondo 1990, Lavie 1990, Visweswaran 1994)
play with the old genres of life history in new ways, and offer us vivid
portraits of persons with multiple identities, allegorical personas, and
complex hidden agendas.

My own contribution to this literature comes from the paradoxical experience of frustration at *not r*eceiving the hoped-for "life history'" from informants I first interviewed with that intention. I began fieldwork with the

Kodi, at the western tip of the Eastern Indonesian island of Sumba, because they lived on the last island in the Malay archipelago to preserve a pagan majority throughout the 1980s. Steeped as they still were in an animist tradition, Kodi narrators could tell us about more radically different notions of self and personhood than those peoples more thoroughly absorbed in Indonesia's rapid development. But the notion of telling one's life directly to another person did not exist in Kodi. From men, especially prominent ones, I often heard a list of accomplishments, offices, or ceremonies performed. From women, the question "Tell me about your life" usually initally produced little more than a list of children. But I did get some insight into personal experience and subjective reactions through a set of interviews that I was conducting on another topic—the history of exchange objects and of ritually important domestic objects.

What I discovered, quite to my surprise, was that I could not collect the histories of objects and the life histories of persons separately. People and the things they valued were so complexly intertwined they could not be disentangled. The frustrations I experienced in trying to follow my planned methodology proved to be an advantage in disguise: I obtained more intro-spective, intimate, and "personal" accounts of many peoples' lives when I asked them about objects, and traced the path of many objects in interviews supposedly focused on persons.

In studying a society so deeply steeped in exchange, a "person-centered" ethnography (Levy 1994) has to be rethought as one that uses objects as metaphors to elicit an indirect account of personal experience. Kodi is a society in which the origins and circulation of valuables are crucial to a sense of time and even of history. The role of named "history objects" in demarcating and perserving a sense of the past and collective memory I have examined elsewhere in some detail (Hoskins 1993a). In this work, I want to move to the more intimate level of individual actors and domestic objects—ordinary household possessions that might be given an extraordinary signifi-cance by becoming entangled in the events of a person's life and used as a vehicle for a sense of selfhood. I argue that the stories generated around objects provide a distanced form of introspection, a way of discussing loaded sexual politics in an ironic mode, and a form of reflection on the meaning of one's own life.

This book explores how identities and biographies are formed around objects in a society that has not been "psychologized" in a confessional tradi-tion. The narcissistic preoccupation with telling and retelling about their own lives is not well developed in Kodi, where direct questions seem either indiscreet or uninformed. But these people, although bashful and tongue-tied when asked to describe themselves, were often great storytellers when asked to talk about their possessions.

Kodi is a language rich both in conventional metaphors (the paired couplets of ritual language) and in idiosyncratic variations on these themes (often "speaking against the grain" of a conventional metaphor to highlight an unconventional meaning). The conventional dualism of ritual speech is gendered, and plays on notions of masculinity or feminity to "finish" an image as somehow composed of both elements. Sexual politics are rarely discussed in Kodi, and sexual feelings almost never. But the nuanced language of gender dualities made it possible for many people to communciate about these things through metaphors focused on objects. In my work on life stories and exchange histories, I became increasingly fascinated by the problem of personal symbolism and the idiosyncratic significance of objects.

A young girl I knew well never confessed her feelings of romantic longing and later disappointment to me directly, but she was fascinated by the story of a magic spindle that flew through the air to snare a beloved. When later her own hopes were cut off, she sent a message to her lost lover through the secret gift of the object. A famous singer and healer who also wanted a female companion composed long ballads to his drum, introducing each ritual session with a history of efforts to cover the drum properly so it could be pierced by a male voice and travel up the heavens.

A respected older man who had served as the Raja in colonial times identified his heritage of spiritual power with the snake depicted on the cloth he chose to be his funeral shroud. Instead of writing an autobiography, he wrote for me an account of his ancestor's encounter with the snake and a gift of cloth that he interpreted as the "basis" of his power to rule.

Another man, famed as a storyteller and bard, said he received his "gift of words" in the simple, woven betel bag he carried with him at all times. His wives, who had sat in respectful silence to listen to him during his lifetime, invited me to hear their own stories after his death—and revealed fables about domestic animals, stories transparently critical of masculinist privilege.

Finally, a young woman who died tragically in a traffic accident was associated with the image of a green bottle, the disposable modern object no longer capable of regeneration. She never narrated her own story to me, but the associations of her death and the disruptive influence of modern technology continued to haunt the area, and my own fieldwork, for many years.

The stories I tell here, and try to make sense of, are stories I played a part in creating, but I did not create the idiom that they were articulated in—it is a cultural propensity to speak about such issues indirectly, and to use objects as a metaphor for the self. I am especially interested in trying to understand how these narratives are constructed, and how the object can mediate for the person.

Sometimes this mediation is direct: In Kodi life-crisis rituals, a spindle or a knife can substitute for a man, a cotton board or a gold pendant can take the place of a woman. A betel bag can be buried instead of a person, and the burial of someone's betel bag in his or her absence can signify their social death—a disinheriting curse by close kin, or a legal sanction by more distant ones. More often, the mediation is somewhat more subtle: A metaphoric alter ego may initially be proposed as part of the elaborate word play that characterizes all formal interactions, and only later come to carry more weight as metaphoric connections are extended to new domains.

A well-known definition of autobiography is "a retrospective account in prose that a real person makes of his own existence stressing his individual life and especially the history of his personality" (Lejeune 1975: 14). By this definition, only some of the stories I recorded in Kodi would qualify, because several took the form of songs or sections in parallel verse, and others revealed their more personal content only through an interpretation of the allegorical message of a fable or folktale. But I prefer to use the term loosely and heuristically, to suggest an autobiographical content to stories that, on the surface, might be said to be about other things as well.

I will try to argue that the Sumbanese narrators of these stories used the objects autobiographically, as the cornerstone of a story about themselves, a vehicle to define personal identity and sexual identity. In a way, the object becomes a prop, a storytelling device, and also a mnemonic for certain experiences. However, such devices are never innocent.

"TELLING ONESELF":
THE RELATION OF AUTOBIOGRAPHY AND MEMORY

Any narrative device does not so much reflect "the truth" as construct it in a particular way. As Frank Kermode notes in discussing his own memoir,

> The honest truth, insofar as this suggests absolute fidelity to historical fact, is inacccessible; the minute you begin to write it you try to write it well, and writing well is an activity which has no simple relation to truth. For memory cannot do the necessary work independently of fantasy; and if it tries, the result will be a dull report. (1995: 37)

Making a life into a story involves crafting it, editing it, giving a form and finality that is always to some extent fictional. Because every book based on fieldwork is also a memoir of shared time and space, my fictions blend with theirs. But most of us who tell stories do so with the intention of offering some truth about ourselves. Freud remarked with surprise, "The urge to tell the truth is much stronger than is usually supposed" (quoted in Kermode 1995: 37), and the popularity of confessional writing in the West certainly bears him out. Though my Indonesian subjects were less overtly confessional, they also insisted on accuracy when it came to autobiographical reflections.

Kermode describes the dominant model of autobiography as St. Augustine's notion that the past can be usefully reworked in present memory, rather than Freud's idea that memory invents a past to defend us against the appalling timelessness of the unconscious. The revelation of unpleasant secrets is not the goal, but the creation of a certain integrated interpretation. "The analyst tries to open the box so that all its contents will eventually fly out; the autobiographer has a notion that his life, as memory reconstructs it, can by certain skills be made to hang together; so, needing the contents, he closes the box and snaps the catch on the lid" (Kermode 1995: 43).

This is an arresting image of why each story has to come to an end. A coherent narrative constructs a unified image of the self out of the disparate, messy fragments of daily experience. It is perhaps significant that the "biographical objects" my informants selected were often containers (the betel pouch, the hollow drum, the funeral shroud), which served as "memory boxes" for holding certain things inside or (in the case of the green bottle) creating anxiety about their capacity to escape.

The closure offered by the well-told story offers "a kind of substitute timelessness, or a time that has a stop, with its own benefits, its own felicity" (Kermode 1995: 43). Kermode points out perceptively that closure is so attractive to writers that "when they go out of their way to avoid it you can tell they are thinking about it but are being rebellious and avant-garde" (43).

In a classic article, the literary critic James Olney defined autobiographies as "metaphors of the self" (1972) and noted that the analysis of life stories now has come to focus less on the *bio*, the events that occurred throughout the lifetime, and more on the *auto*, the construction of self through narrative. In recent years the burgeoning interest in these narratives (Gullestad 1996, Personal Narrative Group 1989, Watson and Smith 1992, Krupat 1985, Linde 1993, Rosenwald and Ochberg 1992) has carried that orientation still further. Perhaps because many of the "grand" narratives of science, progress, and politics have lost their credibility, "little" narratives situated in the particular experience of individuals have resurfaced. Third World authors are publishing their own personal accounts of the rise to nationhood (Rodgers 1995), and "alphabetization increasingly seems to imply autobiographization" (Gullestad 1996: 14). Within the academy, interest in people's own stories has been spurred by a new hermeneutic self-conciousness in criticism and history, and the struggles of feminists and minorities to be heard on a personal as well as a political level.

One of the disappointments of the new trend to reflexivity in anthropology has been the realization that accounts of the anthropologist in the field are still heavily edited and crafted. Indeed, they must be, but the pretended candor of many such accounts can be no more than an engaging stylistic device that makes ethnographies better reading than technical reports are. Anthropology is based on eyewitness accounts, and it is nice to render the immediacy of the field experience, but vividly written first-person ethnographies may hide as much as they reveal of fieldwork dynamics.

The anthropologist writing an ethnography is, of course, telling a tale that is in part an autobiography (Okley 1992). It exists because there was a time when the fieldworker shared time and space with the people who spoke to her, and she shared in their lives. However, if we dismantle the realist position that the life history is the mirror of life events, we must also do the same for the ethnography. Every graduate student trying to finish a dissertation becomes painfully aware of the fact that there is no coherence that dwells within events or social structures themselves. Coherence is imposed by the work of story makers, and much of what the anthropologist does in writing up her material is to try to devise a coherent story line that will shape fragmentary episodes of experience into something intelligible to an academic audience.

Our informants, the people we call the "subjects" of life histories, must go through a similar process when we ask them to narrate aspects of themselves, to give a direction to their lives by explaining them to an outsider. The stories I collected were told in a series of conversations with each of the people I write about. Some include more self-consciously produced "texts"—a ritual song, a long deathbed oration in parallel verse, a fable, or a typed manuscript—but the text is then supplemented by contextualized commentary. In correcting successive versions of stories about themselves and objects, these people were revising and refining their own sense of connection between the events of yesterday and today. As Rosenwald and Ochberg note: "The subjective conviction of autobiographic coherence is intrinsic to a sense of identity" (1992: 6).

They note, however, that from a modern narratologist's perspective, this coherence is an illusion—even a tactical maneuver. We tell our lives in ways that suit the predicaments in which we find ourselves at the moment, and we edit and revise them for other audiences. We may want our listeners to admire us, to understand us, to forgive us, or perhaps to become converted to something that we value very highly. The telling of the tale turns the person listening into someone who may affirm or approve the story told, perhaps even helping to identify and explain discordant accounts.

For this reason, some poststructuralist textual analysts have treated accounts that people give of their own lives as pure fictions, invented more or less of whole cloth. Kamala Visweswaran speaks of "fictions of feminist ethnography" (1994), and Pierre Bourdieu calls the study of life histories "the biographic illusion" (1986). But even if we accept the highly invented and constructed nature of any such narrative, we must address the relationship between experience and representation.

Anthropologists distinguish between a life as lived, a life as experienced, and a life as told. The first refers to what happens to a person; the second to images, feelings, sentiments, desires, and meanings the person may ascribe to these events; and the third to a narrative, influenced by the context in which it is told, the audience, and cultural notions of storytelling (Bruner 1984: 7). More recently, they have also come to define the self as constructed through narrative, in a process of enactment and rhetorical assertion. This calls into question the commonsense boundaries between "self" and "world," and makes it possible to examine individual identities not as unified essences but as "a mobile site of contradiction and disunity, a node where various discourses temporarily intersect in particular ways" (Kondo 1990: 47).

Since a life history is not only a recital of events but also an organization of experience, the way memory is rendered in a narration of the self is a part of both individual style and cultural fashioning. Through an examination of six individuals, three men and three women, I try to see both gender differences and cultural similarities. I look at a way of telling lives that is somewhat alien to Western literary genres but that has enough metaphoric force to be intelligible in translation. I try to explain why objects are important as foils for self-definition and an anchor for the self-historicizing subject. And I wonder, finally, about the relations of persons and objects that underlie these stories.

THE BIOGRAPHICAL OBJECT

In 1989, building on the work of Appadurai (1986), Kopytoff (1986), Strathern (1988), and A. Weiner (1985), I tried to define a new category of "biographical objects," which occupy one pole of the continuum between gifts and commodities and are endowed with the personal characteristics of their owners. My example at the time was an extreme one: the severed head of Rato Malo, a nobleman from Rara who was ambushed by a head-hunting party from Kodi just before the turn of the century. His young son was captured and sold as a slave, but he came to work for the first Catholic mission on the island, where he acquired basic literacy and was baptized "Yoseph." As an adult, he returned to his homeland and began to work for the colonial administration. He used his acquired wealth and political skills to negotiate for the return of his father's skull as part of a counterprestation for bridewealth. The skull was ritually treated first as a female exchange valuable, then "dressed" in male clothes, reunited with the bones of the body, and reburied as a person. The transformations of this "biographical object" show how the lines between persons and things can blur and shift, and also how other inanimate objects (cloth, jewelry, porcelain dishes) are often endowed with the qualities of persons.

The story of Rato Malo's head is a striking example of an object that was once part of a human body and came to be treated as an exchange valuable, and was then ritually retransformed into a part of a person. Its significance for his descendants was easy to understand, and its return was believed to restore honor and fertility to his family. But in arguing that other things (not only those that were once part of human bodies) could also be "biographical," I have to go out a bit further on a limb: I have to transgress the usual boundaries between persons and objects and show how far certain possessions can come to be seen as surrogate selves.

COMMODITIES AND EXCHANGE VALUABLES

The inspiration for my title comes, however, not from anthropological writing about exchange but from an article by the French sociologist Violette

Morin, which deals with the changing significance of objects in modern France. Beginning with graffiti at the Sorbonne during the May 1968 strikes and demonstrations in Paris, it asks how a slogan such as "Object, hide yourself" (*cache-toi objet*) could emerge as an ironic commentary on consumerism.

Has our own subjectivity been lost in the process of marketing new products? Do we objectify ourselves in gendered images? She speculates about its relations to slogans that ask "Inanimate objects, do you have a soul?" (*Objets inanimes, avez-vous donc une âme?*) or speak of women as objects both beloved and despised (*objets cheres et funestes*). A modern image of Faust emerges in the bazaar as a man who petrifies his soul in mechanizing his life, "loving to have so much that he forgets to simply be" (1969: 131).

She discerns in the relations that modern French people have to objects two opposing uses, one that is centered on the person, which she calls *biographique*, and one centered on the cosmos, which she calls *protocolaire*. Though both sorts of objects may be produced for mass consumption, the relation that a person establishes with a biographical object gives it an identity that is localized, particular, and individual, while those established with an object generated by an outside protocol (what we might call a public commodity) are globalized, generalized, and mechanically reproduced. Three levels of mediation are identified as the distinguishing characteristics of biographical objects: their relation to time, space, and the owner or consumer.

At the temporal level, the biographical object grows old, and may become worn and tattered along the life span of its owner, while the public commodity is eternally youthful and not used up but replaced. At the spatial level, the biographical object limits the concrete space of its owner and sinks its roots deeply into the soil. It anchors the owner to a particular time and place. The public commodity, on the other hand, is everywhere and nowhere, marking not a personal experience but a purchasing opportunity. She notes here the difference between an ethnologist's mask (collected as part of a long period of research and deep professional involvement) and the "souvenirs" acquired by tourists or bought at import shops without any significant stay in their place of origin.

Finally, the biographical object "imposes itself as the witness of the functional unity of its user, his or her everyday experience made into a thing" (*sa quotidiennete faite chose*) (1969: 137–38). The public commodity, on the other hand, is not formative of its owner's or user's identity, which is both singular and universal at the same time. Consumers of public commodities are decentered and fragmented by their acquisition of things, and do not use them as part of a narrative process of self-definition.

Biographical objects share our lives with us, and if they gradually deteriorate and fade with the years, we recognize our own aging in the mirror of these personal possessions. Public commodities, on the other hand, project an eternal youth from which the user feels—although always attracted—more and more distant. The anonymous and alienating furnished apartment is compared here with the "lived-in feel" of a place filled with objects that have affective, traditional, or personal ties to their owner. "To meddle in the space between a biographical object and its owner is always, potentially or really, the act of a voyeur" (1969: 133; my translation).

To French eyes, modern American living represents the culmination of consumer alienation. Morin recounts the perhaps apocryphal story of "an American" who got off/on the wrong floor of his building and mistakenly entered someone else's apartment, only to find its anonymous furnishings so familiar that he did not even realize he was not at home. He was a man whose own biography was not invested in any particular object, but scattered through a generalized and replaceable series of modern mechanized products that deprived him of any icon of his individuality. This is the danger, she implies, of substituting the public commodity for the personal possession, the total divorce between physical objects and human identification.

Morin's categories are brought into even sharper relief when they are juxtaposed with those of a society like that of Kodi, in Eastern Indonesia, where objects and their meanings are crucial to the constitution of history, gender, exchange, and social groups. The archive of the past is displayed or at least alluded to through "history objects," the heirlooms stored in ancestral villages and presented as the evidence for ritual rights and prerogatives (Hoskins 1993: 118–41). Marriage defines a flow of goods between wife givers and wife takers that establishes the superiority of the former and the continued indebtedness of the latter. The ancestral cult is centered on the house and its valuables, which must be named in genealogies along with the names of each of the ancestral founders.

Kodi may represent something of an extreme: a society where objects are invested with very great significance, in both the collective representation of the past and the individual storing of biographical memory. The preoccupation that the Kodinese have with things is not, however, unusual in the context of Eastern Indonesia, as many have noted (Howell 1989, Keane 1997, McKinnon 1991, Geirnaert-Martin 1992a) and is not dissimilar from neighboring Melanesia (Battaglia 1990, 1995, Lutkehaus 1995, MacKenzie 1991).

PARTIBLE PERSONHOOD AND GENDERED GIFTS IN MELANESIA

The landmark volume in problematizing all of our assumptions about the relationships between persons and objects in Pacific societies has been Marilyn Strathern's *Gender of the Gift*. Heavily influenced by her as a young scholar, I have struggled for over a decade to articulate the ways I have found her work on this topic both inspirational and frustratingly abstract. She begins by postulating there is a difference between the root metaphors of Western industrial societies and exchange-based Melanesian ones: "If in a commodity economy things and persons assume the social form of things, then in a gift economy they assume the social form of persons" (Gregory

1982: 41). Westerners imagine that "things exist in themselves" (Strathern 1988: 134), while Melanesians see them instead as detached parts of persons, metonyms for their producer. Since a person circulates through his or her work, becoming "enchained" in relations with others (1988: 161), alienation does not occur.

She uses these differences to argue against views of sex role antagonism or the encompassment of female spheres by men: "There are no spheres in that sense, encompassment is relative. There are positions from which people act. And women as much as men are able to construct themselves as reference points for their own acts" (Strathern 1988: 284–85). I am in deep sympathy with an approach that acknowledges that it is "agents, not systems, who act" (328), and that reclaims a measure of autonomy for women even in apparently oppressive circumstances. However, I cannot understand how a theory of "partible personhood" can be advanced without probing the personal relationship established between people and particular possessions. But Strathern deliberately excludes considerations of individual subjectivity or biographic experience from her accounts of Melanesian understandings of persons and things.

In ceremonial exchange transactions, as common in Kodi as in any of her Melanesian examples, she says that "things are conceptualized as parts of persons. . . . These objects create mediated relations. . . . They are apprehended as extracted from one and absorbed by another" (Strathern 1988: 178). She argues that the things do not actually stand for persons ("that is our construction") (178), but that they flow between persons and create their mutual enchainment. But her account does not include emotional affect or trauma as part of this process of "extraction" and "absorption," and the "parts of persons" that circulate are not objects of contemplation or reflection.

I am troubled by the fact that Strathern's Melanesian actors are not concerned to construct a coherent sense of self out of their movable parts, and that little attention is paid to their own narratives or exchange histories. Stories of feeling dislocated, displaced, and fragmented into several possible object-identities were common in my own fieldwork, but the people I spoke to were constantly concerned with telling and retelling their lives around these objects to finally achieve some closure. Even the illusory narrative completion of a "story with a beginning and end" is absent from her accounts of persons and exchanges. Strathern explicitly rejects the idea that a coherent story is needed: "The conceptualization of the person as an individual, a being that worries about its boundaries and searches for a unitary identity, remains an unspoken premise in the anthropology of experience" (1988: 57).

To counter this premise, she proposes instead that Melanesians are not individuals but "dividuals," whose detachable parts circulate freely because there is no indigenous theory of unitary identity. She sees "androgyny" as an initial state, from which women and men are made by detaching parts that make them "incomplete." They reconstitute their selves through the movement of objects, and the objects come to make up their new social identities. The idea of androgyny is proposed to destabilize essentialized notions of masculinity and femininity, and to indicate the possibility of movement. An earlier tradition studied "how women and men experience being women and men" by taking the relationship between the sexes as axiomatic, instead of questioning how these differences could be produced through systems of representation.

But androgyny is so much a concept of the current, gender-bending 1990s that I wonder about its applicability to the traditional Melanesian or Indonesian societies she is describing. Deconstructing the images of "sexual antagonism" of the 1960s and 1970s by substituting more recent versions of "gender trouble" (Butler 1990) does not necessarily being us closer to the lived experience of other cultures. There are a number of other, locally generated models for sexual difference that deserve to be examined—specifically, eastern Indonesian notions of dualism and gender doubling that I will discuss in the next section.

Strathern's exciting formulations of how objects can be complexly gendered and identified with persons can be critically tested in a place like Kodi, because it is close to Melanesia and shares the attributes of ceremonial exchange that she sees as characteristic of a "gift society," but it combines them with very Indonesian dualities and complexities. My own enterprise is not a broad regional analysis, but a thick description of a single society where persons and things are intimately entangled. "Partible personhood," if it is to survive as a viable concept, must also be meaningful at the analytic level of individual lives and strategies, and in the relations between biography and objects. We need to pay more attention to diverse and often contradictory interpretations of the rhetorical value of objects and how they can be "read" to reveal more about the subjects of our investigations, and their own subjectivities.

In an earlier work (Hoskins 1993a), I explored how the public view of the past was represented in objects, and the ways in which heirloom valuables were used to anchor a form of temporality "demonstrated" through things. In this book, I look not at the public world of history objects and founding narratives, but at the smaller scale of domestic objects and the stories told about them, and particularly at how these stories are gendered. Morin in fact pays little attention to narrative, but her definition of these characteristics is very useful for the questions I am seeking to ask.

The categories of the personally meaningful possession, the biographical object, as opposed to the public commodity (or gift, heirloom, piece of ancestral regalia) can lead us to an interpretation of how objects on Sumba are differently involved in the production of selves and identities. Feminist writings about Pacific exchange systems have revealed how complex the process of gender identification can be (MacKenzie 1991, McKinnon 1991, Tsing 1993, A. Weiner 1992), and recent work in history and literary theory has centered on the circulation of goods and its significance for defining new modes of consciousness (Greenblatt 1991). Here, I try to take very personal, grounded narratives and show how they are made up of metaphors involving objects, which tell a story that then provides a unity to a sometimes disparate self. My argument is focused on the Kodi people of Sumba, but its aim is ultimately comparative: to show how a different relation to objects generates differently gendered lives, presenting a model of identification and lived dualism that is an alternative to our own assumptions.

Thomas (1991) has criticized the dichotomy of gift-centered Melanesians and commodity-centered Westerns as oversimplified and essentializing. Strathern proposes the constrast of "gift" and "commodity" as a rhetorical strategy, an heuristic tool, rather than a "fact." But reading her provocative descriptions of Melanesian ideas of personhood and gift giving, one is almost inevitably lead to a homogenizing view of Pacific societies that presents them as inverted mirror images of our own. The strongest argument she makes is that the "gift economies" are not really economies at all, but systems of sociality. What they produce is not unequal forms of value but social relations of a complex kind.

In a rehashing of the Strathern-Thomas debate in the pages of *Social Analysis*, Strathern noted that Thomas "domesticates" the distinction between commodity and gift for a Euro-American context as one between commodity and possession (Thomas 1990: 193): "'Possession' summons all the inalienable qualities of identification that are expressed through the attachment of things to persons by contrast with the alienable commodity" (Strathern 1993: 99–100). She then notes that Thomas fails to question the commonsense realism of the category of possession, which is a cultural category of considerable metaphorical power:

> Metaphors are not detached entities, "things" to be innocently used now in this, now in that manner. Power here rests in the assumption that it is natural for things to become identified with persons (and vice-versa), each in this sense "belonging" to the other, for that in turn feeds into European (and Euro-American) ideology concerning the naturalness of possession itself. . . . Euro-Americans do not need to be reassured that the rest of the world might think in the commonsense way that they do about the naturalness of human possession, of holding on to what you have, of the inevitability of dividing that world into the haves and the have-nots. (Strathern 1993: 98)

If Euro-American possessiveness is colonial and acquisitive, and we need to deconstuct it by contrasting it to other models of the person/object relation, what would then be the content of these new models? Do gifts in traditional societies escape the exclusiveness of other possessions? Or is it instead that case that they have value precisely because they are imbued with the "subjective" attributes of the biographies of their former owners?

Thomas defends himself by noting that he is unequipped to "undertake the historicization of Western conceptions of possession and property that

Strathern calls for" (Thomas 1993: 134; but see Carrier 1990, 1994 as a first step in this direction). He does, however, note that the apparently "subjective" meaning of things in Western industrial societies is established through a process not so different from that of Melanesian shell valuables, which are given a "biographical significance" through the intersection between the life of the shell and the life of the person:

> Such apparently individual or personal appropriations of things are not "subjective." I do not even see that a Euro-American teenager's preoccupation with an article of fashion manifests a subjective valorization of an inanimate object; because precisely what the objects in each case reify are attributes of particular or possible persons and relations. That is, in a Melanesian case the idiosyncratic valorization of the valuable might commemorate a kinswoman. In the Euro-American case it might turn upon a kind of flashness or allure that a singular ornament seems to contain and convey; what is at issue is the embodiment of sexualized and sexualizing attributes, not inanimate things and property metaphors. (Thomas 1993: 133)

The differences between Strathern's view (a radical discontinuity between possessing Westerners and Melanesians whose personhood is made and unmade by the circulation of objects) and Thomas's (who sees parallel processes of appropriation of objects by both sides) will come to occupy us in the conclusion. I have tried to steer a middle path between these two theorists by looking at objects and their relationships to individuals. Thomas's call for a historicized, contextualized account of how things are conceptualized and exchanged is honored by grounding my interpretation of objects in a particular life history. Strathern's more challenging and exciting thinking about an alternative epistemology in the Pacific, where things may take on aspects of agency and be perceived as part of the process of creating identities, is confronted but moved from its highly abstract formulation to the narrative articulations of specific actors and things.

The use of autobiographical materials is also intended to show the moral or affective quality of particular social experiences in Pacific societies in ways that will make these stories recognizable to Western readers even as they seem quite different and exotic. Michael Young writes about Melanesian life histories that "autobiographical narratives offer a salutary lesson by reminding us that conflict is not the only or even the main thing being managed, masked or muted by their authors, and that love too may be seeking an opportunity to express itself" (1983a: 498).

Love is often expressed through an image of possession, a desire to possess another person in his or her entirety that, when frustrated, may be deflected onto the possession of a beloved thing. The search for a love object, a companion or surrogate, is a pervasive theme in the accounts of biographies of things that circulate in Kodi, and its resonances with our own notions of romance and possessiveness are significant.

GENDER AND DUALITY: HOW IS DUALISM LIVED?

I had another reason to be fascinated by the problem of the relation of persons and objects, which stemmed more from my personal interests in feminism than my academic interests in exchange. I was attracted to fieldwork in the area because I knew it was characterized by "dualism." In earlier ethnographic reports, this dualism was described as either a characteristic of formal ritual verse ("speaking in pairs" of metaphoric images; Fox 1988) or social organization (paired villages with opposing ritual tasks; Fox 1980). However, it was also obviously expressed in gendered terms, and I was curious about how a system of what was generally called then "symbolic dualism" would affect the lives of individual women and men. The question is a very complex one, and over the years it seems to me that I have received more clues to its answer by asking about objects than I have by asking directly personal (and thereby indiscreet) questions about people.

I wanted to escape an earlier view of Eastern Indonesian symbolism as totalizing and consensual, in which objects could be lined up neatly in two columns according to their gender attributes, and notions of "male" and "female" then deduced from the characteristics of these columns. Without denying the insights of this earlier tradition and its identification of dualism as an important theme in regional representations (Onvlee 1973), I nevertheless want to emphasize here the significance of objects to individuals and their struggles and the ways in which they are involved in complex negotiations of sexual identity.

Perhaps the most famous early article to tackle the issue of gender dualism was Sherry Ortner's "Is Female to Male as Nature Is to Culture?" (1974). It has been very controversial (MacCormack and Strathern 1980, Valeri 1990), but remains, in my view, one of the most cogent early explorations of the problem of how gender symbolism and people's lives might be related. In a recent reassessment of her own argument, Ortner notes that anthropology has turned away from its interests in universals, but remains concerned with "existential questions" such as the opposition between nature and culture evoked in that article. Moving from the "static parallelism of the categories" to look instead at "the politics of the construction of such linkages," her more recent work involves a much greater emphasis on history and practice (Ortner 1996: 180).

If I return, at this point, to a critical re-examination of what is going on in gender dualism, it is with these new goals in mind. The most crucial flaw in Ortner's argument, as she now recognizes, was its emphasis on universals, including the supposedly "universal" subordination of women. After twenty-five years of more detailed research on gender, few people now would flatly assert that female inferiority is uncontested or invariable. This is partly because, as Ortner notes, "universals are of less compelling interest" (1996: 173), but also because we have come to see that gender hegemonies are very complex. Even in societies roughly described as gender egalitarian, this egalitarianism can be inconsistent and fragile (Atkinson 1990, Tsing 1990, Lepowsky 1993), and even in societies where women seem very "subordinated," they retain the agency to resist, protest, and subvert male domination (Abu-Lughod 1986, 1993; Raheja and Gold 1994). Thus some more complex interaction of historical processes involving notions of power, gender, and embodied selfhood must be at work.

However, another aspect to her argument has not been adequately addressed. Ortner was specifically investigating dualistic divisions as mental structures, influenced here by the work of Lévi-Strauss and Simone de Beauvoir, and most commentators took the nature/culture opposition much too literally as local categories. Certainly, many were able to argue convincingly that the terms "nature" and "culture" did not take the same form in all societies. But Ortner herself notes that the great questions articulated in gender dualism cannot be easily dismissed:

> Gender difference, along with nature/culture, is a powerful question. And the gender relationship is always at least in part situated on a nature-culture border—the body. What I think tends to happen in most if not all cultures is that the two oppositions easily move into a relationship of mutual metaphorization: gender becomes a powerful language for talking about the great existential questions of nature and culture, while a language of nature and culture, when and if it is articulated, can become a powerful language for talking about gender, sexuality and reproduction, not to mention power and helplessness, activity and passivity, and so forth. (1996: 179–80)

In my own commentary on this debate, I argued that in Kodi gender served as an effective metaphor precisely because it was not always the dominant structure of inequality, and could provide a language to express mutuality and complementarity (Hoskins 1990: 305).

Now I would make that argument more complex. The societies of Eastern Indonesia are not simply "gendered," they are saturated with gender, they are "overgendered." There is no practical reason why such a great variety of things should be assigned a connotation of male or female, arranged and rearranged in gender categories, at times even inverted and given a gender-crossing, "transvestite" character. The surfeit of gender in Eastern Indonesia is at one level a pure mental invention, a play of classificatory order, but because it deals with gender—that most human of classifiers—these gender games have serious consequences on the lives of women and men.

Ortner's pioneering insight was that a dualistic opposition articulated in terms of gender ("female is to male as . . .") would necessarily have an impact on the sexual politics of everyday life. In Eastern Indonesia, gender dualism is developed and elaborated to an unusual extent, so rather than arguing that there is anything universal about this, I would instead claim that it deserves analytic attention precisely because it is an ethnographic particularity.

Why are these societies so obsessed with gendered dualities? How does this feature of classificatory logic affect personal experience? Does the "two in one" imagery of paired metaphors in ritual speech also permeate everyday interactions? Do men and women see each other as more dependent on a counterpart than do people in other societies?

To anticipate my conclusions somewhat: Yes, I do think the pervasive complementary dualism of Eastern Indonesian societies has social consequences. I would not describe these societies as sexually egalitarian, and certainly not as female dominant. But several male colleagues of mine who have done ethnographic reserach in the region might do so. (See Lewis 1988 on "maternal descent groups" among the Tana Ai of Flores or Hicks 1989 on the "maternal religion" of Tetum of Timor.) The apparently "matrilineal" societies give women genealogical pre-eminence but usually not ritual leadership, while the more "patrilineal" ones may include (as in Kodi) named female descent groups and a subversive female tradition of herbalism, indigo dyeing, and witchcraft. However, the dualistic dichotomy between matrilineal and patrilineal societies that anthropologists have been so fond of has been shown to have relatively little significance in this region, as people are affiliated to houses through a complex number of different ways, and everything called "descent" must also be confirmed through alliance payments (McKinnon 1991, Valeri 1980).

The consequences of gender dualism lie most obviously at the level of ideology, and they involve the idealization of sexual union. Both men and women believe that their lives are incomplete without a counterpart, and they part with American ideologies of individuality and autonomy by stressing partnership and dependency. The battlegrounds between the sexes that are so readily observable in American daily life (perhaps especially marked in academic contexts) are not drawn in the same way on Sumba. Men and women are not members of opposing teams or clearly demarcated interest groups. They do share some secrets and some sisterly (or brotherly) solidarity, but the cultural norm of double-gendered completion gives a hierarchical priority to the union of male and female.

Exchange valuables in Eastern Indonesia are complexly gendered, as many others have observed (Adams 1969, Fox 1980, Howell 1989, McKinnon 1991). In formal exchanges, they may be marked as male or female gifts. Because such exchanges are hierarchically coded, an object that is "female" in one context (such as women's jewelry) may be "male" in another (when all "male" metal objects are opposed to "female" cloth). The complex hierarchies of formal exchange circumscribe these gendered identities and make them the subject of long, drawn-out negotiations.

The domestic objects I discuss here are also complexly gendered, but I found it impossible to draw up a tally sheet of which objects were seen as "male" or "female" because—instead of oscillating their gender identity as many exchange valuables seem to—these objects were all in some way "double gendered." I define <u>double gendering</u> as a quality that represents an idealized union of male and female rather than their separation or opposition. A doubling of gender is thus quite distinct from the "androgyny" that Strathern and others have described in Melanesia (Strathern 1988, MacKenzie 1991). While I respect this work and do not want to challenge it for the materials they discuss, I do not find it describes the kind of gender fusion I saw in Eastern Indonesia.

In Kodi, male and female are not blended and neutralized but brought together in the reproductive model of parenthood. Male and female are thus intensified and made hierarchically more encompassing than any single gender. An androgynous object is of uncertain sex, while a double-gendered one represents the wholeness of sexual union. The domestic objects I discuss all have, to a greater or lesser degree, a quality of double genderedness that is not "made incomplete" by extractions of maleness or femaleness (in Strathern's model) but instead made powerful by their union. In these objects I read a story of romantic longing on the part of men for women and women for men. Since Freud's early work on fetishism, we have recognized that an idealized longing for human partnership can be projected onto objects that may serve as surrogate companions. Rather than seeing this as as a "pathology of everyday life," I chose to analyze it as a dynamic field for the narrative articulation of identity. It is the longing for completion and companionship that runs as a theme through the different stories told around and about objects that I collected.

In Kodi, individual biographical experience is "made complete" by including within it elements of the opposite gender. Eastern Indonesia is an area that, while riddled with many of the usual tensions between men and women, is not characterized by sexual antagonism or avoidance, and notions of celibacy or single life styles are virtually unknown. Partnership and complementarity are very highly held cultural goals, hard to realize in individual lives, but aspired to by almost everyone. So the complex sexual politics in which objects are entangled revolve around efforts to unify male and female domains, not to separate them.

The biographical object is regendered and re-engendered as a person completed by including missing aspects—an idealized companion with a complementary and contrasting form of experience. From the deities addressed as "Great Mother, Great Father" or "Elder Mother, Ancient Father" down to the small couples of spirits of each sex that guard each door and gateway, Kodi is a cultural geography impregnated with dualism and struggling to resolve the contradictions involved in an often forced combination of male and female elements everywhere.

Individuals strive for a sense of completion through their lives and narrate stories that give them a way to envision this. Men and women tell different kinds of stories, and cultural norms force them to focus them more or less directly on their own personal experiences. Men are allowed to be more overtly self-aggrandizing, but women's uses of metaphor and irony to criticize some of these masculinist patterns are readily understood and need little translation to be recognized by Western readers. These stories are not about "men's and women's worlds," however, but always about a shared world, and efforts to bridging the gap between the sexes to achieve completion and wholeness in a bipartite cosmos.

KODI AS A STRATEGIC SITE
TO RE-EVALUATE INDONESIAN SEXUAL POLITICS

The idea of androgyny, which is often opposed to earlier paradigms of sexual relations that were described as either "complementary" or "antagonistic," has attracted a great deal of interest in recent feminist theory (Butler 1990, Grosz 1994), with particular relevance to struggles for gay and lesbian rights. Its application to exotic fieldsites, particularly where it is posited as an "original state," the basis of a later, socially negotiated, personhood, may, however, be an idealistic projection—a bit like the "abuses of anthropology" in early feminist anthropology that used anthropology as a precedent for modern claims and saw the primitive as bearer of primordial human need: "Women elsewhere are, it seems, the image of ourselves undressed, and the historical specificity of their lives and of our own becomes obscured" (M. Rosaldo 1980: 392).

Judith Butler's critique of the notion of fixed gender identities stresses how selves are constructed through discursive practices:

> The "coherence" and "continuity" of "the person" are not logical or analytical features of personhood but, rather, socially instituted and maintained norms of intelligibility. Inasmuch as "identity" is assured through the stabilizing concepts of sex, gender, and sexuality, the very notion of "the person" is called into question by the cultural emergence of those "incoherent" or "discontinuous" gendered beings who appear to be persons but who fail to conform to the gendered norms of cultural intelligibility by which persons are defined. (1990: 17)

Each society is based on a system of tacit constraints that produce culturally intelligible "sex." Her condemnation of the regulatory practices of "compulsory heterosexuality" in North America and Western Europe is not sensitive, however, to variations on these themes in other societies, such as the many Asian forms of dualism, and specifically the intensified importance of sexuality and sexual union in Eastern Indonesian "complementarity."

Kodi is significant because it has long held a strategic place in the history of theories of social dualism. In 1935, this society attracted scholarly projections based on somewhat different gender models. Dutch structuralism of the Leiden school, inspired by the totalizing theories of FAE. Van Wouden, postulated that Kodi might be the site of the original proto-Austronesian form of dual organization, since it seemed to combine asymmetric marriage rules with a form of "double descent" that included clans traced along both patrilineal and matrilineal lines. Two distinguished anthropologists, Van Wouden himself and his English colleague Rodney Needham, traveled to Sumba in the early 1950s to investigate this possibility. Both were disappointed: The Kodinese do have a form of "double descent" (at least according to the now somewhat dated definition of the term; cf. Van Wouden [1935] 1968), but they do not have a strict directionality of marriage. Van Wouden returned, convinced that evolutionary models had to be opened up to more complex historical interpretations ([1956] 1977), and Needham decided to abandon serious fieldwork in the region (pers. comm.).

But the gender puzzle remained: If Kodi is an area where patrilineal and matrilineal descent are recognized but subject to different ritual and social processing, was this also a recognition of a special form of "double-gendered" personhood? Is this "double gendering" of spiritual beings and objects the same as or different from Strathern's model of "partible personhood" in Melanesia? Are the Kodi not merely a bizarre society whose special proclivities are writ small for the specialists, but also evocative of the problems of gender-confused Americans of the late twentieth century writ large?

The answer is much more complicated than either of these statements. Kodi worshipers of the *marapu* certainly have a cosmology that is classically dualistic. Spirits are invoked in paired couplets, in which two images are juxtaposed to suggest a single metaphor. The Creator is called "Mother who bound the forelock. Father who smelted the crown" (*Inya wolo hungga, Bapa rawi lindu*), suggesting that people were formed by a combination of women's work in binding threads (for weaving) and men's work in smelting metal (for tools, weapons . . . or the hard human skull). All of the most important guardian deities (of the clan altar, the house pillar, and the garden hamlet) are similarly double gendered. The womanly element at times appears "primordial" in these representations: Female spirits are usually named first, so they are called "Elder Mother, Ancient Father" (*Inya Matuyo, Bapa Maheba*) or "Mother of the Earth, Father of the Rivers" (*Inya mangu tana, Bapa mangu loko*).

Below these deities, pairs of female and male spirit intermediaries are found at the edge of the ceiling and the top of the house, at the garden's gate and the edge of cultivated land, and in the graves and tombstones. They skirt the margins and boundaries of human spaces and are given human names. Ancestors are normally invoked as couples, "dead mothers and fathers," and even famed ancestral personalities must be called along with a lesser-known counterpart of the opposite sex. Ra Hupu, the lord of lightning, is said never to have married, so he is summoned beside the name of his sister Tila, who spread out his nets along the shore. Inya Nale, the goddess of sea worms whose annual swarming off the western beaches marks the greatest festivity of the Kodi calendar (Hoskins 1993a: 142–71), is summoned with her maritime companion the Ipu fish, which swarms in a later month.

At the bottom of the spirit hierarchy lie the undifferentiated and gender-ambiguous spirits of wealth and plentiful harvests—rice and corn, livestock, and cloth. Their lower rank is marked by the fact that they are not anthropomorphized or even given personal names. The double-gendered deities are the most "complete" and perfect beings, their paired subsidiaries are somewhat less illustrious (and addressed according to the same etiquette as human ancestors), while the spirits of wealth and crops are more inert and faceless.

Any dualism that plays heavily on sexual difference must have some weight on human lives since, contrary to the assumptions of early binarists, sexuality cannot be reduced to a system of formal oppositions. Women and men are never simply "signs" but also agents, and gender—that most human of classifiers—inflects any system of "complementary balances" with power differentials. The *walla* system of matriclans is said both to precede the history of *parona* patriclans and to encompass it by its size and proliferation. And yet the key political and social offices are linked to patrilineal descent, which also organizes the ownership of land, heirlooms, and livestock.

Kodi is a society that, like several others recently described in Eastern Indonesia (Sugishima 1994, Howell 1995) appears fully "patrilineal" on the surface and hides its "matrilineal" elements in stories of witchcraft, scandal, and incest. Patrilines define the owners of "houses" (*uma*), who worship common ancestors and make up "villages" (*parona*) with complex ritual divisions. Matrilines define marriage prohibitions, relations of "blood," and the inheritance of personality characteristics. A person's patriline is always an object of public knowledge, while the same person's matriline may be a shameful secret. Some matrilines are made up of hereditary witches, others of the descendants of slaves, foreigners, or outcasts (Hoskins 1993a: 16–18). While matrilineal ties may provide access to occult knowledge (especially of the "blue arts" of indigo dyeing, midwifery, and abortion; Hoskins 1989b), they are carefully kept out of the spotlight and alluded to only discreetly, when marriages are being negotiated.

Women must move from their house of birth to their husband's house once a substantial payment of bridewealth (at least ten "tails": five horses and five buffalo) has been made to the bride's parents. However, the wife is "bought but not sold," because once her parents have agreed to accept the groom, they make an equivalent counterpayment in pigs, cloth, ivory bracelets, and perhaps even a slave attendant (Valeri 1994). Women do at times leave their husbands and seek divorce, but in doing so they lose their children, who affiliate patrilaterally once the bridewealth has been paid. Many Kodi wives tolerate physical abuse and younger cowives in order to remain with their children and raise them with their husbands. A wife joins in the worship of her husband's ancestors when she joins his household, and can invoke her own ancestors in prayers only to ask for more children. She retains the right to veto, through nonparticipation, any important decisions about the marriages of her sons or daughters or the transfer of property (land, livestock, etc.), but she rarely speaks in formal negotiations and is almost always on the sidelines.

Kodi gender dualism is not, therefore, an inspiring recipe for female empowerment. It does imply a spiritual and symbolic parity that seems, however, not to be fully realized in the day-to-day sexual politics of the region. In an earlier assessment of gender doubling, I argued that gender duality was used as a "way of thinking" about a variety of relationships not directly structured by gender: The "idealized interdependence of male and female can be diffused over a number of contexts where images of mutuality are needed" (Hoskins 1990: 305).

Now I have become both more concerned about the gaps between this "idealized interdependence" and real sexual inequities, and more sensitive to ways in which women and men have drawn on these images to their own strategic advantage. The completeness of sexual union is desired by all, but the terms that each will accept to gain that desired union vary enormously. Few people are willing to talk directly about sexual politics, which is precisely why only a language of objects and metaphors expressed through things can give us access to these kinds of subjective experiences. Women are themselves "objects exchanged in marriage," so they identify with the domestic animals traded against them. They may fantasize about a spindle that selects a bridegroom, or a buffalo's daughter who founds her own village and marries a prince. Men want to speak with the authority contained in a betel bag, the hierarchical prestige of a python, or the great resonating tones of a man's baritone and his "sweet voiced" drum. Their stories reveal part of themselves attached to the biography of an object, elaborating its history and its characteristics in order to better understand their own needs and desires.

Personal possessions can also be used as a means of conjuring up the memory of an individual. When someone dies, he or she is eulogized by chanting the names of significant possessions—horses, buffalo, spears, knives—which are seen as poignantly evocative of their missing owner. These possessions are believed to be so imbued with the personality of the deceased that they they must leave the house at the same time the dead person does. Some (like the betel bag) may be buried with the body, or sacrificed (like the horse), or broken on the grave. Others may be ritually bestowed onto a descendant to anoint him or her as a successor to a particular role (as a ritual speaker, a warrior, a spinner of fine cloth). When a personal possession such as a headcloth, knife, or betel bag is accidentally left behind, it is believed that a part of the owner's soul (*ndewa*) is lost, and a small rite must be performed to "recall the soul" when it is found and returned.

COMPARATIVE IMPLICATIONS

My central argument is that local constructions of selves on Sumba are tied to the construction amd use of specific types of objects. Within the wider context of debates about dualism in anthropology, objects can become a site for the cathexis of overcoded symbolisms of gender and sexuality. The emotional significance invested in personal possessions gives them a charge of psychic energy, which is given narrative expression in paired verses, songs, and stories. Freud has described things that seem to "take possession" of their owners (German *Besetzung*), and my Sumbanese friends would seem in some ways to be similarly possessed. Complementarity does not mean a weakening of the significance of sexuality in Eastern Indonesia but, on the contrary, may precisely lead to its powerful emphasis.

How widespread is this preoccupation with possessions and gendered duality? This book does not go beyond my own ethnographic research in Kodi, but the idiom is certainly found throughout the island (Forth 1981, Kuipers 1990, 1998, Geirnaert-Martin 1992, Keane 1997) and in neighboring Timor and Flores. Writing about another district on Sumba, Kuipers records, "Listening to Weyewa talk about a powerful man or woman, one does not hear connected, temporally organized biographical narratives about events during a lifetime; instead one hears about clusters of belongings, radiating out, as it were, from a charismatic center" (1998: 155). Writing on East Sumba, L. Onvlee notes, "Personal possessions are singularly linked with the life of their owner. They are not impersonal; rather they are part of the person who owns them and related to his life in a particular way" (1980: 196).

In many other parts of Indonesia, the importance of regalia and magical objects is highly developed, but gender tensions are different. The "syncretic and absorptive center" of the Javanese polity is expressed by the potency of its ruler and occasionally concentrated through ascetic practices, but not expressed in paired polarities (Anderson 1972, Keeler 1987, Pemberton 1994). The evocation of dualism on a more playful and speculative level is reported by Anna Tsing in her witty vignette about the "lessons in structuralism" she received from a mountain shaman among the Meratus of Kalimantan:

> Twice, I watch Uma Adang teach the Dualities as a core secret, a deep structure of the world. Each time, she listed a number of oppositions, including gender, and some of the others [day and night, life and death, maturity and youth], leaving her audiences to chime in as they go the idea with oppositions of their own. "Good and bad," said one man, "big and little, vulva and penis." "Humans and rice," added another. "Rich and poor, " suggested a third, mining this rich vein of thought, he continued: "Gold and diamonds . . . silver and iron . . . silver and lead." The listeners were excited, jumping in with the enthusiasm of university students learning about structuralism for the first time. At each suggestion, Uma Adang nodded approvingly, with the wisdom of a professor who embraces all interpretations. It could have been a send-up of my own training, in which, according to many hoary authorities, dualities really do structure the experience of the native but at such a deep, all-pervasive level that the native cannot explain them, much less invent them as a speculative science. (Tsing 1993: 270)

Her irony underscores the resemblance between the occult knowledge of academic theoreticians and that of village-based religious specialists. While a somewhat similar scene could be imagined in Kodi, no one would teach the Dualities as a personal magical science, as Uma Adang did. Instead, ritual specialists pride themselves on knowing which word must necessarily pair with another, and which object must necessarily be reciprocated by another. Kodi speakers are then able to improvise against this background of conventional pairs, using the dualities less as a secret code than as a shared system of coupled meanings.

Gender dualism is certainly more marked in places like Sumba, Flores, and Timor than in Kalimantan or Sulawesi. Shelly Errington (1990) formulates this contrast as a comparative difference between the "Centrist Archipelago" (which would include Java, Bali, Sulawesi, and Kalimantan) and the "Exchange Archipelago" (which would include most of the other islands). However, the difference is obviously more one of degree than of orientation: Centers and oppositions are part of the conceptual vocabulary of all Indonesian societies. If dualism is more marked on Sumba, it is partially because of the importance of exchanges between houses, which give primacy to the wife giver in an ever-shifting play of marriage strategies.

The key question to be asked, here as elsewhere, is not why finding dualities should have appeared an amusing game, but why it also seemed a legitimate pathway to wisdom and secret knowledge. If Uma Adang chose to draw on dualities as the mark of mystical perception, it was because they had a wider resonance that made this convincing to her followers. And, though I agree that assuming that dualistic oppositions provide the universal substructure of all thought is perhaps a mistake, the meaning of paired contrasts as local categories of experience for many peoples in Eastern Indonesia remains to be explored.

Gender dualism was addressed during the period of structuralism's heyday (when it inspired Ortner's article), but few attempts were made to account for its impact on the experience of actual men and women (Rosaldo and Lamphere 1974, Fox 1980, Maybury-Lewis and Almagor 1989). More recent research on gender in Southeast Asia (Ong and Peletz 1995, Sears 1996) focuses much more on individual experience, resistance, and sexuality, but none of the contributors tries to tangle with a thorny old issue like dualism.

A partial exception within the theoretical literature is Judith Shapiro's essay on "Gender Totemism," which argues that the structuralist binarism often imposed on lowland South America should be reinterpreted as a play of signs and relationships:

> Following the logic of Levi-Strauss' argument, we can say that biological opposition between female and male, like the array of animal species, provides a powerful natural model for representing differences between social groups and oppositions between culturally significant categories. . . . The main point

is to shift the focus from the properties of groups to the nexus of relationships. Instead of focusing on the characteristics of women as a group or men
as group ... [t]he issue becomes one of seeing how a series of categorical
oppositions, including the one between female and male, map onto and
construct each other. (Shapiro 1988: 3)

I might add that it is also necessary to look at the problem of how individuals, in different subject positions, interpret and construct these relationships.
As fathers, daughters, husbands, sisters, wives, brothers, sons, and mothers,
men and women are always complexly related. The question of how gender
dualism is actually lived requires an ethnographic answer, using the particularities of individual lives to understand how they negotiate their own identities against the backdrop of paired cultural categories.

By subjecting the apparent binarism of male and female to a closer and
more nuanced scrutiny, there may also be a way to modify certain other
binarisms that haunt the Western imagination more consistently, such as the
opposition between "self" and "world." Strathern has effectively and persuasively theorized things as reificiations of detachable and attachable parts of
persons and relations. But this "political economy" mode of analysis has had
little to say about experience, subjectivity, or how these "parts of persons"
may be narratively organized to provide at least a temporary illusion of
coherence. In criticizing what has been left out of this picture, Nicholas
Thomas (1993: 132) remembers an argument she made to the Canberra
research group on gender in the southwestern Pacific (in which I also participated) that analytical fictions necessarily produced lacunae as well as pres-
ences. In order to privilege an insight into one area, it is necessary to
privilege a blindness in another.

The insights that I try to privilege in this study focus on the narrative
creation of the self through the vehicle of an object. A number of other
theorists have argued that objects and subjects are mutually defined and
reciprocally constitutive, and they have looked at moments of transaction
and display (Munn 1986, Miller 1987) in which an object's exchange value is
determined. The personal possessions I discuss in this work, while sometimes also involved in exchange, are more significant because of the ways
they are remembered, hoarded, or used as objects of fantasy and desire.
They are used to reify characteristics of personhood that must then be
narratively organized into an identity.

This book, then, looks at six stories, each of them articulated around an
object, which establish the link between person and possession that is part of
the pervasive gendering of persons and objects in Eastern Indonesian sociality. The complex ways gender is manipulated and reinterpreted in these
people's lives can show us an alternative way of looking at female and male,
persons and objects.

2.

THE BETEL BAG

A Sack for Souls and Stories

Maru Daku, chewing a betel quid beside his simple plaited betel bag, with his only daughter on one side and his first wife, Daku Maru, on the other. (Photo J. Hoskins, 1980)

"A story in a sack (*ngara kedoko la kaleku*)? That's what you want, isn't it?" asked Maru Daku somewhat derisively when I balked initially at all the complicated rites needed to elicit a long traditional narrative.

"I got my stories in a betel bag once, but now I don't hand them out that way. To hear the real thing, you must come to our village, share a meal with us, spend the night, and listen as we speak in the dark. Little stories, yes, they can see the light of day. We can tell them even on the edge of the veranda, or off in the gardens. But the real thing, the long ones, the ones we hold from our grandmothers and grandfathers, they need a bit more preparation."

Maru Daku was defending his place and authority as one of the most respected storytellers in Kodi. He was also playing on the problematic "portability" of stories, and their relation to the most portable of Kodi items of everyday wear: the betel bag, which is almost inseparable from its owner. The deep, pleated inner pouches of the betel bag are a place of secrets and can stand for certain forms of hidden knowledge. His own power to speak, the "seeds of wisdom" he inherited from his grandfather (*ha wini wali y'ambu*), was transmitted to him by mouth, in a mixture of saliva and thumbnail wrapped up in a betel quid. He had stored them in a series of small woven sacks that he carried throughout his life, but he was unwilling to open up everything to scrutiny. With these words, he recalled the special status of storytelling, and his special prerogatives as a teller of tales.

The importance of traditional narrative is increasingly challenged by the changes involved in modernization and integration into the nation-state, and Sumba is, like many places, in danger of losing its bards and storytellers. It is significant that, seeing his work under attack, Maru Daku took refuge in the image of the betel bag, and asserted his rights to the ritual required to get access to this knowledge even as he enjoyed the more modern position as my "teacher" in traditional custom and my "research assistant" for the Indonesian bureaucracy.

Betel bags are both intensely personal objects and intensely social ones. Each man or woman carries a small bag over the shoulder, with a supply of fresh betel pipers and areca nut. When alone, the contents of the bag are carefully prepared—breaking open the areca nut and crushing it in a mortar, then inserting it into the mouth with a bite of the betel piper and a small amount of lime. A solitary chew provides a moment of contemplation, and also a spur to memory and concentration, since the betel quid keeps the chewer alert, awake, and staves off hunger pangs so work can be completed or a long story told in full. The exchange of betel is also, however, the first act of any social encounter. Bags are passed from host to guest, from a visiting suitor to his sweetheart, from anthropologist to informant—and in each case, as hands move down into the inner recesses of the bag, the freshness and quality of the ingredients are read as a sign of how welcome the visit really is.

Betel juice is the lubricant of Sumbanese society, and it must be dribbled, spat, and enjoyed at each social interaction, making it more widespread than either coffee or alcohol. To refuse betel is to refuse all social courtesy, to retreat into a world of the self alone. To give it is, on the contrary, to give of oneself, to spread goodwill and knowledge, and to share the vivacious company of one's companions. Maru Daku used the betel bag as a kind of alter ego, a metaphor for his own self, because it was an object that suggested his claims to serve both as a container for ancestral memories and a mediator of new alliances.

The significance he attached to his betel bag was demonstrated in three specific moments of his biography, each one associated with transmission of knowledge across the generations. The first was the gift of words his grandfather gave him as a teenager. The second was the rite he sponsored to call back the lost soul of his brother, burned in a fire that many interpreted as an ancestral sanction for Maru Daku's religious eclecticism. The third was a rite he sponsored to end livestock rustling, aimed indirectly but obviously at the larcenous tendencies of his own favorite son. As a grandson, brother, and father he used the vehicle of the betel quid, stored in the pouches of the betel bag but activated through a shot of lime, to provoke a new moral consciousness and a sense of responsibility.

The betel bag was a significant choice for Maru Daku also because it is an object of local manufacture whose particular form is distinctively Kodi. The particular kind of bag he carried—a simple, lontar-plaited style, rather than the more elaborate bags embroidered with bark thread—also made a statement about ties to tradition in its simplest and most unadorned form. His claims to legitimacy as a storyteller were based on his knowledge of indigenous traditions, but his life had been deeply marked by his periods of assisting foreign researchers. In 1954–55 he worked with Rodney Needham, and in 1979–81 he was my guru besar or "great teacher."

These experiences caused him to be at times the object of suspicion and envy, of rumors that he was disclosing ancestral secrets or profiting from a sacred heritage. He was also accused of adding too many rhetorical flourishes to certain stories, embellishing and embroidering them, so that there were "too many spices in the stew." His choice of betel bag, the same simple style as his grandfather's, was one nonverbal reply to these critics. He also addressed them indirectly in a long lament in parallel verse, recited in my home when he believed himself near death. This lament described his meeting with me and what the real purpose of our research was. In this account of my encounter with him, I will intercut his description of events in verse with my own prose narrative.[1]

THE ETHNOGRAPHIC ENCOUNTER FROM BOTH SIDES

When I arrived on Sumba in 1979 to begin my research, Maru Daku's name was one of the first suggested to me. He was a well-known authority on traditional matters, and even a leader in an incipient movement of cultural revitalization. But perhaps partially because of his established importance as a traditional ideologue, I was initially suspicious. Since he was a former Christian evangelist and local official, I wondered if he was too closely associated with the church and the government, both of which displayed a surface respect for "custom" (adat) but also a very restricted and limited image of what my study of custom should entail. Needham (1960: 232) had called him "as intelligent and imaginative man as I have ever known, and his facility of expression, trained in the daunting subtleties of the Kodi language, was remarkable." But I did not want simply to duplicate the work done by an earlier researcher, and felt that I should immediately immerse myself in learning the local language so I could work with the more traditional village people who at that time still formed a pagan majority. So for the first month I lived in Kodi, although his name was often mentioned, I did not even meet him.

A few weeks after my arrival, I planned a small feast at my house to introduce myself to the community, explain the purpose of my research, and seek the help of local leaders. Maru Daku was among the honored guests invited. As the day approached, I began to hear a number of intriguing stories about him. Christian schoolteachers complained to me that he had backed away from his commitment to the church and returned to the worship of the ancestral spirits. His investigations with Needham were cited as the beginning of an unhealthy fascination with traditional lore, "dwelling again among the marapu." These interests finally led him to drop out of government service and to sponsor an expensive and elaborate series of pagan rituals. Accusations were made that his wandering from the church had brought catastrophe and death on his own family, that it angered not only the Christian God but also the marapu, and that his life was now cursed on both sides. These stories, of course, only served to heighten my interest in meeting him, and I began to hope that he would decide to make the several-hour journey to my house so I could judge for myself.

More than sixty guests came on the appointed day—village headmen, government officials, priests of the marapu cult, and elders in the community—many coming considerable distances to meet the strange white woman who intended to write a book about their customs. The only major disappointment was that Maru Daku did not attend. His advanced age (mid-sixties) and failing health were given as excuses. But, as his own words indicate later, he had decided to delay our encounter for his own reasons.

A month later, I met his son Deta Raya, who was the main singer of work songs at a stone-dragging ceremony to build a megalithic grave near his homeland. Deta Raya was a flamboyant local personality who greeted me with a series of ribald verses in his songs about the "great white mountain" that had come to Kodi, wondering whether any "long black tubers" would ever be planted in it. People giggled at my innocence as they translated some of the words, telling me that sexual metaphors were common in such songs, and Deta Raya himself had particular prominence as a consumer of women. He had a dozen wives, more than anyone else in the district.

When I approached him to get more information, he was polite but not very talkative. "I am really just a child," he said, speaking from his early thirties. "I can sing these songs, but my father is the one who knows the real words, the stories of our ancestors. Why don't you come to meet him at market day in Waiha?" He invited me to his own home, a three-hour walk from the district capital.

I agreed, and arranged to travel by motorcycle to the capital, then walk for several hours and cross a still-unbridged river into Kodi Bangedo. I left early in the morning, but did not arrive until the small market was dispersing. Both Maru Daku and Deta Raya had been there that day, but had returned to their ancestral village along the coast. The ancestral villages are cult centers containing lineage houses, megalithic graves, and ceremonial arenas for major ceremonies. I realized to my annoyance it would take four more hours to walk from Waiha to the seafront village of Wainjolo Wawa. Although I still wanted to meet Maru Daku, I was exhausted and uncertain about whether to make the trip.

A local policeman in Waiha invited me into his home for a meal and offered to lend me a horse and a guide to travel across the hot, wide grassland of the interior to the coconut groves by the beach. As we came in sight of the high-perched clan village of Weinyapu, I began to suspect that our meeting had been planned to take place this way.

Maru Daku did not want to travel to meet me, since that would have indicated subservient status. He wanted me to have to travel (preferably a long way on a hot day) to meet him. He chose as the site of our meeting his ancestral village, where his traditional authority was most evident and where he could welcome us into the hospitiality of his lineage house and cult center. Arranged in a rough circle on top of the cliffs overlooking the southern seas, Weinyapu incorporates twelve clan villages and more than sixty large lineage houses, all with the high-rising thatch towers of traditional Sumbanese houses. Looking out over both the inland valleys and the still-unbridged river of Wuku, it was and still is the most isolated and perhaps also the largest ritual center in all of West Sumba.

Reflecting on this meeting two years later, as he lay ill, Maru Daku points out to his critics that he did not impose himself on me as a local "culture expert" but was specifically sought out for his knowledge. As he said:

Maka ba di wali diyo	So I remember how in the beginning
A kere nggiha ngali nya	At the first diggings with the hoe
Inde hepu hupu mara nggu	I did not cut in front at the tides
Inde tati lombo loko nggu	I did not go across beside the river
A minye bandu bali lyoro	To the duck-woman from overseas
Maka ba di wali diyo	So I remember that then I was
Inde koki ulu monggo ngguni	Not the first monkey to chop through
Mono inde wawi ulu hapu nggumi	And not the first pig to wander in
A minye palokongo loro	The woman who came across the ocean
Tilu wu mangadi	Along the edges of the wide sea
Mono a minye tolokongo	And the woman who crossed over
Limbu wu mandattu	The expanse of deep waters
Na duki ela uma mangu wungga	Who came into my own lineage house
Yila tana nale ngga	In the land of the sea worm rites
La y'Ote ana ratu	Home of Ote son of a nobleman
Na toma la katonga mangu wungga	Who came to sit on my veranda
Yila tana padu nggu	In the land of planting rites
La Hyadi ana meha	Home of Hyadi the only child

My long journey to come to see him, crossing several rivers just as I had earlier crossed the Pacific Ocean to come to Indonesia, highlighted the importance of his expertise and showed how far I had traveled to seek him out. Finally, surrounded by the ancestral spirits of Ote and Hyadi, founders of the clan of Wainjolo Deta, we could meet appropriately.

We were welcomed with fresh betel nut and coffee, and Maru Daku himself came out to sit with us on the front veranda. He was a slight, elderly man with dark skin and piercing black eyes behind wire-rimmed glasses. Dressed in the ceremonial headband and homespun indigo loincloth of traditional Kodi elders, he wore a long bush-knife strapped to his waist. His eyes and prominent eagle nose perched precariously above a red cavern of a mouth, the few remaining teeth blackened by a mixture of tobacco and areca nut, the right cheek caved in completely from a large abscess, the lips curled in a smile of lopsided irony. He hardly shifted position as he spoke, but his hands were in constant motion, grasping the bit of tobacco leaf rolled in corn husk that was his usual prop, pointing here and there, tracing the line of his narrative with the elongated thumbnail of a man who no longer worked in the fields.

"There is much we have to discuss," he told me immediately. "I can tell you about the form of this village, the altars to the harvest of rice and corn, and the harvest of heads. I know the sacred numbers that we use to count out ritual intervals, and the division of tasks between the ancestral houses."

Before he spoke at much length, however, he wanted us to perform the formal betel ceremony that is used when listening spirits must give their consent for a story to be told. A gourd plate was prepared, arranged with dried areca nut and green sirih pipers, and passed to me. I placed a small amount of money (Rp. 10,000, about five dollars) on the plate, and it was passed back to him.

The payment signaled that the interview would be a formal one, and I turned on my tape recorder. He began to recite a catalog of objects, names, and ancestors associated with particular places in Balaghar, pointing out where they were and making sure that I recorded them correctly. He also told a few of the animal fables in Indonesian that Needham had published (1957, 1960), and gave an account of the origins of certain customs, which seemed dry and predigested. He did occasionally cite his sources in the ritual couplets that make up the bulk of Sumbanese oral tradition, but my own inexperience with the language made such references simply obscure.

I was more intrigued by the conversations we had after the tape recorder was turned off, when I and my companion were invited to spend the night. Maru Daku was immensely curious about the outside world. Here in a bamboo house on wooden piles, some ten hours from the nearest paved road and two days' journey from the nearest store or secondary school, he wanted to know if it was true that Paris was the world's most beautiful city. He also asked about the women rajas he had heard about in England and Holland, and the group of people called "Jews" who avoided pork like the Muslims and had been imprisoned by the Nazis in Germany.

I became aware of his lively intelligence as his mind moved from one topic to another in great spirals of exploratory questions, but I was much less impressed by the interpretations and explanations of traditional custom. It seemed all too rehearsed and ready to be served up to a foreign audience.

He had shown me none of the wisdom or flair for storytelling I had been led
to expect, and I wondered whether he might be playing a power game to re-
establish his authority as a traditional sage.

We left the next morning promising to contact him again, but my enthu-
siasm was somewhat diminished. I decided that I had been fooling myself
with the naive vision of a "native philosopher" and that I should not have
been disconcerted to find merely a wily old politician.

For the next few months, I continued to live in a distant garden hamlet
with Gheru Wallu, the first wife of a wealthy village headman. Lack of
privacy, distance from the ceremonial centers, and frustrations with my still-
unfocused research caused me to seek separate housing in a unit originally
built for a rural nurse. It was adjacent to the clinic in the district capital of
Bondo Kodi and closer to the ancestral villages along the coast. I moved
there on New Year's Day in 1980, four months after my arrival on the island.
Since it was only about two hours' walk from Maru Daku's home in Balaghar,
I sent an invitation for him to drop by on market days for some further talk.

On Maru Daku's first visit to my home, I received him as an honored
guest. We killed a chicken and roasted it whole, presenting it to him and his
son along with photographs I had taken on my visit to Weinyapu. At his
next visit I gave him a bright orange headcloth to wear at the sea worm
festivities for the Kodi year, and asked if he could help me to transcribe and
translate some texts I had recorded from the preparations. Within a short
while he began to come to my house regularly after the market, assuming
the role of my teacher and adviser in matters of Kodi custom. He was
accompanied by his nephew, Ndara Katupu, a former schoolteacher who had
lost his job as principal of a Christian school when he took a second wife.
The nephew was to help in translating Kodi ritual language into proper
Indonesian, while Maru Daku himself would serve as source and commenta-
tor on traditional verbal lore.

These sessions provided me with my first solid ethnographic data and
helped me to arrange early impressionistic observations according to a wider
scheme. But I continued to feel a bit uncomfortable about the kind of material I was collecting. This was partly because of the enormous translation
problems involved, since it was still very hard for me to follow anything
more than ordinary conversation in Kodi. Plus, I thought that eventually
this material should be checked with other informants in more isolated
village communities who had not been "contaminated" by exposure to
Christianity and the outside world. I still clung to the romantic anthropological concept of an unblemished, "native" world view. For this reason I was
less sensitive to Maru Daku's real gifts for exploring a matter intellectually
and constructing an extended exegesis.

Later, when I had spoken to a wider range of people, I found my encounters with many of the more isolated ritual specialists unproductive. The real
rato marapu or traditional priests are able to recite extensive prayers and
provide a "rule book" of ritual procedures, but they are neither particularly

concerned with nor articulate in providing explanations. The usual answer given for why a certain object was revered was simply that it was *hari*, "sacred," and therefore must have some special tie with the ancestors. These older men also tended to be suspicious of my intentions and reluctant to divulge their secrets to a foreign white woman. After extensive wooing and repeated visits, I was able to win the trust of one or two, but I still found them concerned more with the politics of interclan prerogatives than with exploring the meaning of their traditional world in a more speculative fashion.

As an ex-Christian who had traveled and had some exposure to the peoples of other islands, Maru Daku had a strongly developed sense of cultural variation and enough distance to be reflective about his own background. He had also become genuinely interested in the enterprise of recording Kodi traditions. He kept his own books, parallel to my notes, in which he would write things down. Often he would have to ask his sons to record things for him, because his eyesight was failing.

Toward the end of my work, we even began to exchange materials. I would lend him a funeral chant or myth recorded from a distant region, and he would get me tapes of feast invocations and stone-dragging songs that his sons had recorded and studied. Deta Raya, his second son, had already more or less been designated as his successor in verbal skills. He had also already begun to assert himself as a prominent local personality, marrying more women than anyone else and then drawing on his extensive affinal networks when he campaigned to be elected the head of Waiha, the administrative ward of the interior of Balaghar.

I was cast in the role of apprentice and "daughter" to this older man, and people came to accept the fact that I paid him a small salary (equivalent to that of a primary school teacher) to come to my home three days a week to work on interpreting texts. The work that we did together began with working over collected materials, but often extended in new directions through our conversations. Stories or rites that Maru Daku knew himself we would transcribe together. Recorded texts that I got from someone else were submitted to his critical and interpretive ear. The ritual verses he used to explain our work present it as an almost archaeological excavation of matters that had been long hidden and need to be "cleaned" and "sifted through" like potentially poisonous cassava roots or bony small fish:

Maka na mburungo la ghobana	So it came down from her mouth
Ba na hama a tuku	The beating to a single beat
Maka na hyalongo la wiwina	So it bloomed from her lips
Ba na mera a bohe	The rowing to a single rhythm
Ole ndende do kinggia, bapa	Be my companion as I stand, father
A kaghero kamihiya	Digging up things which are buried deep
Mono a lunggero kalanaya	Opening bundles of coconut leaves
A hadana kere napu	The customs of the villages at the base
Ole londo do kinggia, bapa	Be my companion as I sit, father

A tepandi codo tana	Sifting the bitter root tubers
Mono a manihini byaghe loro	Cleaning the small river fish
A patana bali byapo	Of the ways of both sides of the bay
Maka ku ndara dola koko	So I was the horse following at the neck
Maka ku karambo manunduka	So I was the buffalo coming obediently along
Maka ku kedeka a kere nggu	So I lifted up my backside
Maka ku panggaka a witti nggu	So I stepped along with my feet
Ku pela nikya loro	I crossed over the river
La wuku wandi cana	The Wuku winding through the land
Maka ku dowa nikya menanga	I came over the bay
La rate woyo nggoko	By the spotted crocodile's grave
Ku tadi calo manu	I wore out the calves of my legs
Ba ku lara li pa linya	As I went along the road
A kalembu lingo winyo	Through the pinang groves and caves
Maka ku monggolo kadalikya	So I exhausted the backs of my knees
Ba ku annu li hamaneya	As I followed along the path
A' marada bala moro	Through fields of green millet

Here, the earlier description of my travels to come meet with him initially is replayed by emphasizing the long walks he made to come to see me. This passage, occurring as it does in a lament declaimed when he had contracted pneumonia, was meant to suggest to me that all this traveling weakened him physically and made him more vulnerable to disease. While emphasizing his devotion to our work and his willingness to walk so far, it was also scripted to make me feel guilty about the demands I placed on a frail old man. The descriptions of his exhaustion do have that effect, even now, as I read over them, and although he received antibiotics and eventually recovered from that illness, this passage makes me again painfully aware of the costs of the research that were born by others.

His position did not become official, however, until a feast I sponsored on my twenty-sixth birthday in April, where I took a Kodi name and publicly named him as my main teacher.

The Kodi name that I took was bestowed on me as something of a joke by an older woman who was my neighbor. She teased me about always wanted to write things down, and said I should be called Inya Tari Mbuku, which would mean (translated into Indonesian and pronounced in the third person) "mother looking for a book." The joke became so popular that I was regularly greeted with this name, which was also the name of various female ancestors. Since my own name was very hard to pronounce (and usually shortened and distorted to "Miss Jen"), widespread sentiment was that the Kodi name should be "feasted on" to make it known. When I began to make preparations for that celebration, I realized that Maru Daku was personally quite anxious that it would also be an occasion to publicly acknowledge his own role in my research.

He coached me to make a brief speech in verse, thanking my hosts for receiving me into their home and stating my own aims through a series of denials ("I am not a foreigner come to raid you or an outsider who steals children . . ."). Then he made his own speech, also in ritual couplets, which in effect dedicated the pigs and chickens that we fed to our guests to commemorating our collaboration:

A minye bandu bali lyoro	The duck woman from overseas
A keketo pahili nya	Decided to establish the position
A rawini ukuna byenge madu	In the way of our ancestors
Rou marupu hodi mono	Offering a packet of leaves (a chicken)
A minye ndeha bali cana	The waterfowl woman from across the land
Na koutaya a deke	Decided to lift me to the post
Na woloni patani lere dinya	With the rites of our forefathers
Pa ramu malla mono	Offering a young coconut shell and a
Pa rangga rabba	Piglet just reaching the trough

I was referred to as the "duck from overseas, the water fowl from across the land" because I come from another island, and traveled to Sumba (as these birds did) after it had already been inhabited. The chicken and pigs killed for the feast were presented in the modest language of sacrifice, where it is always necessary to belittle those gifts offered to the gods, since they can never really be worthy of their recipient. Through this description, the apparently secular feast that I gave on my birthday was transformed into a rite that celebrated Maru Daku as the supreme storyteller of his homeland and legitimated his position through his power to attract foreign researchers.

But even as I became aware of the sophisticated political maneuvers that surrounded our encounter, I was also falling under the spell of Maru Daku's skill as a storyteller. Nine months into my fieldwork, I was finally able to transcribe texts and interview directly in the Kodi language. Separated from the task of constant translation, I began to appreciate for the first time the verbal artistry and traditional knowledge of my teacher. By happy coincidence, his nephew was called back to government service just as our working relationship became more solid, and I started to see how Maru Daku was a magician with words.

His delight in conversation came not from outlining a long ritual protocol, as we had done for many of the past months, but from playing with the paradoxes of ritual verse—the occasionally complementary, usually opposing couplets of parallel meaning whose sense was suspended in a web of dualistic classifications. When I asked for a skeleton outline of a ceremony, I generally got just that: a skeleton, the bare bones of how one passes from one offering to another, with little life or sense to connect the parts. But when I asked him how to speak to the spirits, his small dark face would come alive, and he would recite long ceremonial orations, often quoting particular phrases from famous speakers and integrating them into texts of his own composition.

He presented me with long orations concerning my presence on the island, the eminent authorities in America who had sent me off "like a butterfly that they sent flying, like a bird that they set singing" to study Kodi customs, and the book that would eventually result from our efforts. In less formal sessions he would reminisce through a rich array of anecdotal material, picking out words and images that expressed specific social differences and tensions. While formal paired speech must always be used in addressing the ancestors and other deities, it is not exclusively a religious language. Maru Daku often allowed the couplets to surface in everyday conversation as a sort of rhetorical flourish.

He was also, I discovered, an inveterate gossip. Once I could recognize the names of a number of the key protagonists, I enjoyed his lively accounts of past feuds, vengeance killings, and quarrels over land or women. The precedents used in custom law to mediate such conflicts are expressed in ritual couplets, defining the supposedly unchanging character of the legal concepts that set the parameters for justice in Kodi terms. Because of his skill in ritual speech, as well as his age and social position as head of a prominent lineage, Maru Daku was often called to serve as a mediator at divorce negotiations, land disputes, and meetings to determine brideprice or blood compensation payments. His inside (and often privileged) information was an invaluable contribution to my research.

The longest sessions we undertook were all-night, myth-telling marathons, generally held at his house so that family members and relatives could hear them as well. I had previously recorded several myths from other people and had asked for Maru Daku's help in transcribing the prose sections and in interpreting the allusive poetic language of the songs. Most of them ended with long orations or funeral dirges, where the hero's whole past was recast in traditional couplets.

"Why don't you ever ask me to tell you my own stories?" he asked me petulantly one day. "I know several as good or even better than these." I dared not answer at the time that the trite morality of his earlier animal fables had bored me, compared to the challenges of these elaborate epics.

"I do want to hear your stories," I protested, and then, sensing that something more was needed, I realized that what I should also agree to was to hear them in the proper context. "And I will not ask you to tell them to me sitting here at my kitchen table. I will travel out to your ancestral village and spend the night there, so you can tell them all throughout the night. We will kill a chicken to ask permission of the ancestors, and you will be honored with the betel ceremony." I had remembered with a small pang his earlier remark about stories not traveling well in sacks.

Maru Daku's stories followed the format of other valued narratives in Kodi that are "owned" or "held" by a specific storyteller (see Hoskins 1993a: 82–86, and further examples in chapters three and five). In each myth an initial drama of sibling rivalry (or sibling incest) was resolved through the supernatural interference of one of the parents' souls, reincarnated in a wild animal, and then the hero would undertake a long journey through the seven levels of the sky to find an appropriate bride. All his former sufferings were then retold in elaborate poetic idiom to underscore his present achievements. My teacher claimed that he had hesitated to share any of the longer stories with me for fear that they would bore me (more likely, he feared that I would not be able to understand them). When at last he decided to give me the full-length narratives, I began to be aware of Maru Daku's mastery over the Kodi's rich verbal lore.

I continued to work with other informants on the days my teacher was not in town, supplementing his accounts of the ways of isolated Balaghar with those of ritual specialists from the more centrally located areas of Kodi Bokol and Bukambero. He resented my eclecticism and made a point of telling me that of all men he was the one most qualified to be my instructor on local custom. This was another reason he was frequently critical of the texts I gathered from other sources.

"Why do they pair these images with phrases that should not go with them?" he would complain to me, often suggesting changes in the structure of a passage or ways to vary its meter. His method of literary criticism was intriguing because it was so defiantly provincial, valuing most highly the turns of phrase used in Balaghar and disparaging the others as deviations from the ancestral pattern.

Clan histories, and especially the stories concerning the founding of ancestral villages, are volatile political issues in Kodi, as they provide charters for political prerogatives and ceremonial rank (Hoskins 1993a: 82–87). Competition among clans often worked to my advantage, since representatives of rival groups agreed to give me their own histories in detail, once I told them what Maru Daku had said to me about their position. Maru Daku's alliance with factions on the other side of the Bondo Kodi river caused many people to warn me against relying too heavily on his accounts. They frequently felt obliged to disclose new information to counterbalance what he had told me.

People were also suspicious of Maru Daku because of his ambiguous relationship to the Christian Church and to traditional ritual. "Yes, he can recite the pathway of the spirits, and he knows the ancestors of the various clans, but which way does he look in his own life?" people wondered. "Does he follow the rules of the house of the bitter day (the Christian Church) or does he sacrifice to the local spirits? For someone who was once a Protestant evangelist, he has no business having three wives and holding feasts to placate the deities of the sun and moon." This criticism came from both pagan traditonalists and Christian converts.

They were pointing to a division that ran right down the center of Maru Daku's life and also divided his family. His four older sons were known by Kodi names and sang offerings to the marapu, while the four younger ones were known by Christian names and were schoolteachers, civil servants, and students. Maru Daku was frankly torn between his interest in education, the West and Christianity, and his loyalties to the traditions of his forefathers.

During the course of my work with him, he outlined his life history to me on three different occasions, each time in a totally different way. The first time, shortly after we met, he spoke of his years of government service and his involvement with the outside world: his primary education at a Christian school, his year as Needham's field assistant, his exile to travel to four different islands after an accusation of gold theft, and his later position as coordinator for all of Balaghar, under the independent Indonesian state. The second time he spoke of his family: his four marriages (one of which ended in divorce) and a scandalous extramarital liaison with a woman of the same matriclan, the twelve children born to his first wife (eight sons surviving) and the one daughter born to his second wife. He had me record the names of each of his grandchildren and namesakes, as well as his own extensive genealogy. The third time, impressing me with still another dimension of his life, he told me his ritual history.

The ritual history was the story that was told through the vehicle of the betel bag, and it was, I believe, the most personal and meaningful of the narratives he gave me, the closest thing to an autobiographical rendering of his experiences.

"You see this bag?" he asked rhetorically, holding up a simple betel bag with no embroidery or decoration. "This is how I became a storyteller, this is where my words come from. My grandfather put them in here many years ago, and I go back to this bag if I forget them, if I forget the names of my ancestors, or if other members of my family forget the seeds we store there."

I will explore the meaning of the betel bag first in its very particular meanings for Maru Daku, as a vehicle for personal symbolism. As a ritual alter ego, his betel bag accompanied him in his training as a bearer of traditional knowledge, progressing through his participation in his father's feasts and finally his sponsorship of ceremonies in his own name. When he chose to "return" to the ancestral cult of his forefathers after a Christian education, he saw this as a return to the betel bag, but the reasons for that return were not simply a retreat into the past. On the contrary, his choice to live as a storyteller was a form of intellectual exploration, stimulated by outside influences that made him think again about the world where he grew up.

A LIFE CAUGHT IN THE POUCHES OF A BETEL BAG

Maru Daku was born Maru Mahemba, the first son of a prominent elder and feastgiver, just a few years before the Dutch achieved control of the western part of Sumba, in 1909. From 1911 to 1913 there was a violent uprising against the Dutch army, led by a famous warrior from Bondo Kodi, but the people of Balaghar refused to support the insurgents (Hoskins 1987,

1993a). Maru's father fought to defend Dutch authority on the island during three years of interclan warfare. Once they had won, the people of his homeland were rewarded with one of the first primary schools in Kodi: a small bamboo structure, presided over by a Christian Ambonese schoolmaster, in one of the ancestral villages along the coast.

Maru was a student in the fourth class to enter the school. After completing the first three grades, he was sent to continue his education in the neighboring region of Elopada. Although he had been recommended for a scholarship to attend teacher-training school, his family was reluctant to see him go. The school was in another language area, inhabited by traditional head-hunting rivals of the Kodinese, and he would have to board with a family of strangers. His grandfather, pretending that he needed the boy as an interpreter for a legal dispute, sent word through a messenger that Maru should return immediately. The real reason was that the old man was ailing and felt he did not have much longer to live. He wanted to designate his eldest grandson as his heir in ritual knowledge and verbal eloquence.

He took up his own betel bag, removed a knife from it and scraped off a bit of the fingernail of his right thumb, then mixed it with betel piper and areca nut, adding a dash of lime powder to turn it into a reddish quid. Then he called to his grandson with these words: "Do not go back to those foreign people. There is no one here to replace me in our clan village!" He placed the betel quid in Maru Daku's mouth with this verse (as he remembered it fifty years later):

Njaingo watu wu helu ali	No stones remain for the foundations
Na kikyoko a parona	Our village will be empty and lonely
Ba otu la hakola, ambu nggu	If you go off to school, my grandson
Mono a patera pa helu	And the words passed down generations
A paneghe pa kattu	The speech sewn into couplets
Tana ambu na mbunga	Must not disappear
A maghailo helu koko	You must be the rooster crowing in my place
Helu katanga piyo ela toko mbughu	Strutting about on top of the towering roofs
A pakode helu ndende	You must be the billy goat taking my spot
Helu ndende tanggoda piyo la panu hondi	Standing for me on top of the large stone graves
Kaco pa kadughu ngguni a paneghe ambu	The pointing stick that we extend out from the speech of our grandfathers
Kaloro pa lamenda nggumi a patera nuhi	The rope that we lengthen from the words of our forefathers

He then placed the betel bag in his grandson's hands, and signaled to him that he could keep it. Betel chewing is a practice reserved for adults. Starting to chew publicly marks the passage to social maturity, showing that a boy is old enough to sit in the front veranda for traditional negotiations and that a girl is sexually mature and old enough to marry. The gift of the betel bag designated Maru Daku as his successor and marked him as old enough to represent the family on important occasions.

The lontar-plaited betel bag that he received from his grandfather on that day remained in Maru Daku's possession until it crumbled and decayed. But although the fibers themselves were perishable (and could rarely last more than ten years), the significance of the gift was renewed through a substitute, a new bag made to "hold the words and the seeds of wisdom." His grandfather also gave him a lime flask made of buffalo horn and the small knife he used to trim tobacco leaf.

It was decided that day that Maru, the eldest son, would be trained in traditional speaking and customary lore, while his younger brother went on to further schooling and an eventual government job. In the last years of his grandfather's life, Maru was his companion and apprentice, learning from him a large and cherished store of traditional poetry and oral history. He returned to settle in his ancestral village and married a young woman named Daku. Following Kodi custom, her name was affixed to his, and he prepared to assume a leading position in his clan and lineage.

Yet his interest in education and the outside world continued, stirred by the first Protestant evangelists who came into the area, bringing stories from the Malay Bible. For Maru Daku Christianity was the doorway through which a much wider world could be apprehended. Since he was one of the only people in the region able to read the Bible, he was soon identified with the spreaders of the faith and often invited them to his home. In 1933, shortly after the birth of his first child, he and his wife both converted to Christianity, and he took the Christian name Martinus.

His enemies claimed that the conversion was also motivated by a fear of the traditional sanctions imposed by an oath he swore as a young man. A large gold pendant was stolen from a neighbor's house, and Maru Daku was accused of taking it. When government officials came to investigate, he defiantly declared his innocence, and swore publicly: "If I was the one who took this gold, let lightning come and strike me down!" The court was not convinced, and sentenced him to three years in exile. For the rest of his life, Maru Daku continued to protest that he did not take the gold, but I knew well that he was terrified of thunderstorms. Whenever thunder and lightning came, he would retreat, trembling, under a blanket and wait for them to pass. Later events would come to justify that terror.

Maru Daku continued to identify himself as a Christian during the three years he spent in exile from Sumba, traveling to towns on Flores, Roti, and Timor, where the new religion was already well established and had begun to take on a particularly Indonesian flavor. During those years he also heard the first stirrings of Indonesian nationalism, and he came to see his own customs as only one way of articulating the widespread themes of exchange and reciprocity, honor and social position.

After his return to Kodi, officials of the local church invited him to work with them as a village evangelist. He was able to translate the Malay Bible verses into Kodi ritual couplets, and these verbal skills were important in spreading the Word to isolated areas. In return he was given a small salary and a prestigious link with the authority of the Dutch Church.

His work as an evangelist was restricted during the Japanese occupation, but afterward it continued for more than a decade, taking him throughout the district to explain the Christian view of the world and the laws set down by the church. He also led prayer meetings and presided over Christian ritual feasts, often held for the same reasons as marapu singing ceremonies: to ask for divine help during a long illness or after a misfortune, to bring the Christian God to a new hamlet site, or to consecrate a house or commemorate a death. He told me the need for spiritual mediation came to all people at these times, only the names of the deities addressed and the language used had to be changed.

In 1952 Maru Daku experienced the first overt confrontation between the values of the church and his own family tradition. One of his fellow clansmen had received a Christian burial near the house of the raja. When plans were made to enlarge the raja's kitchens, Maru Daku and his kinsmen decided to dig up the bones and bring them back to their village to be buried in the ways of their ancestors. Members of the local church council forbade the move, maintaining that a church burial was final and no Christian should be pulled back into paganism after his death.

> I told them that in this matter there were three powers at work: the power of the government, the power of the family, and the power of the church. Here, the power of the government [in the person of the raja who had authorized the move] and the power of the family were agreed that our traditions demanded reburial in the clan village of our ancestors. No clan brother of ours could lie underneath the floors of someone else's kitchen. So we simply dug up the bones and left with them. Ever since then I have been refused from the communion table in church. The Bible also tells you to respect the ways of your fathers, but the members of the church council did not understand that.

The quarrel between Maru Daku and the church leadership intensified a few years later. He decided to take a second wife, openly flouting the rules against polygamy that the Sumbanese church had such difficulty enforcing. Although that particular union lasted only two years, he remarried two more times. His sons later followed his lead, marrying often and extensively, which set up a network of affinal ties across the pagan community but undermined one of the only signs of church authority in everyday life.

Maru Daku's skills as a storyteller offered him a new kind of legitimation when foreign researchers came to the island in the 1950s. In 1951–52 he assisted the famous Dutch scholar FAE. Van Wouden in a two-month field survey (Van Wouden 1956 [1977]). Two years later, he spent a full year working with the Englishman Rodney Needham (Needham 1957, 1960).

Both men seem to have been well pleased with his native intelligence and curiosity, and with his familiarity with people on other islands who lived as followers of traditional religions—Christians or Muslims—made him sensitive to differences and variations. He also began to fancy the role of researcher as one that could dignify his lifelong interest in Kodi traditions. A researcher or "assistant" would be able to attend a large number of marapu ceremonies without casting any doubts on his loyalty to Christian ideals.

Soon a small, leather-bound book of notes began to be toted about in his betel bag, mixing the older receptacle of words with a new way of recording them. Maru Daku began keeping this notebook during his year as Needham's field assistant, and carried it with him virtually every day in the early 1980s. As the first Kodi person to write down formal procedures for ritual adjudication, he created a rule book that was referred to at the resolution of important legal disputes. He was asked to bring it to the regency capital of Waikabubak for a conference on custom and land tenure in 1969. He began to develop a role for himself as an authority on Kodi traditions and a culture broker who moved between the world of ancestral mandates and the modern government bureacracy. To signal the shift he switched from wearing the Western costume of the church and office (trousers and a button-down shirt) to the homespun indigo loincloth and bark headband of his forefathers.

At the 1969 conference he scored a victory for the official recognition of traditional costume. Along with other elders, he showed up wearing a loincloth, headband, shoulder-slung betel bag and long tobacco-cutting knife strapped to his waist. Local officials announced that a new ordinance had been passed to ban the wearing of bush knives in the city. The ordinance was designed to reduce the incidence of violent quarrels, since these eighteen-inch knives were often swung about in verbal confrontations and could cause serious wounds or death. Maru Daku told them that each Sumbanese man needed three personal accessories to mark his "essential manhood" (Ind. *perlengkapan laki-laki Sumba*), so it would be impossible for him to remove his bush knife, headband, or betel bag in a formal context. Government officials agreed to waive the rule only for recognized authorities on traditional custom (*petua adat*).

The prestige Maru Daku acquired by serving outsiders prompted him to re-evaluate his own heritage, since these people had traveled so far to study it. Although he still considered himself a Christian, he had quarreled with the church leadership and was increasingly involved in organizing traditional ceremonies. His father had died without dragging a large tombstone fit for the burial of an important man. Maru, as the oldest son, was now charged with gathering together the labor and sacrificial animals required for the task. He had to assume formal leadership of his own ancestral house and gather support from his fellow clansmen and affines.

After the stone had been dragged and consecrated with a full-scale feast, his lineage house fell into disrepair. The social and material expenses of reconstructing these high, towered, bamboo-and-thatch dwellings make the size and condition of the lineage house a good index of the strength and unity of the lineage itself. By 1957 Maru Daku had returned to service as a government clerk, but he was walking back to his homeland in Balaghar almost daily to oversee work on the house to honor his ancestors. This effort was to culminate in a tragic confirmation of all the rumors and suspicions that had surrounded his life.

The frame was finished in October, the end of the Kodi ceremonial season, and guests were invited from all over the region to tie the thatch and celebrate the roof-raising with a feast. To the beat of drums and gongs, men danced in warrior costume and tossed up bundles of elephant grass to be lashed onto the tower. By evening the work was completed, and people were ready to enjoy a meal of twenty-four pigs and eleven water buffalo. Just as the meat was being carved up and distributed, a sudden thunderstorm broke.

In one amazing instant the twenty-five-foot tower of newly secured thatch was set ablaze by lightning. The house, filled with guests, fine cloth, and valuables, was consumed by the blaze almost immediately, and flames were carried by the wind to a second house, which also burned to the ground. Meat dedicated to the deities was never properly distributed, but simply burned up. Fifty people were burned as the blaze spread to the crowd.

Amid all the screaming and confusion, two people were caught inside and perished: Maru Daku's younger brother, the only member of the family who had continued his education in Christian secondary schools, and Mali Ambu, a lineage brother of the only native Kodi minister. In one night the lineage houses of the two earliest converts in Balaghar were destroyed, and two of their number were killed.

Had the marapu spirits refused to sanction the rebuilding of the lineage house? Was the lightning bolt a sign of the anger of the ancestors at the corruption of their rites by Christians? Or was it a delayed punishment for a false oath about stealing gold which Maru Daku made as a young man? Lightning is said to be sent by Ra Hupu, a vengeful, fire-breathing ancestor who punishes violators of traditional law. Followers of the marapu cult debated which of these reasons was most convincing.

Members of the Christian church council interpreted the events in an equally damning but opposite sense. True converts had no business rebuilding lineage houses, so the lightning came from the righteous anger of the Christian God. Maru Daku explained their reaction in these words:

> They said of me that I was trying to worship in two different systems, and so I would suffer the fury of both sides. The marapu were mad at me for reading from the Bible, but because of my quarrel with the church leaders the Christian God would not protect me either. They said that it was only my own pride and vanity that brought about my destruction, because I was seeking to make a name for myself in both worlds.

The complete destruction of his lineage house, the first feast held in his own name, and his younger brother's death had an understandably severe impact on Maru Daku. Crushed by the weight of supernatural disapproval, he resigned his post as government clerk and tried to put his life back in order. He gathered together his remaining kin to bury what charred remains they could at the gateway to the clan village, since victims of a sudden, violent death cannot be brought in among the ancestors until their souls have been called back from the sun and moon. He also committed himself to carry out the elaborate series of rituals required, although he realized he might not be able to fulfill this promise for many years. He accepted the system of payments of debts and obligations to the dead that takes up so much of Kodi life:

> The rebuilding of the lineage house was something I owed to my father, that I had promised to him and to the spirits before his death, just as I had bound myself to drag a gravestone for him. The singing ceremonies and larger feasts to bring down my brother's soul were also a personal debt contracted by the way he died, which I could not fail to pay for the sake of my own honor and well-being. Some people say that we sponsor feasts for our own renown, to make our names great and assure that they will not vanish with the coming generations. But I have put my words and ideas into the white man's books where they will live on after me. So all these feasts were not motivated by personal vanity but are also the discharging of debts that bind me to dead kinsmen whose calls I cannot deny.

His participation in anthropological research was presented as a direct substitute for seeking renown in feasting, but in fact he was again trying to do both: to be remembered as a leader in his ancestral village and as its interpreter to the outside world.

The soul of Maru Daku's burned brother had to be called back with his betel bag (or a newly constructed substitute, given his name), which is placed along with a headcloth and a bush knife on a small bamboo ladder (*pahere*) erected in front of the right corner of the house. The betel bag is said to catch his soul in its pouch when it falls down, accompanied by a loud crashing noise, from the heavens. In Kodi, the rite cannot be held until seven years have passed since the death. For Maru Daku, it was prompted by dreams in which he heard his younger brother pleading for a proper burial and the return of his soul and personal accessories.

In 1965, a new betel bag, headcloth, and bush knife were made, and the first singing ceremony (*yaigho*) was held to try to call back his soul. A famous singer from another clan and two ritual orators were invited to plead all night with the deities of the sun and moon to let his lost soul out of their grip and allow not only the human victim but also the souls of the burned house and sacrificed animals to come down.

Tana hamburingo a uma inya uma bapa	So let us bring down the house of mothers house of fathers
Uma tara manu, uma ule wawi	House of rooster's spurs, house of pig tusks
Hila inya kadu wulla	From hanging on the horns of mother moon
Hola bapa kere lodo	From being stuck at the edge of father sun
Yaigho ela kabihu ba wemu	We sing prayers at the house corner to ask you
Tana hamburuni a kamuri ari Iyoro kalora ari byaba	To bring down the last child at the hip the middle child at the lap
Na kahonga witti wyulla	Who rides the feet of the moon
Na kalete limya lodo	Who sits astride the hand of the sun
Ola lombo ali pariara	At the end of the brilliant rainbow
Ola kere awango hada	At the edge of the colorful sky
Ngarana napingo kalimbyo lali myone	All those who rest on outcroppings of male land
Tana hena bandikya la tundu kabihu	Let them come back along the corner's edge
Ngara na lunango kandoki loko tana	All those who pillow their heads on dry river beds
Tana hena bandikya la tane karangga	Let them return on the roof crossbeam
Tana a ndewa touna no bandikya ela katu pa kalele	So their souls can return to the protective stone circle
Tana a ura dadinya no banikdya ela watu pa kalibye	So their birth crowns can come back to the ring of rock foundations

The calls fell on deaf ears. These prayers, repeated in a dialog format and then set to the rhythm of the drums and gongs, were sung all night long, but the spirit ladder did not shake with the impact of a soul descending, nor did flashes of light appear in the sky or footprints in the ashes at the base. The trapped souls had not been released by the marapu, but guests still had to be fed. Four tusked pigs were speared and a single buffalo slaughtered. Their livers were examined to see why the rite had failed. Diviners said the procedures would have to be repeated on a larger scale.

The family tried to merge this obligation with others, to share the tremendous expense. At rites to establish a garden hamlet at Kalalapo, consecrate a new house, and drag a tombstone for his own grave, Maru Daku made additional entreaties to the deities to let go of the soul they "grasped as the wing, held in the armpit." He re-entered government service as the head of the administrative ward of Waiha. In 1977, he and his clan brothers planned a major feast to move the bones of many people who had been provisionally buried in the gardens into the ancestral village and consecrate the finished tombstone. More than forty buffalo were to be slaughtered and the meat was to be distributed to more than 1,000 guests.

Seven days before, a singing ceremony was held to announce their intentions to the deities and invite them to attend. The singer described all the saving and suffering over the past decade, the hardships that people had endured to make this occasion possible, and called again to the sun and moon. The betel bag named for the lost brother was brought out of storage and bound to the spirit ladder with the headcloth and bush knife. Briefly the morning star seemed to flash in anticipation, but the ashes remained untouched. Convinced he was close to achieving his goal, Maru Daku called the priests back for a second appeal four days later. He hoped the promise of a major feast would persuade the marapu of his sincerity, so the souls of his brother and lineage house could attend the feast in their honor.

The singing lasted until the early hours of dawn. Maru Daku had dozed off in the back of the house when the word finally got through to the invisible listeners. "It has come!" spectators yelled, pointing to what they described as a great disc of light that fell with a thud near the site of the burned house. Running to the spot, the chief priest shouted eagerly, "We've won! The house has come down!"

About half an hour later, after the singing had resumed, the spirit ladder began to shake violently, and the betel bag, knife, and headcloth slipped into the ashes at its base. "The soul has pushed it down! The soul is in the bag again!" they shouted. People found traces of two men's footprints and many pigs and buffalo—all those who had perished in the blaze and been unable to find their final rest.

The ritual cycle demanded by the ancestors was finished. At the larger celebration that followed, all the members of the ancestral village of Wainjolo Wawa were able to rejoice in the lifting of the weight of obligation from their shoulders. The betel bag that had hung on the spirit ladder was placed, along with the headcloth and bush knife, in a stone tomb that also held the bones of Maru Daku's great grandfather. It marked the final resting place of his brother's soul and allowed him to be transformed into an ancestor. As he told me in 1980:

> Before we brought down all the souls of those who died in the fire, we would never have been able to rebuild our lineage house. Our descendants would have had no place to make offerings to their ancestors, and we would be ashamed to receive guests from outside the clan at any large feasts. Now, their souls have come back among us from the upperworld so that weight has been lifted.

The burial of his brother's betel bag closed off one chapter in Maru Daku's life and allowed him to celebrate his victorious reintegration into the world of marapu spirits. Standing now at the head of a large lineage and serving as the ranking elder for his whole ancestral village, he had firmly re-established himself in the traditional sphere. People now said that after death he could be referred to by the title *rato*, a sign of the respect and admiration reserved for a man known not only for his wealth and generosity in feast giving but also for his verbal skills, daring, and mastery of local custom.

At the time of my departure in 1981, Maru Daku and his sons were making plans to rebuild the lineage house so that it faced a new slaughter field (*nataro*), where dancing and offerings could be made and many more people could participate in ceremonial events. The new field would be known as the *nataro rato Maru*, providing yet another physical symbol of the extent of his fame and influence in Balaghar.

Maru Daku's achievements in ancestral ritual only further damned him in the eyes of the Christian community, however. They referred to him as a *murtad*, "apostate." Stories came back to them of instances where he had served as a ritual orator, pronouncing the invocations made with scattered rice to dedicate sacrificial animals. They said he was no longer simply a witness or recorder of Kodi traditions, but an adherent in the full sense of the word. In the traditional verse of ritual speech, they said:

Na pangani jalo nani	He is swimming down too deep
a walla watu kaka	among the swirling pebbles in the surf
Na panene jeta nani	He is trying to climb too high
a tenda rou kamoto	on the bough of kamoto leaves

He had, in other words, "gone too far." If he had finally made his peace with the ghosts of his closest kin, there was no longer any place for him the house of the Christian Lord.

The rejection came in the later 1970s, but in the 1980s the church began to liberalize. The last Dutch minister had returned to Holland fifteen years before, and the organization was now run by native clergy, who tended to be more tolerant of the customary obligations binding each Kodi person to participate in the feasts of his kin group. No longer were Christians forbidden to eat the meat dedicated to the marapu. Native ministers even sang songs of encouragement at stone draggings and kept track of ritual food distributions.

Almost thirty years after his censure by the Christian community, a new chance was extended to Maru Daku because of his prominent social role. Although he was guilty of the sin of polygamy, a recent regulation allowed men of advanced years and positions of leadership in the community to return to communion without losing their wives. They had only to promise not to marry again and to allow their children to be raised as Christians. The former raja, himself an errant ex-evangelist who had married five times, sponsored a large Easter feast at his house to celebrate the first time in three decades that he would be able to consume the blood and body of Christ. Maru Daku, as his friend and an important traditional figure, was invited to join him.

But when the church council came to visit and inquire whether he too wished to walk down to the table and partake of the Christian sacrament, he declined. "You can eat your bread and drink wine in the foreign style," he told them, "but I will stay on the sidelines and chew betel. I have nothing against the Christian religion, and I have encouraged my sons to follow it and baptize their children as well. But it is not the way for myself, as my own life has demonstrated."

The betel bag had played a central role in Maru Daku's inheritance of his verbal skills from his grandfather and in his recovering the soul of his brother burned at the feast. On one other occasion, which also focused on problems in the transmission of patrilineal privileges and obligations, did the betel bag play a central role. That occasion concerned his efforts to control his son while he was serving as government coordinator for the region of Balaghar in 1961.

Deta Raya was rumored to be part of a livestock-stealing racket that was taking buffalo and horses off to distant pasture named Peda Manu where they were sold for export to Arab traders. Realizing that his son was probably guilty but not wanting to confront him directly, Maru Daku decided instead to invite Deta Raya, his favorite son, to a singing ceremony where the marapu spirits would be asked for assistance to put an end to the problem of people's animals disappearing. He instructed the orators to ask all the participants to commit themselves with their mouths—to agree that in accepting betel and areca, or rice and water, they would renounce stealing. If they did not comply, the delicious foods that they took in would turn to poison in their bellies.

Mata doni la mata	Look now with your eyes
Tana doni la tilu	Listen now with your ears
Ngara na tunu hodekongo malogho la kamoto	All of you who secretly roast mice caught at the edge of the gardens
Ngara na palo pipicongo kamboko la kaleku	All of you who stealthily sneak pike fish in your pouches
Nai jongo na ngguku la hadembya na here la kacoka	Those who have escaped the mousetrap and avoided the bird net
Tana ba na mu a ngagha	So eat this rice now and let it be
Mono ngagha bombo witti	Rice to inflame the feet [if guilty]
Tana ba na inu a weiyo	So drink this water now and let it be
Mono weiyo pogho kambu	Water to swell up the stomach
Mu nikya a ngagha mangu ndombona	Eat the rice full of disease
Inu nikya weiyo mangu nggenggena	Drink the water full of spiders

Deta Raya heard these words and, of course, understood their meaning completely. At the end of the rite, he rose to speak and turned to address his father with a statement of contrition that explicitly used the metaphor of the betel bag. Understanding that he had embarrassed his father because a government official should not have to help arrest his own son, he testified that he would now be obedient and respectful. Without ever openly confessing, he accepted responsibility for his acts and promised they would not be repeated:

Ba ku kaleku halili	Let me be the betel pouch tucked in the armpit
Mono kukato paloloni	and the chicken's nest carried about
Ba ku ole mateni mono	Let me be your companion in death and
ole mopironi	your companion in life
Ba ku tonda pa hanggeroni	Let me be the shield held at the shoulder
Ba ku nambu pa lembani	Let me be the spear resting on the back
	of the neck

The declaration brought about a reconciliation between father and son and put an end to a period of great strain. Although Maru Daku indicated that his stern words were helped by violent attacks on the livestock rustlers when they tried to move the stolen animals into Gaura, he did think that these reminders of the obligations that bind fathers and sons and their relation to betel bags had an impact.

An expert at indirection and verbal manipulation, Maru Daku nevertheless also felt that he had been the victim of resentment and manipulation himself, particularly on the part of people who resented his work with foreign researchers. The long verse statement that he recorded at my house in 1981 finishes with a reflection on why many people were made uncomfortable by the position he established with me.

Many people, he noted, wondered why he should make such efforts to walk all the way to Bondo Kodi at his age. "The horse is already old, the dog is already ancient" (*na malupuka a ndara, na kawedaka a bangga*), they said, so what is he doing it for? He protested that his association with anthropologists did not make him dependent or make him neglect his usual obligations: "I do not lean my head back to rest / on the white person's coconut grater / I do not settle my chin comfortably / on the rough tubers" (*Njaku pangada la tanguloya / a kiri jawa kaka / Nja ku pakatulako pa toriya / a lugha kaka alo*). But he also argued that his wider goals in sharing his words with me were misunderstood. He did not seek material gain or fame in the present, but the immortality of the person whose speech lives on and travels far:

Nengyo pa tagheghe anga	The reason the forest fowl has
ate nggu	hidden in his liver
Nengyo pa malogho anga	The reason the mouse has concealed
koko nggu	in his throat
Uru la handoyo mara tana	Is that after a year of dry seasons
Nangga wudi jadi doyo	Like the jackfruit planted in time
A ngara nggu inde moho	My name will not have vanished
La ha wu kalanda tana	From this one stretch of land
Uru la hawunga wulla nale	And after a year of rainy months
Na wulla wudi hyungga do kiyo	Like the moon that appears anew
A ngara nggu inde mboghi	My name will not dissolve
La ha wu kabihu watu	From this one corner of stones

Maru Daku would have liked to travel to America and other places well beyond the boundaries of his own island and region. But he recognized that it was no longer possible. What he asked of me, as we worked together writing down his stories and critiquing those of others, was that his words make the journey for him: His experiences, and the poetic images that he used to describe them, would take his place in traveling back with me "across the deep seas and over the wide oceans" so that his own perspective would reach others who lived far away.

When I was packing to leave, I realized he *had* given me a story in a sack, despite his protestations. My bags were full of notebooks where I had inscribed his words, and now I would carry them away to be unpacked and translated, reinscribed and reprinted in other packages. The modern reproducibility of stories has made them portable but has also famously diminished the art of storytelling. Instead of the mutual engagement of the narrator and audience, we now have more solitary forms of reading or listening to mass-produced information (Benjamin 1969: 83). Stories are not given as personal gifts, caught in a betel bag or held by a particular descent line, which allow for the exchange of experiences along culturally structured lines.

Benjamin argued that in the modern era "the communicability of experience is decreasing" (1969: 207) since we no longer seek counsel in stories. But this view may paint a somewhat falsely nostalgic view of "traditional" societies like Kodi, where storytelling is still of great importance, but experience is not always so reciprocal and shared. In particular, this book examines the ways in which experience is separated along gendered lines and objects are implicated in the sexual politics of their owners.

The stories that Maru Daku received in the betel bag were part of a patrilineally transmitted patrimony. Their container, however, was one of the least gendered objects in Kodi: The betel bag, even in its most prestigious, bark-embroidered form, is virtually identical for men and women.[2] Since it was so deeply penetrated by his personality, even in its most intimate recesses, it became a surrogate self. For Maru Daku, that meant that the bag became a sack for souls and stories. For someone else (even his own wives, whose story follows in the next chapter) it might instead be an empty container, an icon of neglect and sexual frustration.

Recent, detailed studies of the symbolism of objects in traditional societies of Pacific Asia have highlighted the fact that "apparently contradictory world views can be expressed through the same material culture object" (MacKenzie 1991: 201). Debates about the meanings of string bags and gender in New Guinea have focused attention on the complex ways maleness and femaleness are represented through things that can be kept or exchanged. To better understand how the betel bag served as an extension and expression of Maru Daku's identity as a storyteller, we must first describe the attributes of Kodi betel bags and examine why he chose the simplest, unadorned style. Then we can look at the wider context of attempts to understand the relation between gendered persons and possessions.

THE CHOICE OF A BETEL BAG

Kodi betel bags are of two kinds. The simpler one, the *kaleku mboro*, is plaited by women out of lontar leaves (Indonesian *daun gewang*) and carried over the shoulder with a piece of orange cloth. It can also be embroidered with hand-spun thread, usually in a simple zigzag line along the top and reinforcing the corners. In other parts of Sumba, these betel bags are made of plaited pandanus leaves and decorated with commercial colored thread (Geirnaert-Martin 1992b: 64). Such bags are sometimes sold at the market in Kodi, but people do not think much of them.

The term *kaleku mboro* also designates a slave girl, who carries her mistress's betel bag and attends to her personal needs—bathing her, dressing her, combing her hair, but not performing any of the manual labor of ordinary slave women (fetching firewood or water). The metaphor of the betel bag indicates that the slave girl is her mistress's most intimate companion, and in a sense the ultimate personal possession.

The more expensive and elaborate betel bag is the *kaleku kahu*, embroidered with bark-cloth string dyed black with a mixture of indigo and other roots. A fine bark-embroidered betel bag is very valuable, and is sold with the price of a horse (*wali njara*). The finest bags have a very dense, geometric pattern, which forms a dark background to define, as if in a photographic negative, triangles and squares that run in lines across its surface. Three "rooms" (*koro*) or squares occupy the central field of the betel bag, with a top and bottom border of two rows of triangles. The "rooms" are separated by "walls" of vertical lines (*hurato ndende*) arranged within the three fields. The terminology suggests that the betel bag is a miniaturized version of the house, a sort of house for the soul, which is carried around by its owner.

The use of bark fiber to decorate the bag can be interpreted as a tie to origins. The Sumbanese say the first ancestors wore only bark cloth, as a loincloth for men and stiff sarung for women. Cotton clothing has been preferred for most everyday use for at least a century, but during the Japanese occupation (when cloth imports were stopped), many people had to return to the older technology. After independence, the new Indonesian government issued an edict asking men to cut their hair and not to wear bark-cloth garments in public, at markets, or feasts.[3]

Bark loincloths are still worn today by older men when they work in the gardens, fish, or hunt with traditional weapons (the spear, bush knife, and blowpipe). Wild animals are believed to be able to recognize the sounds of a hunter dressed in decorated textiles, but a man in only a loincloth can approach them in silence. I knew no women who wore bark-cloth sarungs, but women can use bark cloth to form the crests of headpieces worn for dancing. The yellow or red bark cloth is tied tight across the forelock (*katipya mandi myata*) so that it hangs directly over the location of the *hamaghu*, or female life spirit. The counterpart male dancing headdress is a long, cotton cloth wrapped not only around the head but also under the jaw (*katali ngenge ngorana*) so that it forms a peak at the crown, where the *ndewa* or male soul is found. Nowadays younger people use cardboard or rolled paper to stuff inside commercial colored cloth, folded in a central flounce and bound across the forehead.

Bark cloth was once used to wrap corpses for burial, with the cotton funeral shroud placed on top of the earlier ancestral covering. A bark loincloth was worn by young boys recovering from circumcision at a secluded hut near the river, but circumcision is now no longer practiced in Kodi.[4] The idea that the stiff, upright tufts of bark cloth which project up to half a meter above the head represent masculinity and virility is often stated. Since a firm headcloth "shows that you are a man" (*tanda kabani*), it is the favored material for the peaked head wraps worn by some elders and priests. A man's head wrap is a rigorously personal item of clothing that is also associated with many taboos, especially if it is made with traditional methods (Keller 1993: 256–59).

The process of making bark cloth must be performed exclusively by men. Bark cloth is made by soaking bark for many hours, then beating it, drying it, and stretching it. The largest bark-cloth item in common use today is a loincloth made from tei kahilye bark, which is suspended over the hearth and grasped by a woman in childbirth. Women's skills in weaving and sewing are explicitly juxtaposed to men's skills in beating bark fibers smooth in a couplet ("beating bark, piercing cloth": *patutu kamballa, pakattu karewe*) that defines the everyday division of sexual labor. Only a few older men still know how to make bark cloth today, however. These are also often skilled at embroidering the bags, and their production of bark-fiber cord is probably the liveliest surviving element of bark-cloth technology.

Maru Daku said that he chose the simplest form of betel bag because his grandfather's bag had been simple, and each new bag that he made was intended as a replica of the bag in which he first received "his words." I accept this interpretation, but think that the associations he wanted to invoke are somewhat more complex.

Plain, totally undecorated bags are sometimes seen as appropriate for older people, since the absence of colors and patterns shows that they are detaching themselves from the world. The very old are sometimes encouraged to renounce all commercially produced products and elaborate clothing to show they have accepted thir transformation into ancestors. The lack of ornamentation may indicate a resignation to approaching death. It can also mark the special office of a ritual specialist, who is less concerned with matters of worldly prestige.

Most of the priests and ritual specialists that I knew, however, carried bark-embroidered betel bags (see the cover photograph of Ra Holo, the high priest of the calendrical rites). These bags represented, for them, their own engagement in the world and the passion with which they clung to life. One notable exception was a diviner and orator, Rangga Pinja, who had become blind. I attended a stone dragging in 1980 when he could still see, and I photographed him with an elaborate, bark-embroidered bag, but when I returned and met him at a funeral divination in 1988, he had renounced it for the simple style of bag. People explained to me that he had lost his sight because "he no longer wanted to see." His son had been accused of stealing, and he was so embarrassed his eyes clouded up so he would not have to confront his son's accusers.

I think that Maru Daku valued the simple, lontar betel bag as a badge of detachment, a sign that he could turn away from malicious gossip and concentrate on higher things. It was also an unspoken reply to those who saw him as greedy or self-serving in his work with foreigners. The bark-cloth fiber embroidery is associated with the search for renown (*kandaba ngara*), a campaign for prestige and public recognition that he came to reject. While the associations with virility and ancestral origins were no doubt attractive to him, he was more concerned to show his distance from trivial concerns, and I think this reason is ultimately what completed his motivations for the choice he made.

CULTURE IN A BETEL BAG VS. A NET BAG

The theoretical terrain linking objects and gender constructs was substantially redefined by the famous debate between Annette Weiner and Marilyn Strathern about the meaning of New Guinea net bags. In a somewhat polemical exchange, Weiner criticized Strathern for neglecting the importance that women's net bags might have in women's exchange and trade (1976: 13). Strathern replied with an iconoclastic vengeance, insisting that "there is no such thing as woman," or an object that is intrinsically identified with women. While net bags were important in New Guinea exchange, they simply did not bear the cultural meanings Weiner claimed for Trobriand grass skirts and banana bundles: "What it means to be a woman in this or that situation must rest to some extent on the cultural logic by which gender is constructed" (1981: 683). Objects cannot be so easily read or identified simply through the process of manufacture and exchange.

A later study of Melanesian net bags suggests that behind this polemic lie important methodological problems for the study of the significance of things (MacKenzie 1991). Many bags made of string net are initially produced by women and then (like the *kaleku kahu*) decorated and elaborated by men, especially in the western highlands. This form of multiple authorship does not erase the productive contribution of women but provides an additional sacred dimension to an androgynous object. The overall form of the bag is traditional and local, but new techniques of looping or knotting are now associated with a pan-Melanesian identity. The gender ambiguity of the net bag both parallels and contrasts with the Indonesian betel bag and its specifically Kodi incarnation using bark fiber.

I argue that Kodi betel bags are not androgynous but double gendered, because they must contain both male and female elements to be complete.

Since the same styles and patterns are worn by both men and women, the bags are not identifiable as masculine or feminine. They are produced by a combination of female and male labor, since only women plait the lontar leaves, but only men embroider the plaited bags. But though their production is similar to that of Melanesian net bags, their contents are not: All over Indonesia, sirih pipers are seen as masculine (in part because of their phallic appearance), while the round, juicy areca nut is feminine. This association seems even to hold true in areas where it is more commonly the sirih leaf, rather than the piper, that is chewed. Betel containers are traditionally interpreted as images of complementarity and dualism and are necessary for all forms of traditional hospitality and especially courtship.

If the net bag in Papua New Guinea does seem to represent women, but it is then the differing constructions of "womanness" in different societies that must be probed, the betel bag in Indonesia seems to represent a conjunction of male and female—but exactly how that conjunction works remains to be established. Keane, writing about the Sumbanese domain of Anakalang, provides a clue to this puzzle when he notes that the betel bag is the "most common instrument of everyday sociality," and thus "seems to embody the boundary and mutual dependence between persons" (Keane 1997: 265).

The betel bag as a "sack for the soul" on Sumba provides a site for the display of dualistic notions of gender identity. Onvlee (1973: 35) describes the Weyewa betel bag as "container for the soul" (*ndewadanja*) and notes that it shares the attributes of other personal possessions in oscillating at times from one gendered polarity to another. Geirnaert-Martin says Laboya bags contain both the ancestral soul (*dewa*) and the vital spirit or breath (*mawo*) of their owner (1992b: 61). Kodi theories of the person explicitly identify the ancestral soul (*ndewa*) as the product of the father creator who formed the hard skull of the crown (Bapa Rawi Lindu), and the vital spirit or breath (*hamaghu*) with the mother creator who bound the hair at the forelock (Inya Wolo Hungga). Thus, each person is made of male and female parts that are joined together in his or her body in an initial doubling of gender. The betel bag replicates that two-sidedness because it brings together both male and female elements.

The betel bag is also a hollow container (and thus an apparently female cavity) that contains a long cylindrical bamboo tube, the lime flask or *katimbu katagha*. Lime is stored as a white powder, which is emptied onto the palm and then tossed into the mouth to "quicken" the quid and turn the combined juices fiery red. This "quickening action" is explicitly compared to the effect of sperm on the coagulated blood of a fetus: It is a male ingredient that "brings the quid to life," just as sperm is believed to "bring the fetus to life" in the mother's belly in about the fifth month of pregnancy. The parallels between the effects of lime on betel and the effects of sperm on fetuses are explicitly spelled out in prayers spoken to help a similar process of "quickening" the dyes in the indigo pot (where lime is added as a mordant), as the production of dark blue dye is compared to the production of children in the womb (Hoskins 1989b). The lime flask, sometimes ornamented with a scratched design, or made of wood or buffalo horn, is the "husband" (*laghi*) of the betel bag, the companion and counterpart that completes the object by including both genders among the containers as well as the contents.

The betel bag is a double-gendered object, but it can be deployed in local sexual politics in ways that privilege one gender over another one. Maru Daku's use of his betel bag was, I would argue, a masculine use. It demonstrated a man's privilege to command attention and compel, if not obedience, at least an audience. Although women carry bags that look very much the same as those men carry, they cannot use them in the same ways. Women's stories (as we will see in the next chapter) show a process of identification with the objects exchanged—cloth, pigs, livestock, gold ornaments—rather than a mastery over them. Betel quids play a role of at least equal importance in the women's stories that follow in the next chapter, since they speak of courtship, adultery, love magic, poisons, and many other "domestic" concerns. The woman's view of the betel bag does not relate to patrilineal transmission or continuity over the generations. Instead, it speaks to the paradox of intimacy and betrayal, closeness established and then violated. It is a domestic politics rather than an ancestral one.

These differences can be best established by reporting a conversation I heard between men and women concerning the symbolism of betel bags.

POLYGAMY AND THE EMPTY BETEL POUCH

"We admit that many wives are hard to manage," chortled Maru Daku in a playful exchange with Raja Horo. "I've had three, you've had five. Each of us has had a lot of trouble, but it is only because we loved women too much."

His companion nodded and added, "We know that you Westerners do not do it. You divorce and remarry, divorce and remarry. But we ... well, even if our gaze wanders to a new woman, we do not lose all our love for the old one. We still care for her, look after her, visit her, even give her some sirih pipers for her pouch. But the wives are never happy with that!"

"Polygamy is condemned by the church. It was why we were kicked out. But we have always thought of it as the sin of love. Women do not understand how men can love them, even several of them. They say love cannot be divided. I say, pick up sirih piper. Notice that before you chew it, you break it off. You can divide it into many parts. Each piece will turn red in the mouth."

An older woman whispered angrily in the dark: "Yes, each piece will be red in the mouth, but who gets the sharp, firm tip of the piper? Who gets the soggy trunk? Do not tell me you can ever divide the fruit equally!"

One of the old men replied: "The best match is the one that is like the areca nut divided into two halves. The man is the inverse of his wife. If the areca nut can be cut in two, so can the sirih fruit."

The reply fed her anger: "The old sticks from the bottom of the pouch! You think that is enough? Your wives will not be fooled by the dry old sirih fruit you offer them, saving the fresh ones for the young girls you chase!" Her words were muffled, however, by the sounds of corn being pounded into meal, and the man never heard them.

This argument about infidelity phrased in terms of the betel basket never escalated from friendly bantering to a direct challenge. While men loved to discuss polygyny with me, always in a faintly teasing mode (by pretending to present an "anthropological" perspective on cultural diversity), women were less vocal but bitter.

Stories of neglected wives come back again and again to the image of the empty sirih pouch, the sirih standing in rather obvious fashion for the penis that could not be in two places at the same time, the man whose affections could not be shared between two women.

The wife who strays and is unfaithful to her husband is portrayed as trying to fill her pouch illicitly, collecting fallen sirih pipers or areca nuts instead of those she is entitled to. There is a small rite that a woman can perform to atone for adultery, which usually begins with a short prayer to ask forgiveness:

Ku koko ani ayaka	I regret it with my throat
A pico rou utta rara	That I picked up the yellow sirih
Ku ate langa ndanaka	I beg for mercy with my heart (liver)
A ghoba labba mone	That I gathered the man's areca nut
Oro ba wolo nggu	Because he used
Kari witti ghyoghi	The lures that catch the crab's feet
Oro ba rawi nggu	Because he offered
Pani kyere ghele	The bait to get the snail shells
A-a nikya a kabani	Perhaps that man had
Moro medako paneghe	Medicine to soften his speech
A-a nikya a lakeda	Perhaps the boy had
Kabali myata patura	Magic to attract the eyes

A man's use of various potions and substances, called *moro waricoyo* or "woman medicine," can help to excuse a woman's sexual misconduct, but not to absolve her completely from responsibility. Although some men were believed to have medicines that made them irresistible, the women they seduced were still condemned for yielding.

The usual practice, I was told, was for a man to put a bit of the medicine on a sirih piper and pass it to the unsuspecting woman. Some preparations could also be scattered inside a lime flask or blown over tea or coffee. The actual makeup of love potions was a strictly kept secret, but there were suggestions that some of the esoteric ingredients included the tears of the dugong, a sea mammal with a humanlike appearance.[5] Women who wanted to attract men and promote their potency, on the other hand, used firm round vines (especially the kyahi kara vine used to lash together the roof beams of houses) and herbs mixed with egg.

Betel supplies are potent symbols of sexual conflicts and longings in neighboring Pacific societies. On Goodenough Island, a Kalauna woman telling her own life story used the language of objects to express a muted protest against a system that, as in Kodi, assures the solidarity of males by dividing and ruling females: "Our name is women,'" she said. "We are bought with limesticks and limepots" (Young 1983a: 492). From the time of courtship and the first exchange of a betel chew, women surrender their freedom when they give in to their desires. Their love is bought and sold, and may later be neglected, while men go off to "seek new betel bags" in which to deposit their lime flasks.

Maru Daku's position was, in part, a testimony to male privilege, and to the ways in which his verbal skills were valued and helped him to be an effective head of a large family. The verbal skills of his wives (which I did not discover until after his death) had to move in the shadow of his own prominent position. Their rather separate development is treated in the next chapter. Maru Daku's life is particularly important because of his position as an innovator in relation to what might be considered the "canon" of Kodi poetics. The specific form that he chose for his longest autobiographical statement—a long lament in paired ritual verse that served as a reflection on his life, a defense of his choices, and a last will and testament to his children—reveals much about what he saw as his heritage and the legacy he wanted to leave.

THE BETEL BAG AS BIOGRAPHICAL OBJECT

The betel bag can be interpreted as perhaps the pre-eminent "biographical object" in Kodi society because it represents the identity of its owner in both a private context and on a ritual stage. When Maru Daku received a betel bag from his grandfather, he was being designated as his successor, "the rooster to crow in his place, the billy goat to take his spot." When he buried his younger brother's betel bag, he finally set his errant soul to rest.

With the same logic, if a father wants to curse his son and cut him off from any inheritance, he would perform a rite called "burying the betel bag" (*konda kaleku*), in which his son would be declared socially dead and excluded from the ancestral cult of his forefathers. The efficacy of the rite (which was once threatened in my presence but never carried out) lies in the powerful social statement it makes: A man is not himself without his betel bag; he loses his identity if it is lost. And if his kin choose to bury the betel bag that bears his name, he will also feel buried. The effect is not magical or automatic, but it is a dramatic way of showing the loss of a social persona.

The metaphor of the betel bag is used to suggest an inseparable connection between two people. It is often a hierarchical link, with one person professing loyalty to his master by assuming the attributes of his betel bag. Intimacy is also connected with possibility of betrayal. The pact made with a wild spirit to obtain wealth and sexual satisfaction is called the tie as "close as the pouches of a betel bag, the folds of the waist cloth" (*ndepeto kaleku, banguto kalambo*), but it is notoriously fragile and fraught with danger. The wild spirit is a bird or snake who takes the form of a beautiful woman and demands sacrifices and regular ritual visits from her human consort. If he neglects her, she erupts into a jealous fury and may "break the bridge leading over the river, put out the flames of the torch by the tides" (*mbata lara lende loko, mbada api hulu mara*), sapping her human husband's strength until he collapses.

Ideas of soul loss along with the loss of particular possessions are common on Sumba, but particularly intense for the loss of a man's bush knife (*katopo*), betel bag, and headcloth. Keller reports the story of a murder in 1990 in the highlands near Laboya that reveals the power attributed to objects. A young man long suspected of cattle rustling was ambushed by a group of people whose corrals he had allegedly raided. They beat him brutally, and then tried to stab him with their bush knives, but his invulnerability magic was so strong that nothing could pierce his skin. Finally, the leader of the group untied his headcloth and struck the captive three times, killing him with the third stroke.

Discussing the case with Sumbanese commentators, Keller notes that "they were convinced that it was the determined personality of the leader which manifested itself through the head-cloth and proved itself to be even stronger than the spiritual powers of invulnerability of his adversary" (1993: 259). It was not the visible weapons that were most effective, but the invisible force of a particular man concentrated into an object.

In similar fashion, it could be argued that Maru Daku's use of the betel quid to receive wisdom from this grandfather, call back his brother's soul, and stop his own son from stealing was not "magical" in any conventional sense of the term. It was an extension of his personality into the vehicle of an object, and a use of the thing as a metaphor for the self.

NOTES

1. I am here retelling the story of Maru Daku's life a bit differently from the way I published it in 1985. Readers interested in seeing the complete text of Maru Daku's apologia pro vita sua are referred to the earlier publication, which reflects on his words as an innovative poetic expression of his life history. Here, I try to probe the context of his statements and their relation to the betel bag as a vehicle for identity.

2. In other parts of Sumba, betel containers may be more gendered. Kuipers (pers. comm.) says that Weyewa betel boxes are "almost exclusively" women's, while betel bags—which women carry all the time—are still viewed as "male." Geirnaert-Martin (1992b: 68) says that Laboya bags decorated with a mamoli are

only for women, but both women and men carry shoulder bags. The bright yarn decorations in red, yellow, and black that are favored by young people in Laboya (but not in Kodi) are less popular among their elders. Onvlee (1973: 35) describes an East Sumbanese betel box and the West Sumbanese bag, but does not link these differences to gender.

3. Edgar Keller (1993: 247–63) has published a detailed history of bark and cotton clothing on Sumba, focusing on the ritual and personal significance of the bark headcloth in the Laboya district.

4. Keller (1992: 255) reports: "Laboyans still maintain today that the protecting, healing, cooling, and fluid-absorbing qualities of bark-cloth are unrivalled by the available alternatives. Probably for this reason the production of bark loin-cloths, for use by the initiates during the seclusion period of the circumcision ceremony, is still widespread in Laboya nowadays."

5. Forth (1989: 189–228) has published a narrative from East Sumba that suggests certain reasons for the dugong's appropriateness: In the narrative, a woman is brutally beaten by her husband for allowing their daughter to eat a shark's liver, which she should have saved for him. She goes to soak her wounds in the sea (suggesting female moistness) and turns into a dugong. She cannot suckle her baby boy anymore, so the son and daughter turn into monkeys. The monkeys resolve to steal food from humans, and the dugong to refuse the bait on a fishing line. The dugong is the most human creature in the sea, as the monkey is the most humanlike creature on land. Since the dugong has breasts and can suckle, it is seen as a fallen woman, a displaced mother, and its tears reflect its rejection by the husband. Its human origins and exile to the sea represent the sorrow of abused love. Forth does not say whether the East Sumbanese story was told by a man or woman, but it would seem to fit the themes of the "women's stories" of domestic abuse I collected in Kodi. He does tells us that the story is a "parable" that belongs to the public domain, and not one of the ancestral stories that is the property of a specific village or clan.

3.

DOMESTICATING ANIMALS AND WIVES

Women's Fables of Protest

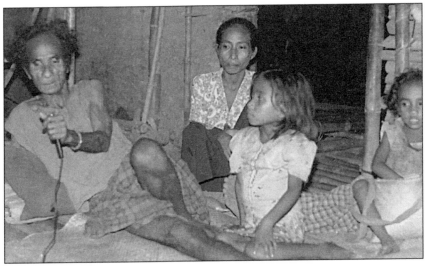

Maru Daku telling a myth, with Ra Mete, his second wife, and her daughter sitting beside him in his house. (Photo J. Hoskins, 1980)

People's folk tales are their autobiography.
—Ruth Benedict, *Encyclopedia of the Social Sciences*, 1931

Women in Kodi society are exchanged between houses, traded against livestock and gold, and travel along with pigs, cloth, and ivory. They are often described as objects of exchange: The daughter-in-law is the *wei haranga*, "what is received for the livestock," and her value is measured through her brideprice. Women's autobiographical reflections appear most often in narratives that focus on possessions that are not "objects" in the strictest sense, but domestic animals. I interpret them as a form of subordinate discourse that uses the language of possessions in a distinctive way—to highlight feelings of neglect and abuse, which they project away from themselves onto other household creatures. Domestic animals are so important in women's stories because of their use in bridewealth and as symbols of the possession, even pseudo-ownership, of wives and daughters-in-law.

The narrative preoccupation with animals and domestic objects as a reflection about the self is found in a number of other "indirect" auto-

biographical accounts collected in Pacific Asia. Saying she was only something "bought with limesticks and limepots" (Young 1983a), a woman on
Goodenough Island accounted for own life by talking almost exclusively
about the achievements of her husbands and brothers. Her references to the
temptations of the betel chew (and its associations with marriage payments)
was a muted protest against the ways in which her life had been marginalized by male preoccupations.

Kwaio women in the Solomon Islands described an idealized "virtuous
woman's life" and tried to explain their deviations from this model (Keesing
1985, 1987). Commenting on these women's refusal to reveal the personal
information often found in men's accounts, Susan Gal notes, "Their insistence on moral justification of womanhood evokes a parallel strategy in
Western women's autobiographies, in which a recurring figure of divided
consciousness can be read as the authors' awareness that they are being read
as *women* and thus judged differently in their self-constructions" (Gal 1991:
190). This leads her to conclude that anthropology's long focus on "muted-
ness" as a structural product should be replaced with a focus on "the
processes by which women are rendered 'mute' or manage to construct
dissenting genres and resisting discourses" (190).

The stories I heard from women in Kodi can be seen as a "resisting
discourse" that uses as its central image the abuse of domestic animals. This
image is appropriated to make a political point: That even the apparently
silent or muted inhabitants of a household should be listened to, but perhaps
we must learn to listen differently to what women have to say (Geiger 1986).
This was a lesson that I also had to learn in Kodi. Although I was interested
in feminism and wanted to record women's lives when I began fieldwork in
1979, I did not manage to do so until 1985. The young girls who lived with
me in several households offered giggling confidences but, given my own
unmarried status and "professional" research goals, most older women maintained a dignified silence. Even those I had known for several years were
cordial but reserved when I tried to tease out their perspective.

As is often the case in anthropological fieldwork, I did not not find the
specific genre of "women's narratives" by looking for them but by stum-
bling on them. Maru Daku died a year after my departure, in 1982. When I
returned to Kodi, one of the things I knew I must do was make a visit to the
ancestral village where his tomb was found to pay my last respects. His
house, located just beside the stone tomb where his body lay, was still inhabited by Maru Daku's three wives. Daku Maru,[1] the first wife, was tall and
dignified and the mother of eight sons who were carrying on their father's
tradition of ritual and social prominence. The second wife, Ra Mete (Christian name Rachel), had only one young daughter, and was much shyer and
more reserved. The third wife, Maha Dita (unbaptized), was a girl of only
nineteen who was already negotiating a new marriage.

Daku Maru received me graciously, introduced me to her newest grandchildren, and invited me to spend the night. That evening, as the new

daughter-in-law prepared a meal, Ra Mete told me that she remembered my staying in the house many times to listen to stories told by her late husband. "Now that he is gone, and we are only women here, I will tell you our women's stories." And she sat beside the sacred house pillar, where storytellers, diviners, and ritual specialists hold dialogues with the invisible spirits. Speaking in a soft whisper, but showing a fluency and composure that surprised me, she proceeded to narrate three stories—all involving female protagonists with some mixture of human and animal characteristics. The first, and the most elaborate, was the story of "Kahi the Buffalo Girl."

About halfway through the story, I realized that an account of a poor girl who is beaten by a jealous stepmother, given magical gifts by a wild spirit, and sought out as a bride because of a forgotten sandal had strong parallels with the familiar tale of Cinderella. At the same time, however, it was an unfamiliar story, featuring animals who gave birth to human children, beheadings, and horse chases, and an unusual assertion of female autonomy and independence in the context of traditional Sumbanese society.

After recording, transcribing, and translating the story in my home, I decided that it was—in a sense—a veiled version of her own life story. It was not a direct autobiography, but recent commentators have noted that the genre of autobiography is problematic in any case, both because it is culturally specific to the West, and has been shaped by a gender ideology that assumes a male subject (Rosaldo 1976, Gal 1991). The points at which Ra Mete[2] obviously identified with her heroine were many and often poignant. The points at which her own life diverged from that of the narrative were also notable and reflect a series of tensions centering on the issues of polygamy, female economic contributions, child rearing, and the meaning of brideprice payments and postmarital residence.

What Ra Mete was giving me, in an engrossing and appealing story form, was a commentary on "woman's experience" in Sumbanese society. It was a commentary intended for my ears, for those of her cowives who also listened, and—through the sacrifice and invocation of a chicken—for the listening ghost of her dead husband, who had been summoned to join the audience that gathered around her at the base of the sacred house pillar. But it was a performance that probably would not have been possible during his lifetime, since he—as my official teacher—had monopolized the spotlight and could not, in that social setting, silence his own voice to allow her a chance to speak.

CHARACTERISTICS OF WOMEN'S NARRATIVES

"Now that our husband is dead, the house is silent and lonely," they told me. "He used to fill it with the sound of his words, his stories, his songs, and now we can only tell our simpler stories to get ourselves through the night." The content of these "simpler stories" was, however, markedly different from men's ancestral narratives, even when—as in the "Kahi the Buffalo's Daughter" narrative—many of the conventions were the same. Men's heroic narratives told the story of the acquisition of heirloom objects associated with ritual office, the founding of new patrilineages and new ancestral villages, and the division of ritual tasks. Women's stories were less specific in their physical setting and focused more on the psychological conflicts of domestic life.

Both men's and women's stories followed a plot sequence that began with the birth of the protagonist and a series of traumatic experiences including the loss of a parent, and finished with marriage and a triumph over earlier enemies. But the orientation to the audience was different: In addition to the actual narrative, a number of rhetorical comments were made by storytellers to show their awareness of the story's implications. For men, these were references to "proof" of the story's authenticity by citing descendants ("This was the ancestor of those people who now live by the bay"), physical markers ("You can see the marks left on the tree where they stopped"), or valuables ("This is the sword they gave us"). For women, they were parenthetical comments on the proper care of children, decent treatment of wives, and the ownership of household property. Men presented their stories along with the historical evidence of veracity. Women cited instead moral precedent and the didactic function of instilling ethical values.

The division between the storytelling styles of the two sexes was based on criteria of *appropriate narrators* rather than knowledge of the plots or poetic refrains. Most of Maru Daku's stories were known also to his wives, who could correct mistakes in transcriptions or provide missing lines from the songs and poems. They did not feel, however, that it was appropriate for them to narrate the stories themselves. Their husband's successor as a bard and storehouse of traditional lore was Deta Raya, his third son, who was already a famous singer and orator. Married to twelve women, he had already outdone his father as a consumer of wives and established himself as a flamboyant social personality whose traditional authority was based on the idea that he had "inherited the seeds of wisdom from his father" (*diyo na pa helu ha wini wali byapana*).

In other villages, some women told ancestral narratives and even sang long invocations (*lodo ndandu*) in the center of the village during feasts. But these were unusual, and the shorter, homespun stories that Ra Mete shared with me were, I discovered, a more common genre of "women's narratives," and one that was in fact quite widespread. Once I knew about them, I found it much easier to ask women to tell me their "stories" than to tell their "lives"—but one led to another since the stories and lives were always intermingled and intertwined, for complex psychological reasons that we are equally aware of in our own society.[3]

CINDERELLA ACROSS CULTURES

The Cinderella story is perhaps the most widely documented folktale in the world (Cox 1893, Rooth 1951, Dundes 1982). Variants of it have been found from Africa and Egypt to Polynesia and Iceland. Our own familiarity with the version published by Charles Perrault, and adapted into popular forms such as Disney animation, a musical, and several films and television screenplays, may, however, blind us to the real variety of themes that can be expressed within a recognizeable "bundle" of folkloric motifs.

This Sumbanese version of Cinderella gives us insight into women's lives and women's aspirations in a manner very different from the "classic" Perrault story. In popular writing, especially a best-selling book by Colette Dowling, the "Cinderella Complex" has become associated with women's hidden fear of independence and the tendency of modern American women to wait passively for something external to transform their lives (Dowling 1981). The "deep yearning for dependence" and the covert "wish to be saved" is ascribed to the myth of a Prince Charming who steps in to provide a form and shape to women's lives that would be empty without him. This myth has many resonances in contemporary women's experiences, which may help to explain its continuing popularity. However, it is not the only message that can be gleaned from the story. In its Sumbanese version—and in many other variants connected from other societies—Cinderella is a remarkably independent woman who breaks cultural rules about residence, descent, and marriage, and succeeds brilliantly both in establishing her own autonomy and taking a gruesome revenge upon her enemies.

The Sumbanese Cinderella story offers an extended commentary on problems of female rivalry, especially in the cowife situation of polygynous households. It proposes an alternative mode of relation between women, based on the bonds of sisters, mothers, and daughters, which triumphs over the schemes of the jealous wife and her offspring. The Prince Charming character is found, but his role is strangely passive, as is the figure of the loving but ineffectual father. I argue that it can be interpreted as a parable about female relationships, in which men figure less importantly than women, and female power is idealized and represented in ways that are deliberately at odds with prevailing social institutions.

RA METE'S STORY

The first violation of gender codes in this version of the Cinderella story is in the separation of male and female spheres of labor, specifically the heroine's identification with the male sphere of pastoralism. Sumbanese households divide labor along gender lines. Women care for chickens and pigs and do routine garden work such as weeding and collecting tubers and vegetables for cooking. Men take care of the larger domestic animals, horses and buffalo, clear new fields by burning old crops, and help to plant and harvest rice and corn.

Ra Mete's story begins with an account of the father's attachment to the cow, the first cow he ever owned (*kapunge pote*, the "source of the herd"), who was the beginning of his move to wealth. The sexual relationship between the man and cow is only discreetly suggested at this stage:

Rato Ndelo had a wife named Randa Peda. They had a small herd of livestock, who lived in corral beside the house. His favorite cow was the first cow he had ever owned, and he guarded her very carefully. He guarded her so carefully that whenever the cow went to urinate, he went with her. That was how he guarded her and took care of her, day after day.

Then one day, the cow got pregnant. She was pregnant with a human child. After ten months, the buffalo cow gave birth to a human being, a baby girl.

After the girl was born, whenever they herded the buffalo out to pasture the girl would follow along to nurse from her mother. Rato Ndelo became very fond of the little girl, who was the daughter of his favorite cow.

So the little girl gradually grew up. And Rato Ndelo did not leave her at home when he herded buffalo, but always brought her along. When she was hungry, she would nurse from the cow. The cow could suckle the human child well, and she knew when she was getting hungry, so she would offer her udder full of milk.

So then the girl became old enough to do household chores. At his home, they said to Rato Ndelo, "Don't take the girl along with you to the pastures anymore, because we can use her here to help out." That was said by Randa Peda, the wife of Rato Ndelo.

"Let her come with me, so she won't be far from her mother," said Rato Ndelo.

"It doesn't matter. We want her to stay in the house," said his wife.

But Rato Ndelo did not want to leave her behind. He really loved the girl, who was the daughter of his buffalo cow. Because after all she was also a human being.

The girl was born after a cow's ten-month pregnancy, but emerged fully human in her physical characteristics. In a dramatic difference from the Perrault tale, she was not kept in the house as a scullery maid but allowed great freedom, following her father off through the fields and escaping the domestic work usually expected of girls.

When the girl reached marriageable age, her stepmother's jealousy grew greater and she refused to eat anything, claiming that she was sick. When her husband asked what he should do, she demanded the sacrifice of his favorite cow to pray for her recovery. After some resistance, her husband agreed, and Kahi Buffalo rushed off to warn her mother:

The buffalo's daughter, hearing that they were planning to slaughter her mother the next day, went to nurse one last time at her udder. "Mother!" she said.

"What is it?" said the cow.

"They are planning to slaughter you tomorrow. What will happen to me then?"

"They are planning to slaughter me tomorrow?" said the cow.

"Yes. They say they will slaughter you for sure," said the daughter.

"If they slaughter me tomorrow, ask your father to give you my entrails afterwards," said the buffalo cow to Kahi Buffalo, her daughter.

"Agreed," said the girl. She went back to the house and slept.

The next day, they slaughtered the first cow of the herd.

"Father!" she called to her father, Rato Ndelo.

"What is it?" he answered.

"Please give me my mother's entrails, father," she said. So when they butchered the cow they gave her the entrails. She brought them to the seashore and cleaned them out. She went straight to the seashore, Kahi Buffalo, carrying the entrails. She did not wait for her share of the meat.

When she came to the sea shore, she opened up the entrails. As she did so, she saw a gold ring—a ring to spin at the end of the index finger (*taghuru lombo dodoko*).

She took the ring out of the entrails and put it on her hand, where it fit perfectly. "This is why my mother told me to take the entrails," she said. Then she cleaned the entrails, emptying their contents into the water. Once she had cleaned them out, she set them on top of the sand. She said, "I'll bathe first, because my body is still covered with buffalo excrement."

She took off her sarung and folded it on the sand, and placed the ring on top of her sarung. Then she went to bathe. But she didn't know the buffalo entrails still had something more inside them.

While she was bathing, out came another daughter of the buffalo cow and took the ring. There were in fact two young girls who were inside the buffalo's entrails. They had not been visible earlier. When they were in the water, they looked like fish, but when they came to get the ring, they had a human form.

The two girls refused to give Kahi Buffalo the ring, but told her she could always come to the seashore to receive help from them. They provided her with beautiful sandals, a blouse, a sarung, gold chains to wear at the throat and wrist, and silver bracelets.

When she returned with this finery to her home, her sister was jealous. The sister was a deformed double of Kahi Buffalo, crippled at birth so that she could only limp feebly, and was called Kahi Twisted Foot (Kahi Kabenggelo). The step-mother, Randa Peda, asked how she acquired this wealth, and when she heard it was given to her as she cried on the seashore, she and her own daughter went to the same spot to try for themselves. Although Kahi Twisted Foot cried for many hours, "until her eyes were swollen with tears," no one came to her assistance. They returned home and began to beat Kahi Buffalo, saying she must have stolen her fine gifts.

Fearing for her life, Kahi Buffalo ran off to her father, who apologized for the bad treatment, but said, "I don't know what to do for you, daughter. I can't simply let you go away, because I love you too much. I felt sorry for your mother too. It was only because they forced me, since they wanted to get back at you, that she had to be slaughtered."

Kahi Buffalo sought the advice of the two sisters from the sea, who told her to ask her father for some land off in a distant pasture, where he could see her as he herded his buffalo. He agreed, and a house was magically built for them by the sisters, who flew inland from the sea in the form of birds. Her father came to live with her in the pastures, further angering his wife and other daughter.

Four days after they moved there, Kahi Buffalo saw a good-looking young man chasing a runaway horse as she sat sunning herself wearing her fine sandals. She deliberately dangled the sandals enticingly from her ankles, crossing and recrossing her feet as the young man watched. When he approached, she ran into the house and closed the door because her father was not at home. The young man picked up the sandals and took them home to his father, who was the king (*raja*). He spied on the girl from on top of a tree, trying to see her again and totally forgetting the runaway horse. That night, he told his father of his vision of a strangely independent woman:

"Father . . ." he called.

"What is it?" asked his father.

"There is a girl who lives in an empty pasture. A pasture that has no inhabitants. Maybe she lives all alone. She lives in a very fine house. I think that if I could settle down with her, I wouldn't want to move again. I am very attracted to her. I would simply move my work over there and stay with her."

"Whose daughter is this girl?" asked the raja.

"I don't know. I never saw her before. This is the first time," said the boy. And when they gave him food, he didn't eat. They saw the way he was acting and understood that he was in love.

Father and son went together to return the sandals, and to ask Kahi Buffalo's father for her hand in marriage. He agreed, but warned the suitor that his daughter "has had a hard life" because her mother was slaughtered when she was just a child: "My daughter has already lost her mother, so she needs someone who will love her. Remember she is not the daughter of a human being, but of a buffalo cow. Maybe later people will make fun of her and say that her mother was just a cow."

Although warned about her ancestry, the raja's son persisted in his proposal, and promised to come back with a magnificent brideprice. Four days later, he and his father arrived with so many buffalo and horses that they covered the whole area, and "all you could see in any direction were the raja's livestock." The marriage was completed, and at the feast that followed the son announced that he would not take his bride home—as is the custom once brideprice has been paid—but move in with her in the house in the pastures. This violated the usual pattern, suggesting that Kahi Buffalo and her descendants would break away from the raja's ancestral village to form their own splinter group.

Nine months passed, and Kahi Buffalo had a child, a little girl. Four days after she gave birth, her husband went off to work, and she received a visit from her stepmother and stepsister, who said they came to see the baby and help with the chores. They prepared some food, and Kahi Twisted Foot boiled a huge pot of water to offer her sister a warm bath. At first, Kahi Buffalo protested that she would bathe herself later, but her stepsister insisted. "This is the first time we visit since you left our home, so you must let me bathe you, or I won't feel right," she said. Kahi Buffalo took off her clothes and waited for the bucket of water, warm mixed with cool. Instead, her sister emptied the boiling pot directly on her head and scalded her to death. She threw the body into the bushes and took her half-sister's place in the bedroom with the baby.

The spirit sisters saw all this happen as they sat on the rooftop in the form of birds. They went to revive her body, but stopped to watch Kahi Twisted Foot's pathetic efforts to play at being a wife and mother:

Kahi Twisted Foot came back and took up the little baby. She bathed the child in warm water, dressed her up, and lay down with her in the room of her half-sister. She tried to nurse the baby, but there was no milk, so the baby began to cry. She tried to give her the warm bath water, but the baby would not take it. How could you give water to a child so newly born? She had been in the world for only four nights.

The crying baby would not go to sleep. It was already very late. The father of the child came home as the sun was setting. "Open the door!" he called. She went to open the door and quickly returned to the sleeping room. She went directly to the room where Kahi Buffalo slept with her husband.

"Why don't you give me any food?" said the husband.

"Just take it from the hearth shelf and eat it," she called. From the sound of her voice he knew it wasn't really Kahi Buffalo. "This isn't my wife," he said to himself. "Why should she already be different?" He asked her loudly, "Why do you sound so changed?"

"Don't bother about that. Just eat now and then come in here and sleep," said Kahi Twisted Foot.

Covering her foot, Kahi Twisted Foot went to sleep beside the husband and the child crying in hunger. The birds told her husband what happened, and added a note of reproach: "You left your wife alone, and she was killed horribly. It is only because of us that she can come back to life, and that your child is still well." He was told to take revenge on this false wife once her ruse was revealed in the light of day.

The next morning, he dragged her out and revealed her twisted foot. She cried and confessed that she killed her half-sister in order to take her place beside her husband. He cut off her head and tossed it into the sea.

Once her enemy was dead, Kahi Buffalo was brought back to life and joined her husband again in their house. A feast was planned to celebrate her return to life, and then the final stage of her revenge was completed:

They invited people to come to a feast. Kahi Buffalo's stepmother came along with the other wifegivers. As soon as they arrived, they slaughtered buffalo. They hardly wasted any time in speaking. They gave them a buffalo calf with horns an inch long to carry the slaughtered meat. And as for her father, they told him to stay with them, and gave him a calf.

They had already spoken to the calf. Once the party left the feast and came to a place with no trees or anything to block the way, they told him, "Turn on that woman and stab her with your right and left horns!"

When they came to an empty pasture, Randa Peda saw the calf turning toward her and coming to stab her, first with the right horn, then with the left. She was deeply gored and died in the empty pasture.

CONTEXTS AND SOCIAL COMMENTARY

[Ra Mete's story was a way of narrating certain events from her own life indirectly, and also of expressing goals that she had (such as a dream of acquiring her own house) that it would not be tactful to state publicly.)The goals were easily recognized by women, and when I played back the tape of her story to friends, they immediately commented on its hidden meanings. "This story is about a cow, but it is really about a wife," said one woman. "The buffalo wife has made Randa Peda jealous, like a spirit wife (*ariwyei myarapu*)," said another.

In early modern Europe, when Perrault's version was culled, supposedly from peasant sources, a high mortality rate meant that remarriages and stepmothers were very much a part of family life, and the neglect of extra and perhaps unwanted children was an issue of high concern. On Sumba, the stepmother becomes a jealous cowife, and her envy is particularly acute because her rival is not even human. The often absent husband, who seems to prefer the company of his cows to that of his wife and daughters, is a familiar theme in Sumbanese households. And it is often the case that a husband who is gone too often to the pastures is suspected of carrying on liaisons in these isolated spots, and perhaps even secretly supporting another family there. The social stigma associated with Kahi's birth is even greater because the union between her mother and father was never sanctioned by brideprice payments, so in Kodi legal arrangements she should in fact be matrilaterally affiliated, that is, "one of the cows" rather than "one of the human beings." The story presents an account of how she achieves humanity by resisting the insults of her sister and stepmother, and finally by contracting a good marriage that *is* sanctioned by a full brideprice payment.

I played the tape of this story to several groups of listeners, some of them all female, others all male. Men and women differed on their interpretation of the animal wife theme. Men explained it to me literally, saying that because of high bridewealth levels, many young men suffered from sexual frustration and had to "use animals instead of women" until their families had amassed enough wealth for them to marry. The father had a continuing sentimental attachment to the cow as his first sexual partner and the beginning of his herd. Women, on the other hand, were unanimous in seeing the buffalo cow as a metaphor: She was a first wife who had been "treated like an animal," and left behind in a home that was "no better than a corral." It was her husband's neglect that degraded her to the status of livestock—even if in the story he appears attached to her.

RA METE'S LIFE: AN OBLIQUE MIRROR

Ra Mete was herself a second wife, who had to live many of her days in the shadow of an accomplished and well-established first wife who had borne twelve children, eight of them sons who survived to adulthood. Since her only child was a daughter, she had produced no descendants for her husband's lineage, but she had raised a girl who could serve as her companion. Five years after her daughter's birth, her husband took a third wife, a very young girl who took her former place as her husband's closest personal attendant and the one who "chewed betel for him," since he had lost many of his own teeth.

Ra Mete had neither the authority usually given to the first wife nor the special indulgences reserved for the youngest and favored wife. She would have liked to have a house of her own, as Kahi Buffalo did, near her husband's pastures, since it was also near her own natal home. She was also obviously envious of Kahi Buffalo's seductive power to lure the raja's son her way by playing an erotic game with her sandal. She certainly had many bitter experiences of female rivalry with Maru Daku's other wives, so it is easy to imagine that Kahi Buffalo's revenge on her half-sister and stepmother might have corresponded to her own fantasies of retribution.

COMPARATIVE NOTES

This version of the Cinderella story is quite different from the Perrault version most familiar to European audiences, but it is recognizably within a wider tradition of "family resemblances" in the Cinderella cycle. The fairy godmother figure is often an animal mother: Ralston ([1879] 1982: 33–35) reports a Serbian version of the tale where the mother is turned into a cow and slaughtered at the stepmother's request; Mills (1982: 181–89) reports a version from Afghanistan in which the girl kills her mother but is later helped by a yellow cow who comes to take her place. The cow is killed to heal the sick stepmother, and from her bones magical objects appear. As in the Sumbanese story, the shoes are made of gold, and male characters are of relatively little importance: "The father and prince are almost completely passive prizes of the women's struggle, male brides" (Mills 1982: 191).

Themes of Cinderella's independence are also commonplace, often by resisting a forced marriage or taking the initiative to find her own husband. As Yolen (1982: 303) has pointed out, the mass-market image of Cinderella promoted by Disney's film—an "insipid beauty waiting for Prince Charming"—is a falsification of the predominant moral tone of the tales, which are feminist fables of resourceful heroines who trespass into men's territory.

The dead mother who takes the form of a cow and helps the Cinderella figure with some magical object is a common theme in Europe and the Near East (Rooth 1951: 151–52), but versions of the story collected in Sulawesi (Adriani 1894: 8; Wilken 1863: 295, 304) replace the cow with a fish or tortoise. A version from the Tontemboan islands north of Sulawesi also features a cow (Schwarz 1907: 81), and the Kodi variant suggests that Buffalo Girl's magical ring comes from sisters who spring from the entrails washed in the sea and take the form of both fish and birds.

Where the Kodi story is unusual is in its protracted account of the sexual rivalry between the two sisters, one beautiful but born to an animal mother, the other deformed but born to a human being. Some form of revenge on the stepsisters occurs in other versions (in Grimm's account, the sisters first mutilate their own feet by chopping off a heel or toe, and then have their eyes plucked out by birds (Grimm 1982: 28–29), but this vision of multiple murder, one punished by a beheading and then a goring of the mother, is particularly bloodthirsty. The buffalo calf, perhaps a relative designated to be the agent of Kahi Buffalo's revenge, reminds us that she is avenging her stepmother's demand that her mother be put to death—and that her allegiances are still partially in the animal world.

The special features of this Kodi version can alert us to ways in which widespread themes are reinterpreted in a local context to reflect the most compelling concerns of Sumbanese women's lives—the problems of polygyny, the relegation of women to the domain of domestic animals, their exclusion from the male world of sacrifice. The story is infused with wish-fulfillment on both a biographical level (because of the particular life experiences of its narrator) and as a form of submerged discourse protesting what could be called "the female condition" in this historical and political context.

This discourse takes the "victim's perspective," playing on the identification of women and domestic animals, both of which are "kept" by men. Rather than seeing a triumphant duel between virile males who struggle to steal animal vitality to perpetuate patrilineal identity, female commentators see the potential for exploitation and misunderstanding in human/animal interactions. In their stories of triumph and revenge, men are pushed aside or used as simple counters in rivalries between women, and the abused domesticated animal finally receives her due.

THE BUFFALO CORRAL AND THE FAMILY HOME

Both men and women talk at times of the family home as if were a buffalo corral, but they deploy the image in strategically different ways.

"Wives have to be managed, to be led, to be tended, and to be cared for," an older man told me, attempting to temper the continuing discussion of the morality of polygynous households. "Yes, I have three wives, but I see that each is well fed, each is given her bit of pasture, each is brought in in the evening and taken out in the day."

Talk of the husband as the "good shepherd" who handles his household the way he handles his flock was common among men, but fiercely resisted by women in their separate conversations, conducted not on the public space of the front veranda but behind the hearth in the shadows.

"A home is not the same thing as a buffalo corral," countered a salty older widow who had listened to their talk. "Your cows you can herd here and there, leading them by the rope through their noses, but your wives are not always so easy to handle." She then continued, in a furious whisper:

"Yes, it is true that taking several wives is our custom. But according to custom, each wife should have her own house. Each wife should have her own home to raise her children, her own hearth, and her own life, while it should be the husband who moves around.

"What do we have here? Husbands showing up suddenly with new wives in tow, nowhere to put them, no fields for them to work in, no looms for them to weave on. Husbands think they can bring in a new young wife as a plaything, like a child's cotton toy. And will the new wife help with the cooking, the gardening, or the housework? No, she will ride off behind him to the market, spend her time traveling and gossiping, chewing betel and filling her sirih basket while we are home with the children.

"Or the husband leaves for overseas, to study, to work for the government. Does he think of his wife left behind? Does he send money or cloth, a little something to show he remembers her? No, the sirih pouch sits empty, the woman is forgotten, and she still has to feed her children and send them to school."

This older woman's outburst confirms my point: The docility of the buffalo cow, a huge animal absurdly submissive to a smaller but craftier master, is regularly used to suggest obedience without understanding, a long-suffering trust in male authority that may be mistaken.

Wives do not directly defy the institution of polygamy, but express discontent with the way they have experienced it, the hardships they have suffered, while grudgingly allowing that perhaps—if properly handled— there could be a sharing of husbands in separate space.

MORE FEMALE PROTEST: THE CAT AND HEN STORIES

We encounter similar themes, inscribed perhaps more forcefully still, in the two simpler stories of the cat and the hen that Ra Mete also told.

The Female Cat ("Bei Wyodo")

One day a female cat went into her master's garden. She did not go into the woven bags of freshly harvested paddy. She would sit each evening on top of the largest woven bag so that no mice would come near them. During the day, she went to sleep somewhere else. Then, out came the chameleons and the gekko lizards, with all their friends. They began to wiggle around and squirm on top of the rice bag, until it tipped over and spilled on the ground and the veranda. The master came home from the garden and saw the paddy scattered on the ground and the veranda. "Hey, what is it with this cat? Why does she let them fool around here on top of the paddy, so that it falls on the ground and scatters on the veranda?"

At the urging of his wife, Kahi Leba, Rato Ndelo decided to sell the cat because he blamed her for tipping over the rice bag. He set off on his journey, but heavy rains and floods made it impossible for him to continue. So, he returned home to sleep once more. That night, he heard the cat singing a song of lament:

Mengau, Mengau	Meouw, meouw
Wuku wei karinungga	He is bringing misfortune on himself
A mori bei kabani	My master the great lord
Ngaho wei karina nggama	He is simply asking for suffering
A maramba mangu langu	The noble of great renown
Aya home pinja kyombo kahi ryara	When it was really the fault of the
Kyombo kahi ryara	Golden chameleon named Kahi
Na kandi lipye loti liango	Who guards the opening of the cave
Aya home pinja	When it was really the fault of
Ryake ri patola	The gekko lizard with royal spots
Pandali witti wyodo	Who trips under the cat's feet
Kana ndewa witti mboghi	So that my soul has rotten feet
La malende lerani nbei ba weda	He wanted to sell me to the winds
Inda ngola wangga mandoka la kapepe	But he got no gold coins in the basket
La hamahani hema ba wedangga	He wanted to bring me to the market
Njana kole waingo marara ihi bengge	But he got no yellow at the waistband

Rato Ndelo was impressed by his cat's song, and decided to set her free in the gardens. This time, when the gekkos and lizards came out to play, she shook them until they died, and everyone returned to find their bodies there. Later, her master concluded:

Ghala maka emeni	Fortunately there came
A waingo ha katana	The sudden floods
La mangada limbu njamu	From the darkest depths of the river
Maka nja ku palako	So I could not wander on
Ghala maka emeni	Fortunately there came
A ura rende loko	The rains that beat the water
La mangedi li manjamu	With the strongest currents
Maka nja ku palara	So I could not follow the path

The cat's eloquence and spiritual power averted an injustice.

The Hen ("Bei Wyodo")

A poor hen was badly cared for by her master, who did not feed her regularly but left her to scavenge on the ground. He did not provide a nest for her to lay her eggs, so she had to lay them in front of the house, and she had to brood over them on the ground, since there was no brooding perch (rambi) where they could be safe.

As a result, she laid her eggs and had lots of chicks, but the hawk swooped to gobble up her chicks, and there was no one who shooed him away. Soon all of her chicks were eaten. So his wife proposed to sell the poor hen, because none of her chicks grew up, and she wanted to use the money to buy a new sarung.

But that night as she was bound to the foot of the housepost to be taken to market, the hen sang a touching song of lament, and this song was overheard by her master, who realized how he had wronged her. The next day, he cut down coconut leaves to plait a little basket for her to lay her eggs in, and built a wooden platform for her to perch on while she brooded on the eggs, so they would be safe. In her own nest and perch (keko), the eggs hatched, and her master scared away the hawks, throwing rocks at them so they could not swoop down and gobble up the young chicks. She had twelve chicks who grew to adulthood, six roosters and six hens. Her master decided to sell the six roosters and keep the six hens, who were already laying so many eggs that he could eat some and sell some others. He sold the roosters and eggs for pigs, then sold the pigs for buffalo, and his wealth increased dramatically.

So finally they had a big feast, roasting four of the roosters and slaughtering them to celebrate their new prosperity, which came only because they learned to take proper care of the hen, their first hen.

The theme that female voices are often not heard or heeded is especially clear in these tales. Both the cat and the hen did their domestic tasks responsibly, but their master did not realize this until he heard their songs. The tales are a testimony to the power of poetic speech.

But, the reader may wonder, did I not try to listen to this speech before? Now is the time to tell the story of the women's song that I did hear during Maru Daku's lifetime.

GETTING ACCESS TO WOMEN'S STORIES: HUSBANDS AS GATEKEEPERS

About a year into my dissertation fieldwork, I began to realize that although I was allowed to study ritual speech with virtually no impediments, despite my gender, I had recorded almost exclusively male speech. Apart from a few teasing courtship songs sung by older women at the sea worm festivities, almost nothing of what I transcribed was said by women. Although probably most of my time was spent with female companions, the conversations were informal, sometimes noted in my notebook but apparently "off the record."

I asked Maru Daku to tell me if he knew of any women who could sing songs or knew stories. Yes, he knew one woman who told fine stories, and we began a lengthy process of contacting her through her husband. He also told me that his own wife had composed a rather moving little song that I might hear at his house.

"She might be embarassed to share it with you," he said, "but I'll tell her it is all right."

She agreed to record it at night, holding a grandson on her knee, since, as she told me, "the song is really a lullaby, and it needs a child to hear it. It is a song we sing to calm our children and make them sleep, but also to calm ourselves." Her seventh son, Matheus, had been a tiny "red baby" (*ana rara*) when she was moved to compose the song, so he was its original audience. In soft, caressing voice she began to sing:

Ndi myata mala wemu	Dry your tears my little one
Ana mete mata woya	Dark-eyed child of the crocodile
Ambu hoyo mangadi ngadi	Do not cry on and on
Baba nggu ba wemu	"Take me on your lap" you asked him (your father)
Otu pango la lembero pa duki	He went off visiting to another home
La kapandu pohe myalo	In the evening darkness
Baba nggu ba wemu	"Take me on your lap" you asked
Otu pangu la palako hamama	He left to chew sirih and areca elsewhere
La kandeghu wulla taru	In the light of the full moon

Listening at this point, I tensed with the realization that the song was protesting the departure of her husband on a courtship errand. The betel idiom was unmistakable, as was the tone of reproach, projected here from the unhappy mother to her child.

Lara li pya li pyanikaya	The path that he chose to take
A kumero wewe tattu	Wound through deep undergrowth
Annu li hya mane pyani	The road that he followed
A katoki cana mahi	Crossed along the seashore
La kaderi woleko harama	Going to see the great feast
Ole lete oro mburu	At the steps that he came down
La tabeku mamba mayo	The cliff where Mamba came
La haranga woleko harama	Going to witness the celebrations
Ola binya oro lohona	At the door that he came out (village of his maternal origins)
La tawada rate nggaro	The incline of the Gaura man's grave (couplet name for Ratenggaro)

Her sad story began, she related, when her husband went off a great buffalo feast (*woleko harama*) sponsored by Muda Daru of Ratenngaro.

Di moka diyo ana	But there is something I must say, child
Ba ku ndilu tilu	Which came to my ears
Lyolikyo paringi	News blowing in the wind
Nangga wudi jangga	(Like) the young jackfruit which appears
A ngendana kamboko ghobo kura	He acted like a red buffalo calf
Kali lyokongo kaduna	Swinging his horns back and forth
La homba tana rara	In the swampy yellow land
Rongo la nyaluho kapote	Heard in the swirling dust storms
La helu wulla wudi hyungga	(Like) the rising new moon
A tudana wawi mbyara langge	He played the pale ribbed piglet
Waghehongo kikuna	Shaking his tail wildly
La kalibye watu kaka	Over the heap of white stones

There she says she heard reports that he misbehaved, using idioms of "horny" young calves and "tail waving" young pigs, familiar as euphemisms for sexual misconduct. The account continues, however, to register a further protest.

Ndi mata wemu	Dry your tears, my little one
Ana mete mata woya	Dark-eyed child of the crocodile
Baba nggu ba wemu	"Take me on your lap," you asked him
Otu pangu la kalunggu rongo	But we heard that he went off
La wolongoka kawica olengo hamenga	To act like the squid with filthy ink
La rawingoka kura tadungo teinya	To be like the shrimp with shit in his head

These lines use terms in ritual speech reserved for incestuous sexual relations because the woman Maru Daku met at the feast was a member of the matriclan Walla Mbera, the sister of Ra Mbolu of Rangga Baki. She was a young widow who had been married to Lengga Kendu of Hali Kandangar, and was Maru Daku's *dughu*, or maternal relative. His matriline, Walla Mbiri, was related to hers, Walla Mbera.

Their relationship was considered to be in violation of the rules of matriclan exogamy, so it could not be sanctioned by exchange payments. The two of them persisted, however, to meet secretly, even though her family refused to allow him to propose to take her as a second wife. He was working as a Christian evangelist (*guru injil*) and so was not supposed to marry more than one woman. She got pregnant and gave birth to a son, and Maru Daku came to stay with her when their child was born, saying defiantly that he wanted to stay with her anyway. The child was sickly, however, and died before a year was over.

Other people said the maternal blood lines were too close, so no healthy child could be conceived. Finally, the two of them separated, becoming "embarrassed" at the passion that had led them into an inappropriate union. Maru Daku told me she never married again and went back to raise her children in her former husband's hamlet. Twenty-two years after the scandal, he met her again at another feast, and they saw they both were toothless.

"I had loved her," he told me, "in spite of the shame, and I had wanted to stay with her. But her family would not agree, and she remembered her children, so she returned to them. When I saw her again, we laughed, and we cried, and she told me she still thought of me although she was now an old woman and I was an old man."

The tie that a mother feels to her children was the theme that Daku Maru emphasized next, explaining to her own son why she remained a part of her husband's household:

Ba di wyali yayo	But as for me now
Ana mete mata woya	My dark-eyed child of the crocodile
Yimonggaka tiku nja wena	I stay here without saying anything
Yila karaha bapa yanno nggu	By the ribs of my father-in-law
La canggu hola ndara	The stallion with many burdens
La Ote ana rato	Among the descendants of Ote the nobleman
La Hyadi ana meha	And those of Hadi the only child[4]
Yimonggaka mbaha nja wena	I stick it out in silence
Yila tidi inya yanno nggu	At the side of my mother-in-law
Yila Kyaka bapi lyeko	The white mare with the sweet name

Although she remains dutifully in the home of her parents in law, she does sing of her ambivalence:

Ku pangga ndana atekya	I step but my heart holds me back
Maka di wyali diyo	It is only because of this here
Ana mete mata woya	Dark-eyed child of the crocodile
Nja namo pighumi	And those others I remember
Hambule pare mboghi	Who filled my belly like decaying paddy
Ndaha walu	Who were like layers in my intestines
Maka ku banda loro koko	So I try to make my throat patient
Ku kamodo baka mangga	I want to wait beside the bushes
A ando koti lighya nggu	For the post my ginger vine creeps up
Nggallu mbaku haghu nggu	For the one who encloses my small tobacco patch

The thought of the children who once filled her womb binds her to her husband, who is referred to somewhat ironically with the ritual names of his position, suggesting his duties to provide support (the post for the vine) and protection (the fence around fine tobacco).

In the final verses of her song, Daku Maru turns to register almost a curse against him for these actions, noting that the marapu will punish him on their own for violating the incest code:

Ate deke wu banikya	The heart will take its own share
Ba na maliti jo konggolo	If he returns to the banyan trunk
Koko deke wu banikya	The throat will take its own share
Ba na mali byangga kaheka	If he goes back to the scene of the crime
La kataku loko mbunako	The headwaters where the river swirls fiercely
La mata rende kabaro	The source of cloudy swamp lands
Maka angga lai doyaka	And he will surely also be summoned
Ela dulango paneghe	To the formal negotiation
Ola bapa na tepa todo tana	By the father who sifts the root tubers
Angga lungga do donikya	He will have to go to meet them
Ela pandengo patera	At the place of official speech
La mengahu naj panuni	By the stallion who can't be crossed[5]

In addition to supernatural sanctions (which may have taken the form of the death of the child he conceived with his mistress), she indicates that her husband will be called to appear in front of the Raja to present a *kanale* payment. The payment is a fine for sexual misconduct, which men describe as "throwing away livestock without even getting a wife." It can be required by the family of the wronged woman, and usually consists of five head of livestock to "restore the woman's honor" (*habali a mekena*) and allow her to return home in good standing.

In this case, Rangga Kura, the woman's father-in-law, did suggest that a fine should be paid, but after the death of the child he decided simply to allow his daughter-in-law to return home to her children without insisting on a livestock payment.

After she had finished singing the song, Daku Maru made no further comment. It was her husband who filled in the details, providing the context for these events and admitting his own guilt. Later, in the privacy of my living room, he helped me to transcribe the words and provided the usual painstaking exegesis of ritual terms and vocabulary.

At one point I turned to him and asked the obvious question: "Is this hard for you?" I allowed for the question to appear ambiguous, as if it could refer either to the difficulties of translation or the emotional burden involved in rendering such a personal text.

"No, I knew her feelings well," he responded directly. "I know she loved me and was moved when I heard the song. She learned many of these words from me, but she has combined them in her own way. My sons are lucky to have an intelligent mother. But sometimes a husband has to take his own path."

These comments seemed to encapsulate a common masculine perspective in Kodi. Wives are valued and loved, and their abilities may be respected. But they should not seek to limit male freedom, including the sexual freedom to seek out other women. While Maru Daku had been briefly ostracized and threatened with punitive fines because of a liaison that was considered incestuous, he did not suffer the same fate as that of a woman accused of adultery.

I may seem unfair to have focused this chapter on domestic unrest specifically on two of Maru Daku's wives. I would not argue, in fact, that his wives were any less happy than those of many other men. The reason they were chosen is simply that I became familiar with them over the two years that their husband was my teacher, and they were articulate. It was in part because he was so generous in allowing me to transcribe one song from his first wife that I also dare to include the story from his second wife.

MALE INFIDELITY VS. FEMALE INFIDELITY

Women were expected to remain faithful to their husbands throughout their lives, while men expected to want to stray, allowed to take as many wives as they could afford, and forgiven if at times they entered into a relationship that could not be sanctioned by exchange payments. The dangers that haunted female infidelity were not simply the social ones of being beaten by a jealous husband, but also the threat of death in childbirth.

I encountered this threat one evening when I traveled to a small garden hamlet to wait for a singing ceremony (*yaigho*) that was supposed to begin that evening. It was quickly explained to me that the ceremony could not take place, because a young wife had gone into labor the previous day, and although the birth had been expected by that evening, something was blocking it, and the child could not be born.

The young woman was seated by the hearth, holding onto a strip of bark suspended above her head. Two older women assisted the birth, one holding her from behind and massaging her belly vigorously to "loosen up the child," the other sitting in front of her spead legs to receive it when it came. The young woman held her back and moaned, while the other women in the house came up to her and whispered urgently, "You must name your lover! Tell us who he is!"

"If she doesn't say his name," one older woman explained to me, "the child will never come out, and the dark blood inside her will kill her. If she says his name but does not tell the whole truth, perhaps we can get the child out safely, but still the placenta (the *ghagha* or 'elder sibling') will not come out."

The young woman, obviously terrified, said nothing, but sat with her damp eyes wide open, breathing painfully and staring into the fire. Her face was pale and covered with sweat, and her hands trembled as they clasped themselves over her heaving belly. Her sister asked me if I had brought any medicines with me, and I sadly reported that I had not.

The tone of the other women in attendance was sympathetic to the young woman in labor, but also critical. They were convinced that the birth canal would not open up until her guilty secret spilled out of her.

"Are you sure there is a lover?" I asked one of her sisters.

"Yes, there always is in cases like this. I do not know who he is, but I hope she will tell them."

"Sometimes the girls will die rather than tell the name. It could be someone related to them, or the husband of another woman in the house. They feel very ashamed, but it must be done."

After a day of labor, the husband had sent for a midwife from a more distant village. His wife was complaining of intense back pain, but her waters had still not broken. The new midwife arrived, and pulled the husband over to the side.

"Do you want the child more, or the wife?" she asked. "I may not be able to save them both." The husband told her to do what she could to save his wife; they could have another child if she lived. The midwife took a pointed piece of bamboo and used it to pierce the water sac. Both women massaged the girl's stomach very violently, and after an hour or two we heard a small cry from the back of the house. I had not seen the birth itself, and tried to rush back.

"Don't go," said one of the women, restraining me. "They are washing her up now, and the child may not be well." They knew I had not yet had a child and told me there were things I should not see.

The child, a small, wrinkled little boy, was shown to us about an hour later. He had a dark stain on his forehead, a kind of birthmark, which they said was what was left of his mother's shame.

"Did she ever say her lover's name?" I asked hesitantly.

"She said something to her husband. We don't know what it was, but I think he allowed her to open up to give birth," I was told. The exact content of their words remained private, but their moral was clear: Whatever the moral value of terrorizing mothers at childbed, this father was more interested in holding onto his wife.

This was not the only case where "custom" seemed to prescribe censor and punishment, but a man chose to believe in the goodness and innocence of his wife.

The very different kinds of risks which men and women ran always seemed profoundly unfair to me.

"Why don't men fall sick if they are unfaithful or commit incest?" I protested. "Why is the afflicted body always female?"

The older woman I asked this of looked at me is if I were incredibly stupid. "But where do you think adultery takes place?" she said. "It is in the woman's body, after all. Men are only there for a moment, and then they are gone. But what they leave behind, the liquid from the penis, it stays and is like a poison to her."

The idea of the poisoned vagina and the poisoned sirih pouch were linked. The man could leave behind some love magic, which would make the woman powerless to resist. He could also leave behind his semen, which might poison her womb and kill her or her child, but his own body remained unaffected. In fact, extramarital sexual adventures served only to demonstrate his power that could weaken and even kill women.

BUFFALO AND HORSES, WOMEN AND MEN

The identification that women express with the sacrificial animals (buffalo, pigs, and chickens) is paralleled by an even clearer identification of men, especially important men, with their horses. A prominent man is addressed, as a gesture of respect, by the name he has given to his stallion. The name is usually chosen by him at a rite to mark his maturity (often the first feast where he offers an animal for sacrifice as an adult head of household), and it attributes a part of his own biographical experience to his mount. Thus, a quick-tempered man took the horse name Ndara Katupu, or "feisty stallion." A man who felt he had taken on too many family obligations chose to call himself Ndara Tanggu Holo ("the horse who carries other peoples' burdens"). Someone who was appointed to a high government office took the name Ndara Kaha Deta, or "the horse of the tall tamarind tree."

Horse names can also be "inherited" from a grandfather, if the man is interested in marking his relationship to an important ancestor. In effect, most of the young men and boys addressed as "Ndara" in Kodi at the time of my fieldwork were "carrying on" an ancestral name and had not yet achieved the ritual right to carry that name into the sacrificial field.

Women also have, on occasion, a named mare, but in most of the cases that I heard of the name given to the mare was not of their own choosing. The former raja of Rara, Yoseph Malo, gave horse names to four of his five wives, but each name reflected on his own experiences rather than theirs (Hoskins 1989a). Raja Horo had a grandmother who was called Rato, and had a horse name to parallel her husband. I also heard of a woman in Parona Baroro who was a famous dancer and was known as Bei Mu Karaboko, or "The Mare Who Eats Dust," because of the small duststorms she kicked up with her pounding feet. This example is the only one I encountered of a horse name that celebrated a female achievement independently of a male one. In most cases, both the horse and the woman are simply vehicles to highlight the achievements of their owners.

A horse is not a sacrificial animal in the usual sense; it is not killed to provide "food for the ancestors" or meat to be distributed on ritual occasions. Its body is never "read" through a divinatory examination of the entrails or liver (Hoskins 1993b), and it is not used as a medium of communication with the spirits. A man's or woman's favorite horse may be killed at a funeral as a "companion" to carry the soul of the deceased to the afterworld. Sometimes the flesh is simply discarded (or scavenged by people from other islands). At other times a horse may actually be buried inside a separate chamber of a great man's stone tomb.

Women's identification with pigs, cats, and chickens is metonymic: These animals are tended and fed by women, in the back of the house. In small-scale women's sacrifices to the spirits of indigo dyeing or childbirth, chicks or piglets can also be killed. Women's identification with buffalo is metaphoric: Although buffalo are herded to pasture by boys and always exchanged and sacrificed by men, they share with women characteristics of silence and subjugation.

A Kodi story about the origins of pastoralism illustrates this point well. It is said that once all animals were wild and lived alongside people in the forests. Buffalo were able to talk and would often come into people's houses and speak to them as equals. When they visited, however, their large, clumsy bodies wreaked havoc on the delicate bamboo construction of Kodi houses: Rooftops were pushed upward (the peak of a Kodi roof is still called the "house buffalo"), and floors collapsed under them. Finally, the buffalo asked people to help them by building a corral, and leading them down to the water each morning and back to their home in the evening. They willingly placed themselves in a subordinate position and surrendered to the lead rope. At that time, they lost both their voices and their sexuality. They became silent, and people began to geld them (which they do not do to stallions) and pull them around by the rope through the nose. Once they were no longer able to speak themselves, they were used in sacrifices to carry messages to the ancestral spirits (Hoskins 1993b).

There is no equally explicit parallel story about the subjugation of women, but the identification of women and domestic animals in Ra Mete's story shows that women also feel they have "lost their voices" and been relegated to an inferior status. A neglected wife is someone who is "treated like a buffalo cow" (*pa karimyoyo*) and no longer listened to or allowed to speak. They may sing in protest, like the cat or hen, or like Daku Maru, who crooned her protests to her newborn son. But these songs will fall on deaf ears unless the men who love them but also abuse them take heed.

The fables of protest that these women narrators told portrayed themselves as chattel, personal property, or domestic animals whose needs were not tended. Underneath the idealized rhetoric of complementarity that is used in gender dualism, subtle differences in power and the ability to act lie veiled. In telling me these stories, these women showed me their identification with possessions and used it to subvert masculinist privilege and express a dissenting viewpoint. The subordinate discourse was an indirect assertion of the rights of the object of exchange to tell her own story and become a biographical subject as well as an object.

NOTES

1. Marriage in Kodi brings a change in the term of reference for both men and women. My teacher, born Maru Mahemba, was called Maru Daku after his marriage to the woman born Daku Lendu. Her Christian name, taken at her baptism when she was about twenty-five, was Juliana. A husband and his first wife have names that are inverses of each other, and both may be designated with teknonyms referring to them as parents of their first child. Subsequent wives do not change their names, but may also be called with teknonyms once they have borne a child.

2. In 1996, I attributed this story to Ra Muda, thinking that because of the personal nature of the narrative it would be better to use a pseudonym. I have since realized that no one in Kodi would be fooled by a false name and might in fact be offended by one, so I have chosen in this book to use a real name when the person is certain to be identifiable.

3. Gal notes that if we are to find that women are not always silent and inarticulate, we must seek out and understand the genres and discourses that women produce: "Especially revealing are genres created by speakers themselves, to reflect on their own experience, that are not primarily a product of the ethnographic interview" (1991: 192). My efforts to collect life histories directly fell flat, but precisely because of that I feel I am justified in treating these stories about animals as suggesting a strong autobiographical content. The narration of the Buffalo Girl story in this particular context shows not only the diffusion of a widespread folkloric tradition but also a strategic ploy to bring attention to women's concerns and to displace the male monopoly on public storytelling.

4. This is the couplet name of Wainjolo Deta, Maru Daku's ancestral village. The references to the "stallion with many burdens" and "white mare with a sweet name" are the horse names of her father and mother-in-law, Muda Mbeiyo and Kaka Muda.

5. This is the couplet name of Raja Horo, combining his horse name and a phrase indicating the research that he must do to resolve each dispute that comes before him, like the work of sifting through root tubers and cleansing them of poisonous fibers.

4.

THE ROYAL SNAKE SHROUD

Local Weaving and Colonial Kingship

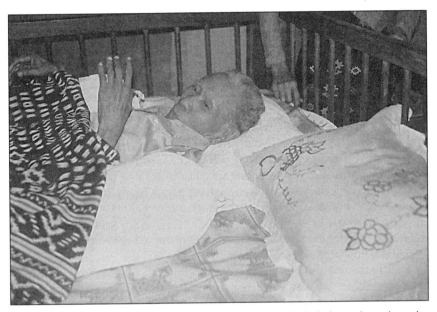

A man's cloth with the snake motif (*hanggi nggoko karaha kaboko*) is brought to the bed of a dying man (here, A. W. Bulu) as a possible contribution to the shroud. (Photo J. Forshee, 1993)

Kodi cloth is the most famous export of the western part of the island. It does not have the large figures of lions, unicorns, skull trees, and deer that represent the glory of the royal families of East Sumba, but its complex design, with diamondlike nets in the center and undulating lines at the side, is representational in a more abstract format. The finest Kodi cloth is a *hanggi nggoko karaha kaboko*, a man's mantle or loincloth with a pattern called the snake's rib. The snake is an uncurled *Python reticulatus*, glossed in Indonesian as *ular patola* or *ular naga*, both suggesting links to Indian trade cloths and Hindu ideas of divine kingship. The pattern appears geometric, but its name shows the influence of both the scaly shapes on a python's skin and the designs on Indian silks. Other important cloths are the women's sarungs with ikat-tied designs (*lawo pa wolo*) of parts of buffalo, horses, and the gold ornaments paid in brideprice, and the striped *lambeleko* pattern or the embroidered *pa humbi* style. Pairs of men's and women's cloths are presented to reciprocate for a brideprice payment, to express grief at a funeral, and at other ceremonial occasions.

In the early 1980s, when I returned to Kodi and stayed as a houseguest in the home of Raja H. R. Horo, his wives showed me a number of very fine snake cloths. One in particular was woven of hand-spun thread and had exquisitely detailed indigo designs and a fine border contrast-dyed in rust. I was interested in buying some cloth to take home, and asked about that one.

"No," my host told me. "This one is a royal cloth—it is a cloth I could wear for my final journey, when I cross over from the world of the living to that of the dead. This is the cloth we are saving for my funeral shroud (*ghabuho*)."

"Why must it be this particular cloth?" I asked.

"These cloths are used by only the highest nobility at funerals. They bear the signs of royal privilege, the mystical power of kings (*kesaktian raja-raja*). For me, this cloth is especially powerful, because it depicts the guardian spirit of my ancestor, Rato Rangga Ramba Deta."

The name was familiar to me as that of the founder of Rangga Baki, the raja's ancestral village. But I had not specifically associated his name with the patterned cloth before, or realized that the Horo family saw this as a royal cloth. I asked him to explain what the cloth meant to him.

"You know the reasons for this already," Raja Horo said with a note of reproach. "I gave you a copy of the history of my village from my files, and it explains how important this snake image is to us."

Raja Horo was the only person I knew in Kodi who kept his own files, and who wrote down stories from the oral tradition. The "history of his village" was in fact a narrative of its founding by Rangga Ramba Deta, accompanied by notes about his own relationship with the guardian spirit who took the form of a snake. The snake cloth symbolized an invisible inheritance of the power to heal and reconcile, to restore potency and settle disputes. This story of an ancestor can be interpreted as an indirect autobiography, an account of the source of his own authority, and the basis for his legitimacy as ruler of Kodi and at one time the whole island of Sumba.

The snake shroud became a biographical object for Raja Horo because it brought together local traditions concerning magical snakes and imported notions of divine kings. The most famous snake in the mythology of West Sumba is Pala Kawata, a giant python who lives in the wet rice fields of the highlands and gives abundant rainfall to those who sacrifice to him in the proper way. Two villages in Kodi have a special ritual relationship with him and can be approached during a drought to ask for rain. Pala Kawata is said by some to be the father of the sacrificed rice maiden, Mbiri Kyoni, who is reincarnated with each new crop (Hoskins 1993a: 98–99).

The python that Raja Horo claimed as his benefactor and ancestral guardian is not Pala Kawata but instead a kind of *yora* or "spirit wife" (*ariwyei marapu*). She can take the form of a beautiful woman, and has appeared to him most often in his bed. She is the source of his famous medicine to treat impotence, and his power to conjure her up in his imagination has helped him to restore the virility of many other men who have come to him for treatment.

But the snake is also important in the iconography of Southeast Asian kingship and can be interpreted as a symbol of royal or even divine status. The snake was depicted on the "throne" constructed by Dutch officials for the ceremony to install him as raja, and is said to visit him on auspicious occasions to announce a new honor on the way. Because of the ways Horo and his family celebrated the heritage of the snake and its depiction on the ikat cloth, this pattern has become an emblem of nobility that some linked to the colonial cult of royalty and an autocratic "feudalism."

Raja Horo's story provides a point for the intersection of rivalrous local models for the control of spiritual power with more hierarchical external ideas, which he learned about in his travels overseas. Relations of privilege on Sumba are encoded and elaborated with reference to both indigenous and outside (primarily Javanese) models. By focusing on a man important in the transition from colonial rule to Indonesian independence, we draw on a wider context of impinging forces that inflect local politics from a distance.

First, we must set the stage by outlining the context in which Raja Horo's stories were told and letting him lead us into the exploits of his famous ancestor.[1]

THE "FEUDAL" RULER OR THE GRANDFATHERLY LEADER

Raja Horo lived in a house that wanted to be European but had long since seen its glory days. The house in the district capital of Bondo Kodi was, like many of the homes of colonial rulers, a decaying wooden frame, grand enough to show the pretensions of European architecture at the front, but simple and rather dilapidated in the back. A large corrugated iron roof hovered, as if on wings, over the living room and reception area, which had a waxed concrete floor and European-style couches and chairs. Large armoires housed a collection of papers, photographs, manuscripts, and documents that were the district's only surviving historical archive. Pictures of Raja Horo at official ceremonies were framed and hung along the wall, along with fine traditional cloths and a small portrait of one son who had become a university professor in Jogjakarta.

The four rooms of the front house were the master bedroom (where Raja Horo slept with each of his three resident wives, on a nightly rotation), the guest room, and the bedroom officially assigned to the "Older Mother," his most senior wife. There was also a hall with a large table to serve meals for guests. Behind the house were two smaller structures with bamboo-plaited walls, one containing an outhouse and bathing room, the other several cots and looms used in weaving. Then a short path led to the two houses of his younger wives, both with simple dirt floors and several large, canopied beds, where they lived with their children.

In the late 1970s, when I first came to Kodi, there were already a number of more modern stone houses, built for the government-appointed district head (*camat*) and other officials, that made Raja Horo's house seem shabby. It was dwarfed by the house next to it, which had been assembled from materials shipped to the island from Java and had once been the home of a real European, the Dutch minister who lived in the district in the 1930s and again in the 1950s. The minister's house (as it was still called a generation later) had tiled floors, glass windowpanes, and a much higher roof. Since his departure a quarter-century before, it had been used as a temporary clinic, housing for health workers, and a practice room for dancers training to perform in the regency capital.

The expectations I had for a raja's residence had been formed by the splendid sultan's palaces of Java and Balinese royal pavilions, so this hybrid wooden structure was initially disappointing, with none of the "royal" glamor I had anticipated. But the Raja himself was very warm and welcoming of foreign visitors, having heard of my arrival in the market town of Kory some days before. A short man with a broad face and a black *pinci* (the brimless black hat popularized by Sukarno and associated with Indonesian nationalism), he was eager to tell me about foreign researchers who had come before and to show me his guest book and correspondence with Needham, Van Wouden, Onvlee, and others. The father of more than twenty daughters, he said he was especially glad that Kodi would now be studied by an educated woman, so she could be a role model to his own children.

A large part of Raja Horo's authority derived from his association with foreigners, especially the Dutch. Unlike the hereditary rulers of East Sumba, the rajas of West Sumba were the sons of important families who were given an elementary education in Dutch schools and then appointed to their positions. Because the Netherlands Indies government was interested in using traditional forms of legitimacy, they carefully prepared genealogies for each of the rulers they appointed, and they selected from the largest and wealthiest ancestral villages. But in West Sumba it could be said with some accuracy that an aristocracy was *created* by the colonial government, rather than simply incorporated into it. Whenever anyone questioned Raja Horo about his family or his prerogatives, he gave two answers.

The first was to cite his most famous ancestor, Rangga Ramba Deta, who had the encounter with the snakes. "Aren't I the grandson of the man who was once the wealthiest person in all of Bangedo?" he would ask. The second was to cite the authority of the Netherlands Indies government. "Just ask the Dutch officials! They collected my genealogy, they wrote it down. They did all the research, and they were the ones who appointed me raja." Ancestral mandate was thus wedded to colonial authority, combining to make up the two-stranded legacy that justified his rank and position in postcolonial Indonesia.

Titles and prerogatives are not easily lost in the Malay archipelago.

Although after independence, the colonial rajas were redefined as civil district officers (*camat*), they continued to be addressed with the title raja, as a gesture of respect. Indonesian speakers in the regency capital would speak of Raja Horo or Raja Kodi, while villagers speaking Kodi called him the *toko*, holder of the *tongkat*, or the golden staff given to all royal figures by the Dutch authorities. But remaining a raja in a period characterized first by the fierce populist nationalism of the Sukarno era and then by the increasing state penetration of Suharto's New Order was not a simple task.

As I spent more time in Kodi and became familiar with the often vicious local politics of status anxiety, I came to realize that Raja Horo was also grateful to have me come listen to him. He was, without a doubt, one of the most knowledgeable authorities on Kodi's recent history, its colonial administration, and all the many changes it had gone through (under his leadership) in the past few decades. But he was also a sometimes lonely older man, no longer directly involved in government, whose voice was respected but not always heeded in contemporary events. His own children told me apologetically, "He keeps remembering the days when he was a raja under the Dutch. It cannot be like that anymore. This is the age of independence, that was a time of feudalism."

Feodal was an invective which could be hurled against members of the family whenever they seemed to presume aristocratic prerogatives that others resented. A fistfight once broke out between groups of young boys practicing traditional boxing (*patukengo*) because one of Raja Horo's grandsons referred to the members of his family as *putri Rangga Baki* ("the little princes of Rangga Baki"), instead of simply the sons of the village. The label also appeared in a police report in the early 1980s that censored one of Raja Horo's sons for beating a runaway slave. (The slave, it should be noted, was found by the police and returned to his master, but with instructions that because slavery was now illegal, he should be treated "with human respect" as a poorer relative.)

Raja Horo's reaction to the term was a palpable shudder. His *pinci* identified him with Indonesian nationalism, but he had been the target of nationalist and populist crusades against "feudalism" in the mid-1960s, when his ancestral village (and a splendid lineage house he had erected some years earlier) was burned to the ground by arsonists. In the early 1980s, his family opened up a small kiosk, and the name he chose to epitomize the spirit he wanted to promote was Toleransi. He saw himself, in so many different situations throughout his life, as an advocate not of privilege but of tolerance, a reconciliator who helped both sides to see their weaknesses.

This role was a legacy from his famous ancestor. In 1978 he composed a short manuscript, which he asked his wife to type; it was intended primarily for family members to defend the honor of Rangga Baki against doubts about its legitimacy as a "village of kings." I quote here from the typescript he gave me titled "The History of Rangga Ramba Deta":

Raja Horo's Own Text

Rangga Ramba Deta was the only son of Rato Leko Botodadi of Waindimu. He was orphaned, along with a sister, when he was about twelve years old, left with only two buffalo, one male and one female. He decided to go stay with his mother's brother Rato Loha in Ngahu Watu, and he took his buffalo out to pasture near there.

One day he fell asleep under a pandanus tree, and woke to see two large pythons fighting before his eyes. One of them was a white python from the sea (*kaboko kaka*), and the other was a black python from the land (*kaboko tana*). Their bodies were so violently twisted together that it looked like they would finish each other off, strangling in a mutual deadlock.

Moved by feelings of compassion but afraid to pull them apart, Rangga Ramba Deta took his own headcloth and tore it into two pieces, laying it on the snakes and saying "Here, my Lords, take this cloth as a sign that you must separate, or else you will surely kill each other." Immediately, the snakes fell apart and turned into two splendidly built men.

"Don't be afraid," one of them told him. "You have made peace by offering us the cloth, and we have received it. What can we do to reward you for your sacrifice?"

"I am just a poor orphan, grandparents, so I would accept whatever you wish to give me," said Rangga Ramba Deta.

"Then we will give you riches from the sea and from the land," said the snake men, then they both disappeared. Rangga Ramba Deta went home to his mother's brother's house and told him what had happened.

When he was old enough, Rangga Ramba Deta set up his own corral near the garden hamlet called Bala Moro. He built a small wooden fence around it, and his two buffalo were so tame that they would go out by themselves during the day to eat grass and come back on their own in the evenings. But then something strange started to happen. When the bull went to drink from the source at Wai Kapeke, he came back with five or six other buffaloes whose horns all turned down (*kamburu kudu*). When the cow went off to drink from the source at Wai Mallu near the coast, she came back five or six other buffaloes with the same horns. This didn't happen if they went to drink water anywhere else. It was the special power of these sources.

Everyone was amazed, and no one could claim the animals because they had no notches in their ears (to mark ownership). Soon Rangga Ramba Deta had so many buffalo that he built a village, called Rangga Baki. It had the form of a giant corral, surrounded by a stone fence, and was known as "the village to watch the buffalo and tend the horses" (*parona eli kari, dagha ndara*).

He took up a wooden plate, and decided he would put a notch on the plate for each corral that he had filled with one hundred buffalo. There are eight-eight notches on the plate, so he once had 8,800 buffalo. The plate is now an heirloom in Rangga Baki. It cannot be used by Rangga Ramba Deta's descendants or by their guests, but only by his daughters who marry out. When they come back to their origin village to scatter betel nut on the tombs of their ancestors during the sea worm festivities (*nale*), then they can eat from that plate and receive his blessings.

There are two possible ways to analyze this narrative: One (which I followed in Hoskins 1991) is to "read" its general cultural messages in a classificatory sense. The second is to look instead for more personal, idiosyncratic meanings.

In the first mode, we can simply observe how the story suggests interpretations of the iconography of the snakeskin cloth. The secret of wealth and of rulership lies in the ability to end conflict and bring together complementary opposites in a peaceful rather than antagonistic way. Light and dark are expressive of other divisions (male and female, land and water) that must also be brought into the relationship in order to produce descendants or crops. The two pythons are powerful creatures whose fierceness needed to be tempered by the cool wisdom conveyed by cloth. As recipients of a sacrifice, these snakes showed their gratitude with gifts of wealth. The story can be read against the background of other stories about snakes presented as the makers and consumers of human sacrifices. In this model, a man can achieve a transcendent, encompassing status by reconciling opposites and thus demonstrating hierarchical authority. The narrative suggests that the excesses of either sexual passion (the coupling of a male and female snake) or blood lust must be moderated by exchange.

In the second mode, however, we can try to read this text as showing Raja Horo's complicated personal ambivalence toward his ancestral heritage and his commitment to Christianity and modernity. Ramba Deta's fabulous wealth may be represented as originating in peacemaking, but it was also so divisive that it caused his death. A conflict over bridewealth payments with the headhunting village of Ndelo erupted suddenly, and Ramba Deta, left behind by sons, was wounded in the leg. When his sons came to his bedside, they urged him to divide his livestock immediately so there would be no further conflicts about inheritance. Horrified at their greed and lack of concern for him, he packed up all his gold and hid in a small garden hamlet near Tossi. There, he instructed his personal servants to bury him secretly, wrapping all the finest ornaments inside his funeral shroud. He cursed his immediate descendants, declaring that no one should reveal the location of his grave for seven generations.

Raja Horo, his great-grandson, was now a great-grandfather, so in the Kodi of the 1980s it should finally have been possible to determine the gravesite by divination. A large stone megalith, pulled by his grandson Rato Longo, stood in Rangga Baki ready to receive the bones when they were found, and Raja Horo sang me a few lines of doggerel verse (*lawitti*) that supposedly protected the treasure from plunder by local grave thieves. But although Horo believed that he was the beneficiary of the powers of the python that Ramba Deta had encountered, he also had not been able to find the buried wealth. Whenever bones are dug up for reburial, the gold and ivory found there go by rights to the descendants. His ancestor's soul was, he said, apparently still embittered and not ready to share his riches with the new generation.

Horo's text is followed by an additional commentary (written in the third person, like a government report), which offers an interpretation linking the story to sightings of the snake at important times in his life, and providing a moral justification for the veneration of the python and the way his ancestor addresses it as "grandfather" (*ambu*) or "Lord" (*mori*):

> There are also stories about snakes in other traditions, such as in the Bible in the Old Testament, the snake in the Garden of Eden who spoke to Eve, so we should not be so surprised at this story. The power of snakes is so well known we have the proverb that says as sneaky as a snake and as mild as a dove.[2] It is not the intention of this description to present the snake as something that we worship like a god, but there are real events which are related to the snake's legacy that we must recount:
>
> 1. When Raja Horo had a big feast in 1953, a snake as large as your big toe and very tame came up into his bed to watch the festivities. He came down to watch people butchering the pigs, and played around in the middle of the thousands of guests, even climbing up on top of a gas lamp.
> 2. When the Raja of Kodi became the Head of the Council of Rajas in 1948 the snake came again to his bed, and someone then told him to go away, and he vanished we do not know where.
> 3. When the Raja of Kodi was very sick in 1968 and brought to the hospital in Waikabubak, after he had left the snake came and curled up on the cushion, in exactly the same place where he had been sitting earlier.

The commentary indicates something of a compromise: A pagan story is introduced and framed with references to the Bible. While Raja Horo denied worshiping animals, he accepts that the snake was at times a protector and guardian to him, and says that the snake wanted to be near him on these occasions of both his greatest triumphs and his greatest suffering. The snake who came onto his cushion when he was sick was expressing its concern, and he says in fact that when he was told this at the hospital, he immediately began to feel better.

In January 1980, Raja Horo told me a few other snake stories. His son Cornelius trained as a Protestant minister and did not respect the snake. Once he saw him at his house in Jakarta and chopped him in two pieces. Other family members were horrified, telling him that "to kill that snake is like killing your own grandfather." Cornelius then collected the two pieces in a blanket and apologized, asking forgiveness from the snake's spirit. The next day, they opened up the blanket and the snake was whole again, and slithered away. But Cornelius never enjoyed much prosperity after that day.

When they wanted to move the bones of Raja Horo's mother from an earthen grave into a stone tomb, the snake marked her grave for them. First, they dug in the wrong place, and couldn't find anything. Then people in their ancestral village told them they had seen the snake coming to sun itself on another heap of stones, and when they dug them up they found her coffin and grave goods. Her body could then be moved into the stone chamber prepared for her husband.

Raja Horo added that on several other occasions the snake came into his bed, both in Bondo Kodi and in Waingapu, the island capital. Once, he noticed that it was sleeping under his pillow and had gotten a bit flattened. "Oh, excuse me, grandfather," he had said, and the snake had gone on its way. After that, he was appointed head of the Council of Rajas (Ketua Dewan Raja-Raja). On another occasion, it climbed on top of the mosquito netting over his bed and watched him from above. He knew something of great importance would happen, and a few days later the transfer of sovereignty from the Netherlands to a new independent Indonesia was announced.

In Kodi terminology, the snake would be called his *yora* ("wild spirit familiar") or *ndepetona* (literally, "the pouches of his betel bag," figuratively, his bosom companion). This is a very special and intimate relationship, with complicated obligations on both sides: The wild spirit offers gifts of wealth and success in love, but requires regular payment in the form of sacrifices and the respect of particular taboos. The spirit is represented as a jealous wife (*ariwyei marapu*) who may place restrictions on her human partner's relationships with other women, the way he dresses, or the houses he lives in. In conversation, Raja Horo acknowledged the complex commitments involved in this relationship, but his comment at the end of the printed text plays down these aspects, seeming to reduce this special veneration for a snake familiar to tolerance for all small creatures:

> Our understanding of these events is that although we people have been given the right by the Lord God to rule over the other creatures on the earth, still they need to be able to come close to us as long as we are not cruel to them.

To fully understand how the snake's blessing was expressed in his own life, we must turn to that life, and in particular to five specific themes: his father's death and early hardships, his Christian education and polygamous marriages, his difficulties assuming command of the region during the Japanese occupation, efforts to find Rangga Ramba Deta's grave and build a public tomb for him, and his activities as a healer and maker of medicines after retiring from government office.

A COLONIAL CHILDHOOD

The future Raja of Kodi was born in the first years of the twentieth century as Rangga Horo, the son of Pati Katoda and Ndengi Wallu. His father's ancestral village, Rangga Baki, was locked in a feud with his mother's village, Ratenggaro. When Rangga Horo was just a small boy, his father was killed in battle by a man from Kodi Bokol who fought for Ratenggaro, and he was taken into the house of his grandfather Rato Raya. Rato Raya rode onto the battlefield between the two villages and was struck by a spear that pulled his lungs completely outside his chest. Because he had medicine that he had received from his ancestors, he was able to push his lungs back into his chest and ride home. The story of his miraculous recovery made him famous, and he became one of the most important men in Kodi.

When the Dutch army took political control of Sumba in 1909, they sought to appoint a local leader who would work with them to administer the island. A meeting of the elders of the different ancestral villages of Kodi Bokol ("Greater Kodi") was held in Tossi, and Rato Loghe Kanduyo was selected and given a gold staff to designate him as raja (Hoskins 1993a: 127–28). Rato Loghe came from the ceremonial center of calendrical ritual, but from a house associated with the enforcement of traditional garden boundaries, not the one that "held the year" and owned the most sacred heirlooms. Notions of precedence interacted with a diarchic division of powers to delineate an original source of power and its executor, with the executor delegated to negotiate with outside powers.

For the smaller population of Kodi Bangedo, however, the ritually central village of Waindium was not the one where government power came to be located. A number of prominent men were asked if they would accept the silver staff of the Raja Kecil. Among these were Rato Raya of Rangga Baki and his archrival Rato Poka of Ratenggaro, but neither of them would swear to stop their feud to cooperate with a new Pax Nederlandica. Rato Tende of Parona Baroro became a friend and ally of the Dutch but did not want the staff. It was finally given to Rato Hembo of Hali Kandangar, a small village that had split off from Waindimu a few generations earlier. No figure associated with a ritually important house was approached.

In just two years, the region was torn by civil war because soldiers of the Netherlands Indies army were accused of raping a local woman and beating laborers on a project to build a bridge between Kodi Bokol and Kodi Bangedo. Four soldiers were killed in an ambush, and the Dutch retaliated by burning the royal village of Tossi. The Dutch commander fled to Bangedo and was sheltered by Rato Tende, while Wona Kaka, a famous headhunter from Kodi Bokol, began a three-year resistance struggle. The first Kodi raja, Rato Loghe, rode to Parona Baroro to negotiate the payment of bloodwealth, but he was pulled from his horse, tied up and beaten, and made to march two days to a Dutch prison, where he soon died. His nephew, Ndera Wulla, was appointed to take his place.

The armed struggle against the Dutch came to an end in 1913, when Wona Kaka and four other leaders surrendered their weapons and were sent into exile. Rangga Horo watched them lay down their spears and ride off on a white ship, and he was very impressed by the power of the colonial rulers.

When Dutch officials came to recruit the sons of important families to go to a new elementary school in Tanggaba, he eagerly agreed to travel to the Weyewa district to do so.

In the 1920s, he became the only student from Kodi to attend a small theological seminary in Karuni that would train village evangelists (*guru injil*). One of the most treasured momentos in his later life was a photograph of the small class of six students at this school, who (not coincidentally) later became the native administrators appointed by the Dutch to carry out colonial policy. He appeared in this photograph as a short, full-faced boy, studiously copying lessons out of a schoolbook, while beside him sat the taller, lankier boy who later became the raja of Memboro, one of his closest friends and rivals.

The Dutch brought to an end the period of intraregional feuding and interregional headhunting that had claimed the life of his father and almost his grandfather as well. They found in Rangga Horo, now baptized "Hermanus," their most diligent student: Of all the native administrators, he was the only one capable of writing reports in the appropriate style, and the one most skilled at recordkeeping. He adopted Western dress, and after independence in 1950 decided that one of the best ways to "modernize" Kodi was to require that men should cut their hair and that women should wear blouses or kabayas on all public occasions. His enthusiastic embrace of all the trappings of Dutch *beschaving* ("civilization") provoked criticism from some quarters in his own society, but allowed him to rise to the very top of island administration during the colonial period.

Hermanus Rangga Horo began to work for the Dutch Reformed Mission (Zending der Gereformeerde Kerken) in 1927, when he was a new husband and father. He remembered the period as one of great hardship, because shortly after the birth of their fourth child, his first wife left him for another man. He was left to raise the children on his own, with no assistance.

"It will bring tears to your eyes to hear how we suffered!" he told me. "I had to fetch water with my tiny children, since no woman would do it for me. My oldest son, Sam would carry one end of a bamboo pole, my daughter Reta the other end. Since Sam was taller than Reta, the water would always spill out before we reached home."

He sought the hand of Mina Moto, the daughter of a Javanese trader. His attraction to her came partly from the fact that she was Javanese, and so was tied to a wider world that he hoped to learn about. Although her father was Muslim, he agreed to allow his daughter to marry and be baptized as a Christian. They set up their new household in the 1930s, and Mina Moto cared for the four children from his first marriage and eventually nine of her own.

The Dutch appointed H. R. Horo to assist the raja of Kodi, Ndera Wulla, in administering the new kingdom (*swapraja*), which included both Kodi Bokol and Kodi Bangedo. His duties included keeping records on the population and submitting written reports on litigation involving land or cattle, to help the older raja and subrajas of Bangedo,[3] who were all illiterate.

Raja Hermanus Rangga Horo, wearing the nationalist pinci hat, attending a marriage negotiation with Marta Mete, his fifth wife, on the left and Mina Moto, his second wife, on the right. (Photo J. Hoskin, 1980)

To mark his newly important position in government service, Horo rebuilt his ancestral house in Rangga Baki and sponsored a two-day buffalo feast (*woleko wongo weiyo*) to consecrate it. He had planned to call down the soul of Rangga Ramba Deta to witness his new position and share in the sacrificial meat. However, when he and his wife consulted a group of priests (*rato marapu*), they were told they could not summon an ancestor if they were Christian. The most sacred invocations to this ancestral founder were not performed, but when I interviewed Mina Moto in 1986 she told me about a moment when she was touched by a "mystical experience":

> As a new daughter-in-law to Rangga Baki, I was supposed to go down into the village square and dance to honor the ancestors. But my Javanese father had never let me learn Kodi dancing, so I was very nervous. They dressed me in fine jewels and a sarung, then something came into me, that made me very beautiful and special. I became like a forest nymph (Ind. bidadari).
>
> My father gave me a gold ring that came from Java, and I dropped it onto the dancing ground to ask permission. It fell with a little noise—plunk!— and then I felt the gold heirloom mamuli that they had hung around my neck. I raised my arms, and I was able to move with almost no effort. I slid around gracefully, my feet beating out the rhythms of the gongs. Although I had not learned to dance, the marapu made me dance. I felt so happy. And when my

father gave a buffalo calf for the sacrifice, people told me that they were very impressed. I moved just like a Kodi girl would have, as if I had been dancing my whole life.

The passage vividly illustrates her ambivalent position: the daughter of a foreigner, yet someone who had grown up in Kodi, a Muslim by birth and a Christian by conversion. The Javanese gold ring and the locally smelted mamuli pendant gave her a feeling of power and grace that she described as a kind of possession. But she followed this glowing story with its more sobering consequences:

I felt blessed then, but there may have been a hidden cost. After the feast, both my husband and I became very sick. We were taken to the hospital and had to stay there for several weeks. People said it was because the feast was not complete, it did not involve the most important ancestors, who should have been invited even though we were Christian. Yes, the marapu let me dance, but we had to pay another price.

Her comments reveal the still-shifting terrrain, between fearing the sanctions of the marapu and celebrating a new faith, that she and her husband had to navigate.

THE JAPANESE OCCUPATION
AND THE GHOST OF RANGGA MAHEMBA

In 1942, Japanese soldiers invaded Sumba and deported all Dutch citizens and their families to internment camps. A very large occupying force of 8,000 soldiers was sent over, which placed heavy demands on the island's population of about 200,000. Local people were forcibly inducted to construct air strips and bunkers along the southern and western coasts of the island to prepare for a possible invasion of Australia. Churches were closed, and religious instruction in schools was stopped. Sunday became a work day like any other. All of the power that Europeans had seemed to command evaporated in an instant.

The islands of Eastern Indonesia were placed under naval control because they were regarded as "politically primitive and economically essential to Japan" (Ricklefs 1993: 199). They were governed in a manner that was the most repressive of all. The Japanese commander in Kodi is described by all who remembered him as a tyrant. He required local government officials to provide him and his troops with rice and meat in a period of great scarcity. All imports of food, cloth, and metal goods were stopped, and many people wore rags. Local herds were decimated by the slaughter of forty head of livestock each month to feed the soldiers. When people did not show up for forced labor service, they were fiercely beaten. Hungry, weakened laborers who did not work fast enough were also beaten.

The Japanese commander even asked the local community to supply his men with sexual services. Horo described to me how deeply troubled he and Raja Ndera Wulla were by this request: "We told him no, we were sorry, this was not Java. In Java we knew there were women like that, women who provided that service for money. But here on Sumba we didn't have anyone like that, only our own wives and daughters. We pleaded with him to bring women from Java for the soldiers."

Some outside women were brought in, but some ugly incidents involving Japanese soldiers occurred during the occupation. Many Sumbanese were imprisoned and humiliated, and no one believed the Japanese propaganda that they had been sent to liberate the Indies from the oppression of Dutch colonialism.

In 1943, Raja Ndera Wulla died, some said as a consequence of his sorrow at not being able to relieve the suffering of his people. Hermanus Rangga Horo was appointed to succeed him, taking leadership during a period of incredible tension.

He had to assist the occupying forces to extract food from a starving population and to enforce order over proud and provocative personalities.

His most difficult moment came, he told me, when a close relative from his own village, Rangga Mahemba, was accused of stealing cigarettes from Dutch storage units.

> They came to me and told me they had caught the person who had been stealing. They found packages of cigarettes under his bed. Rangga Mahemba denied that he had done anything wrong. He said someone else had put the cigarettes there. The Japanese tried him, convicted him, and sentenced him to be shot in the regency capital. Rangga Mahemba protested his innocence, and refused to wear a cloth tied over his eyes when they led him out to the firing squad.
>
> "I want to see those bullets before they hit me," he said. I had to stand and witness his execution, with all my family standing beside me, including his own brothers and children. I told them all to be calm, we didn't want more people to be executed, we had to accept it. I cried afterward.

Rangga Mahemba's defiance of his executioners became enshrined in popular legend. In 1986, when I returned to Kodi with my husband, people told us they wanted to give him a Kodi name that belonged to a hero. The name they selected was Rangga Mahemba. Many people told us again about his bravery, and they detailed plans to call back his soul and provide him with a new tombstone in the ancestral village.

As my husband and I were sitting in the Horo living room discussing this story, an absurd coincidence brought it to life. Someone knocked at the door, and in came the Japanese commander, returning to visit Kodi forty-two years after he had left. Assisted by an interpreter, he explained that he had fond memories of Raja Horo, especially of the times that they had gone hunting together. He produced a photograph of himself and the Kodi Raja standing in front of a jeep, with rifles over their shoulders and a few birds strapped to their backs.

"The former Japanese commander wanted to revisit the island where he had spent such pleasant years," explained his interpreter. "He is now retired, and he would like to give a gift to the community that received him so well."

People excitedly ran out to fetch the current district admininistrator and other notable figures who could receive this foreign guest in Raja Horo's absence. The Japanese commander had brought bags of pens, candies, and toys to give to children, who soon scrambled to take them. Adults, however, kept their distance, and even moved out of the way when he approached them.

"That was my uncle he had shot," a schoolteacher whispered as he watched from the sidelines.

Food was prepared for the guests, but all of the people from Rangga Baki who had been at the house left before it was served. The "gift" that local government officials thought would be most appropriate was a meeting hall, which would make Bondo Kodi look more "modern" by adding another stone building among those of wood and bamboo. Arrangements were made for him to send money to the district capital, where it would be erected to mark the friendship of Japan and Indonesia.

The Japanese commander stayed only a few hours. There were few other names that he remembered from his time in Kodi, but no one could be found from the period of the occupation who was willing to meet him. He said he was very disappointed that Raja Horo had passed away, because he had been so "hospitable" during his time in Kodi. In his rented Jeep, he visited the seashore and the new bridge that the Indonesian government had constructed to replace the one built by the Japanese.

Once he had gone, I asked people what they made of this "nostalgic" visit. How could Kodi people and this Japanese commander have such different memories of that period? The most trenchant comment came from Pati Cora, a nephew of Rangga Mahemba's who was also a ritual singer.

It was Rangga Mahemba's ghost which sent him back. He heard his name being mentioned when your husband came, and he realized no bloodwealth (*tapo*) had ever been paid. In our custom, a death has to be washed clean with gold. The Japanese commander is getting old. He wanted to pay off his debts before he died. He gave this money because he must have seen Rangga Mahemba in his dreams. The money should not be taken by the government. It should be used to call back his soul from the sun and moon.

He then finished his conversation with an invocation in ritual verse of what he thought was the real message of this visit:

| Wakico pa dimbyani mono | Digging up things which are pressed down |
| Rapico pa dalo nggani | Lifting the thatch to look inside |

A bandalo makana mono	When the rifles were fired and
A panna pa kalakona	The bow let loose its arrow
A ndeha bali cana	The ducks from over land
Mono a bandu bali lyoro	And the wild fowl from over seas
Ba na heda dengeni mono	Killed him without cause
Ba na mate dengeni	Executed him for nothing
Maka duki bandi hondi wu panduku	So they should bring him back to the row of tombstones
Tama bongoka ela rate wu palolo	Return him back to the graves in a line

The bloodwealth that should be paid to the families of the victims of violent crimes is believed to make a killer feel responsible, causing a "guilty twitch" which will drive him to return to the scene of the crime. As long as this debt remains unpaid, the killer cannot be assured of good health or prosperity. Once he has made the proper payments, however, the soul of the victim can be recalled to the village ("brought back to the row of tombstones/returned to the graves in a line") and peace can be re-established between the two groups of people.

Though it is highly unlikely that any of this money will be used for these purposes, his comments reveal something of the obligations that bind one generation to another, and that continued to haunt Raja Horo as he tried to find a way to honor the legacy of his ancestor Rangga Ramba Deta.

THE COLONIAL CULT OF ROYALTY

In 1945, Japan surrendered, and Indonesian nationalists issued their own declaration of independence. The Netherlands did not accept this, however, and returned in force to Indonesia. Five years of bloody fighting began in Java and Sumatra, but the Dutch ministers and administrators who returned to Sumba were welcomed. In 1946, the state of Eastern Indonesia was created at a conference in Denpasar. It was headed by a Balinese prince, Soekawati, and based in Makassar. The Dutch intended it as the beginning of a new federation of states for the Indies, but opponents saw it as a puppet government whose initials NIT (Negara Indonesia Timur) really stood for *negara ikut tuan*, or "the state which follows the [Dutch] master."[4] Although Horo had taken over the administration of Kodi in 1943, he was not formally installed as raja until the Dutch returned to power.

In 1945, Rehi Calei, an important elder in Tossi, challenged H. R. Horo's right to hold the raja's staff, claiming that Tossi had always been the ceremonial center of Kodi, and now that the Dutch were back on the island it was time to return the staff to its rightful owners. With the help of a local schoolteacher, Rehi Calei sent a series of letters to the regency capital in Waikabubak arguing that he be appointed to succeed Raja Ndera Wulla. The situation was complicated by the fact that Tossi and Rangga Baki, rivals in status, were also affines. Raja Horo's oldest daughter, Margareta, was married to the son of Rehi Calei. She remembered the situation this way in 1984:

I was engaged to Martinus Calei when we were both children, and my father was working with Raja Ndera Wulla. Our families were both important, and the brideprice was set at two hundred head of livestock. When I was fourteen, the people from Tossi became afraid for my safety, because there were so many Japanese soldiers around, and all the unmarried girls could be approached by them. So they brought dozens of buffalo and horses to my father's house as the *haranga londo* (the payment to allow the bride to live with her husband) and I moved to Tossi.

Then, while I was living in my father-in-law's house, he began his feud with my father. He accused him of corruption during the Japanese occupation, saying he made money off the suffering of the people. Letters went back and forth, people went back and forth, and for a while I was afraid I would not be able to see my family anymore. I cried and wanted to come home, but my father told me stay with my husband. My father-in-law said the people of Tossi had a hereditary right to be raja because they were the "mother-father village" for all of Kodi. My father answered him with the same words Raja Ndera Wulla had used. He said, "No one is born holding the raja's staff in his mother's womb!" The Dutch resident was the one who had to decide.

Resident Schuyler reviewed the case, and called on various other important people in Tossi to offer their own testimonies. Ra Katupu, Rehi Calei's rival within the village, said that Rehi Calei was descended from Uma Nale, the center for sea worm ceremonies, which was "the house of priests, not the house of government." He denied, as Horo had, that there was any traditional hereditary right to rule, and asserted that diarchic principles should in fact prevent one man holding both spiritual and temporal power.[5] The Dutch also hesitated to give so much power to an older man with only an elementary-school education. The compromise eventually suggested was that Martinus Calei, who had a Javanese secondary education, would be nominated for important government offices, but his barely literate father would stand aside. Raja Horo would keep the gold staff, and the marriage of Margareta and Martinus would be celebrated in a large Christian wedding, which would also show that their families had made peace with each other.

In 1947, Resident Schuyler planned the ceremony to install Raja Horo as the raja of Kodi in what he may have already realized would be the island's last opulent expression of the colonial cult of royalty. Raja Horo was dressed in the most elaborate form of traditional costume, supplemented by a few colonial touches: His head was bound with many meters of bright red, orange, and black cloth, and he wore a starched Dutch white shirt. His loins were wrapped with a fine indigo snake cloth, and similar cloth was draped around his shoulders. Attendants had to help him put on and tie the cloths; it had been so long since he had worn Kodi clothing, he had forgotten how to put it on. A new pair of wire-rimmed glasses were prepared for his eyes, and new leather shoes were placed on his feet.

A wooden throne, a sort of palanquin, was constructed for the occasion. Like the litters used by Balinese kings, it was carved and painted with a pair of snakes. The snakes were identified as the benefactors who helped Rangga Ramba Deta, but, as Jessup notes in a catalog of the *Court Arts of Indonesia*, "Paired nagas are a royal symbol and in addition have a deification implication" (1990: 241). The platform was carried by eight men from his ancestral village of Rangga Baki to the district capital at Bondo Kodi, more than an hour away. When guests arrived at Rangga Baki to see the beginning of the ceremony, a mock battle modeled on the calendrical jousting of the pasola was staged between the villages of Ratenggaro and Rangga Baki. Several hundred riders rode about in full war costume over the terrain where his own father had been killed and his grandfather wounded. Then the procession formed, gongs and drums were beaten with the victory rhythm used after a successful headhunt, and dozens of dancers, spectators, and animals being brought for sacrifice began the trek to the capital for his installation.

After a formal ceremony in Dutch and Indonesian, dozens of buffalo, pigs, and goats were slaughtered to feed several thousand guests at a night-long carnival (*pasar malam*). Chinese storekeepers from the city brought gas lamps and city foods—satay, spiced curries, medicinal wines, beer, packets of boiled rice, and coconut beef. Many villagers who had never tasted more than the usual boiled meat of Kodi cooking sampled these exotic national dishes for the first time. There were both traditional dances and Western dances, Christian prayers and marapu blessings. Spectators say there had not been anything to equal it until the companion ceremony carried out thirty-eight years later when Raja Horo died and a funeral procession carried him—in an exact retracing of his earlier itinerary—from his home in Bondo Kodi to his tombstone in Rangga Baki.

In 1948, Raja Horo was moved from Kodi to the coastal town of Waingapu to become the head of the Council of Rajas for the whole island. He traveled, as Sumba's supreme sovereign, to a meeting of other native rulers in Makassar, where he became very taken with stories of the mystical attributes of rajas:

> On Sumba, I had not heard much about the sacred power of rulers (*kesaktian raja-raja*), but in Makassar they told me many stories about magical kerises, healing potions, invincible weapons, and the splendid treasures that each raja should have, with all the finest things in the kingdom. I met princes from Bali and Sulawesi, and sultans from Ternate and Tidore. Like the Biblical Solomon, these rajas had many wives and fine palaces, and all their gold gave them special powers. They could heal the wounded and cure the sick, restore fertility and potency. I wanted to bring back some of that power to my own island.

Entranced with an image of royalty that he then attached to himself, Raja Horo copied what he could on the somewhat less opulent scale of a remote eastern island. He took a second wife, a Savunese girl who came to live with him at his official residence, while his first wife and thirteen children remained in Kodi. He began to buy gold objects, or at least to "borrow" them from people who needed quick cash, and established a royal treasure. Although many items were pawned rather than fully owned by him, the simple presence of gold in his possession was believed to endow him with a certain numinous quality.

He brought a goldsmith from Makassar who could smelt gold and silver into the forms of traditional Sumbanese jewelry—the mamuli pendant and marangga breastplate, gold chains, and half-moon head ornaments (see photograph of him showing me part of his gold treasure in 1984). He needed to have a storehouse of gold to prepare for the marriages of his daughters, who were being sought by the sons of important families from all over the island. Over a hundred horses and buffalo were pledged by the raja of Memboro when he came requesting the hand of Salome, and another hundred were offered for Nona Kapu by a royal family from East Sumba. Gold and ivory were needed, along with pigs and fine textiles, to "match" these brideprices with an appropriate counterpayment.

Despite receiving hundreds of buffalo in bridewealth, Horo never approached the wealth in livestock enjoyed by his ancestor Rangga Ramba Deta. His own corrals were modest, and often raided or plagued by disease. I heard him make several speeches reproaching his sons for not caring well

Raja Horo seated in his living room, showing the author some of his gold treasures: a half-moon shaped tabelo headpiece, gold chains, and the crossed horns design of a marangga breastplate. (Photo M. Mete, 1984)

enough for their buffalo herds, and others remarked critically, "Raja Horo wants to be a gold Raja, a foreign prince, rather than a Kodi Raja, whose wealth would show in his corral." Entranced by external images of sovereignty, he sought to aquire the metal jewelry, weapons and regalia that were seen elsewhere as defining features of royal rank. Some of his neighbors saw these innovations as disloyal to his Kodi heritage, and argued that he would not recover the good graces of the pythons who had once blessed him if he did not respect traditional values. "Why, he even goes out to buy cattle with money for his own sons' bridewealth payments," they argued.

Wealth in livestock was locally seen as more legitimate because it was public: Anyone could see how many animals were in a corral, and it would be difficult for a man with many buffalo to refuse a relative in need with arguments that he had nothing to give. Wealth in gold or money, on the other hand, could be hidden away, and kept a secret from those who wanted it. Raja Horo was rumored by some to be fabulously wealthy, and he was disparaged by others as a pauper with princely pretensions. The family kept information about its financial situation strictly private, increasing speculation in both camps.

The most public investment that Raja Horo made was in the education of his sons: His oldest son, Sam, studied law on Java and eventually became a judge in Jakarta. Mina Moto's son Alex Ramba Deta (named after the ancestor who had the snake encounter) studied English (completing a master's degree at the University of Leeds), and became a professor of literature in Jogjakarta. Marta Mete's son Ibrahim finished a law degree and worked in a government office in Waingapu. Almost all of his other sons completed a high school education and qualified to become civil servants, drawing salaries and rising to positions of some influence.

These changes in notions of wealth and power came at time when Indonesia was preparing itself for independence. In 1950 the long war between republican and Dutch forces waged in other parts of the archipelago came to an end. Some people wondered if Raja Horo, a Christian educated by the Dutch and obviously influenced by them, would be loyal to the Netherlands Indies or stand with the revolution. In fact, his feelings were probably very ambivalent during the five years of armed struggle. But when it became clear that Sukarno's Declaration of Independence would become a reality, he did not hesitate. Raja Horo was the one who authorized the final lowering of the Dutch flag in Waingapu and the raising of the flag of the new Republic of Indonesia. He could thus claim with some justice that he was not only a surviving figure from the period of colonial royalty but also the "midwife" who helped the new nation to be born on this remote island.

POSTINDEPENDENCE CONFLICTS OVER POLYGAMY

Indonesia's first few decades were marked by residues of the struggle against colonialism and a visionary nationalism that sought to unite its widely scattered people in a single imagined community. One result was that questions of ideological purity became especially charged in a number of arenas. Local Protestants decided to separate from the Dutch Calvinist mission to form the independent Christian Church of Sumba. They wanted to define a new style of Christianity, cleansed of the stain of colonialism, which would offer moral leadership to the island's inhabitants.

At each synod of the new Independent Church of Sumba, polygamy was discussed. In 1947, the synod decided that men guilty of polygamy could no longer take communion in the church. Disagreement arose about baptizing women in polygamous marriages, and discussion on that topic continued throughout the 1950s. In 1954, the church decided to allow these wives to be part of the Christian community, and in 1958, a more detailed rationale was provided: "The added wife comes from a pagan community, and just like a blind person, she has been deceived by her husband, so that she allowed herself to be convinced by his courtship. Now that her eyes are open and she knows Jesus, she realizes her sin, but she still cannot simply detach herself from her husband, since their marriage is already official, and her husband would be furious if she tried to leave him. She is welcome to come to the Church and to raise her children in it" (Gereja Kristen Sumba 1974: 7).

For the man who had been baptized in the church and attended it regularly, however, the sin of taking an additional wife was more serious: On the one hand, the church said he could not be forgiven so easily, but on the other they recognized that he should not simply abandon the wives and children that he had accepted responsibility for. Their recommendation was that the polygamous husband should be excluded from active participation, but encouraged to baptize his children and be a "social Christian" by supporting church construction and activities.

Raja Horo had, in speaking to me, justified his taking additional wives with the argument that polygamy had to be seen as "the right of kings" (*hak raja-raja*). But though it could be argued that it was a part of traditional statecraft to forge alliances with other peoples through marriage, it was harder to make such an argument after independence. Mina Moto, who had not been told about her husband's new marriage, was surprised and not at all pleased when the Savunese wife was brought back to Kodi, and the whole household was thrown into disarray. Raja Horo returned as a district head (*camat*) under the new independent government, but his leadership was now challenged by those who claimed he had betrayed the Christian faith.

These sanctions hit Raja Horo hard, because they defined a contradiction between the splendid "rights of kings" (which he had learned about from serving the Dutch colonial administration) and the Christian church (which he had also served for twenty years). He was deeply disturbed that he himself was not invited to be part of the community of people, many of whom he had personally baptized. The new Protestant church in Bondokodi was built directly in front of the raja's house. On Sundays his wives and children made up about half of the small congregation, but he himself stayed at home.

The paradoxical result of this censure was that it made Raja Horo decide to marry even more women. "If they decided to exclude me for marrying one other wife, they couldn't do more for additional ones, could they?" he noted. In the late 1950s, he took two younger wives, Korilina from Balaghar and Marta Mete from Bondo Kawango, Kodi Bokol, bringing his total to five. The small bamboo houses behind the large wooden house were built then, for them and their children, who started to come almost immediately: Korilina eventually had seven, Marta four. Both were skilled at designing ikat textiles, and they contributed to the household economy by selling Kodi cloth to pay for school fees and uniforms for their children.

But a large polygamous household is a considerable challenge to adminis-ter. After his fourth and fifth marriages, Horo's third wife became unhappy and ran off, returning to the Savunese community in Melolo, where she lived with another man. Her children were left behind, and became the responsibility of Mina Moto, as the most senior wife. Soon the wood-frame house had several dozen children moving in and out of it, and the family had to rent another house in the regency capital for those who were attend-ing school there.

Marta Mete, the youngest wife, had been his secretary at the camat's office before their marriage and had a secondary education. She became, as time passed, the most vocal of his wives and the most socially assured. She accepted his argument that the betrayal of his first and third wives justified his taking additional wives "to be sure there would be someone to raise the children," but she also told me that she regretted bitterly not holding on to her job in the civil service after her marriage. She also made it clear that Raja Horo had not followed Kodi custom. Most polygamous men kept their wives in separate households, one in the ancestral village and another near the gardens. The complex of small buildings in Bondokodi was a breeding ground for conflict and jealousy, while if each wife had had her own home (shared at times with her husband), family relations would not be so strained.

The raja's polygamous household contrasted with the increasing number of monogamous Christian households in the district capital of Bondokodi. Conversion to both the independent Protestant Church (Gereja Kristen Sumba, now separated from the Dutch Calvinist mother church) and the Catholic Church went up in the period after 1965, when anyone suspected of leftist leanings felt under pressure to show commitment to a monotheistic faith, since the Indonesian state took the position that "the making of believ-ers was the unmaking of Communists" (Thomson 1993: 8).[6] In the 1970s, the number of Christians stabilized at about one-fifth of the population.

In 1981, the Sumbanese Church leadership began a new campaign to increase conversion by relaxing certain restrictions. They decided to forgive the "sin of love" (dosa cinta) for those older men who promised not to marry again and to raise their children as good Protestants. Raja Horo was invited back to the communion table to drink the blood and eat the body of Christ.

He sponsored a huge Easter banquet at his house, in which the whole Christian community of Bondo Kodi was invited. It was, for him, a vindication of his leadership and a proof that his combination of "traditional" family politics with "modern" Christian values had ultimately triumphed.

THE SNAKE'S LEGACY: IMPOTENCE AND FERTILITY MEDICINE

Raja Horo's many children and many wives were the basis of a reputation he established as a healer who specialized in treating impotence and infertility. The medicines that he used were traditional combinations of plants, which he had learned from his grandfather Rato Raya. The most important ingredient was a thick, rather phallic vine called the *kyahi kara*, which is used to lash together bamboo in constructing Kodi houses. The firmness and tenacity it was supposed to produce were obviously related to the suggestive power of sympathetic magic. In a secret combination, Raja Horo took these traditional ingredients and mixed them with ash, coconut oil, and *jamu* (commercial herbal remedies) bought on Java.

He prided himself on a high success rate, and a number of clients rewarded him handsomely for his treatment. During the three years that I was able to observe his practice, three children were born to men who had previously complained of impotence. But because everyone knew what he treated, there was a certain stigma to having been a patient of Raja Horo's. A young man from a wealthy Weyewa family came to Bondokodi to get the medicine, and then tried to marry a local girl. She refused him adamantly, maintaining that "no medicines last forever," and she ended instead as the wife of Raja Horo's Makassarese goldsmith.

Raja Horo's ability to perform a cure depended not only on the medicines themselves but also on his own experience as a *tou manura*, or herbalist, and a vocation that he received in a dream. After the trip to Makassar, he saw the snake benefactors of Rangga Ramba Deta, who told him that he should make this gift available to others. He first treated only family members, and did not receive outside patients until after he retired from government service.

Many other impotence treatments sold in Indonesia are quite literally snake oil. Traveling peddlars, often from "exotic" places like Kalimantan, sell these preparations at markets. In 1980, I remember the visit of a flamboyant peddlar who was accompanied by a tattooed Dayak who performed feats of strength to show the efficacy of his medicines. I experienced a certain ironic pleasure in joining a crowd of Kodi spectators who recognized many of the "primitive" aspects of Dayak culture paraded before them (tattoos, symbols of headhunting, feathered headdresses) as their own, but still came to gape at an exotic "Other." Raja Horo invited the man to dinner to discuss his preparations, and the man bought a small bottle to sample.

Raja Horo's eclectic interest in medicines extended to modern ones as well. He asked me repeatedly if I could get testosterone for him, since he wanted to be able to give his patients hormonal treatments. (He was disappointed and perhaps unconvinced by my arguments that I could not get it without a doctor's prescription.)

Perhaps he had better luck with his grandson, the son of Martinus and Margareta Calei, who returned to Sumba in 1987 from a medical school on Java and set up a local practice.

THE SACRED POWER OF THE KING'S CLOTH: IMPORTED OR INDIGENOUS?

Horo's account of how he tried to "bring the sacred powers of rajas" back to Sumba at the end of the colonial era is just one moment in a long history of contacts between the island and the kingdoms and sultanates to the west. Indigenous social institutions, especially those that express hierarchical difference, have long been conceived and legitimated in terms of external political powers. A great many of the heirloom valuables stored in ancestral villages are imported objects (swords, spears, porcelain urns and plates, gongs), and histories of foreign origins are also attached to things made of wood or stone which could have been locally made (Hoskins 1993a: 29).

What makes these efforts particularly interesting to me, however, is both that we could hear about them directly from Raja Horo, speaking as an important actor in Sumba's history, and that it is possible to make explicit which aspects of Javanese and Balinese "high culture" were being imported at the middle of the twentieth century. Horo became particularly attached to the notion of *kesaktian*, a form of "sacred power" with no equivalent in Sumbanese languages.

Wiener, describing the ideas of magical power attached to Balinese kings, says:

> Power, *kesaktian*, results from the generation or maintenance of connections between a person and the invisible world, especially (though not exclusively) the gods. In the broadest sense, *kesaktian* is the ability to achieve any goal . . . it is synonymous with efficacy. . . . *Kesaktian* suggests more than human capabilities: an ability to prevent rain or . . . to know (and potently affect) the bodies and feelings of others. Phenomena Euro-Americans would ascribe to chance, coincidence, luck or charisma—words whose English definitions are essentially confessions of ignorance—are treated as meaningful messages to and about persons with power. Persons with endless good fortune, whose presence is sought by others who happily do their bidding, are regarded as tuned to the invisible world or *sakti*. (M. Wiener 1995: 58)

Sumbanese speak of power with reference to ancestors and to objects, to divisions and oppositions, but with no reference to a unitary source. The Dutch missionary Onvlee, looking for a way to translate the Christian notion of "holy," despaired that he could do so only by invoking either the hot, dangerous spiritually charged domain of the forbidden, or the cool, calming, but ultimately disempowering domain of the permitted (Onvlee 1938). People who had unusual success in life were said to *mangu marapu*, "have a way with the ancestors," and objects that were particularly charged were *hari*, "taboo." But persons could not control or call on invisible powers themselves, and even potent medicines were part of ancestral legacy, not individual charisma.

The particular relationship to the invisible that was believed in Bali and Java to be concentrated in royalty was organized differerently on Sumba, where rituals defined an oscillation of hot and cold, bitter and bland, and these powers tend to be dispersed throughout a number of different clans. Notions of rank and hierarchy are more clearly defined in East Sumba (Forth 1981, Hoskins 1996d), but even there traditional rulers did not have the importance that they did in Bali or Java before colonial control. Though the Dutch did not introduce ideas of hierarchy to the island, their appointment of native rulers transformed and reoriented local notions of power in important ways.

Horo had to reconceptualize his own view of his past and present in dialog with a number of outside interlocutors: first, the Dutch ministers who trained him in schools and converted him to Christianity; second, the Dutch adminstrators who employed him in colonial administration; third, the "other rajas" from Bali, Lombok, Sulawesi, and other parts of the province of Eastern Indonesia whom he met with in Makassar; fourth, the nationalist and populist leaders who criticized the "feudalism" of the colonial period and tried to introduce new republican ideals.

Horo's vision of his snake "spirit friend" as establishing a heritage of healing and mystical power (*warisan kesaktian*) was constructed from both an indigenous tradition of ancestral gifts and the historical fact of his service to the colonial government. The idea that the snake cloth was also a "royal cloth" (*kain raja-raja*) had a similarly complex genealogy. The Dutch administrator, familiar with the sumptuary rules about certain forms of batik on Java, had asked what kind of traditional clothing would be appropriate for a raja. While "royal clothing" did not exist as a category in West Sumba, men of high rank did show this through wearing gold ear pendants and ivory bracelets. The appropriateness of the snake cloth for the elaborate ritual of his installation seems to have come from its associations with the transition to another world and another status:

> Formerly, when a nobleman felt he was growing old and believed he would die soon. he would ask his eldest wife to make the necessary arrangments so that a *wola remba*[7] could be prepared for him as a shroud. The woman would call his granddaughters who were of marriageable age to the centre (*natara*) of the village and order then to start spinning. The old lady's major task consisted in encouraging them when their thread broke, something which happened often because the girls were thought to be inexperienced. For every fully spun spindle, the grandmother would reward the spinner with small presents. Because of

their so-called lack of experience, the girls were supposed to produce a coarse but strong thread which would make a thick cloth. The thick material was "like a thick skin and would not wear out easily." The deceased would take the cloth with him on his travel to the realm of the dead. Like reptiles, the dead, at least the wealthy ones, were provided with "an extra skin" ready for use when they chose to live again, that is, to come back to earth. The custom is recalled by older women in Kodi and seems to have been followed up to the 1930s. (Geirnaert-Martin 1991: 37)

The funeral cloth spun by young girls was considered a fitting garment for another kind of "rebirth" to a higher status, in a ceremony that turned Horo into a raja rather than an ancestor. Because its production was so costly and drawn out, this type of cloth could be used only as a ceremonial mantle or funeral shroud for men of the highest rank.

From a primeval sense that pythons brought rain to more mundane instances of encounters in the forest, pythons are emblems of fertility and power. They can be dangerous to the uninitiated: A girl's fertility can be damaged by being "scared" by the sight of a python fully open on the path, and although girls are told to spin the thread for the funeral cloth, they are not allowed to attend the secret ceremony where the threads are dyed with indigo to establish the pattern (Hoskins 1989b). A particularly sacred cloth (such as the one used to wrap Horo's body) should not be seen by young girls when it is fully spread out, as it may make them blind or ill (Geirnaert-Martin 1991: 37). Familiarity with the snakeskin pattern presumes sexual experience.

The representation of the python on man's cloth (worn as both mantle and shroud) might seem a domestication of this power, but it is also a harnessing of it to serve a specific social purpose—the glorification of a descent line and aristocratic leadership. It might be useful here to look somewhat more broadly at the magical and mythological traditions that link snakes and cloth in other parts of Indonesia.

In defiance of classical Freudians, snakes in much of the archipelago are not phallic symbols but instead are associated with sexually alluring women. The snake is a female ancestress, a powerful giver of fertility and rain, but also a sometimes dangerous and capricious woman. Remembering a childhood in West Java, Alit Veldhuisen-Djajasoebrata writes (1991: 51–52):

On my way to school I often saw a sawah-snake slithering over the path. We children then held our steps until the snake had vanished in the sawah dike. *Yang punya, tuh*, said one of the boys. I understood: "the one who owns it all," referring to Ibu Pertwiwi again, or Nyi Pohaci: identification with a grand snake or the thought of mighty snakes as protective beings came naturally to us and its relation with rice and rice-plants was easily made. You had to treat it all with proper respect. A snake was to be killed only if it proved injurious. And you felt awe for the small room in which rice was stored, where the cook entered as respectfully as when she was summoned by grandmother, each time she had to take out the ration of the day.

Both rice and the cotton plant are said to have originated from the body of Nyi Pohaci Sanyang Sri, who can take the form of a snake, especially a python (*ular naga*).

The ancestral mother of Javanese royalty, Dewi Nawang Wulan, had a cloth patterned with a scalelike motif called Antakusuma (after the snake-shaped god Dewa Anta) that was stolen from her while she was bathing. She remained on earth and married, giving birth to a daughter who married the last ruler of Majahpahit, and their offspring gave birth to the founder of the Matarm royal dynasty, according to legend. Although she supposedly later returned to the heavens, an heirloom jacket also called Antakusuma has been worn for centuries by Javanese kings when they ascended the throne (Veldhuisen-Djajasoebrata 1991: 52–53). The jacket has a patchwork pattern, and was worn by several sultans in the nineteenth century, as well as traditional priests in the Hindu enclave of Tengger, East Java. A Jogjakarta wayang story mentions a multicolored wool garment that could revive the dead (Veldhuisen-Djajasoebrata 1992: 53).

The Sumbanese *hanggi nggyoko* repeats these ideas of snakelike scales and a mixture of colors, transferring them into ikat technology and using hand-spun cotton instead of silk or wool. Raja Horo traveled frequently to Java and was particularly taken with the Javanese belief in the mystical power of rulers, so he relished such stories and sought out parallels in Sumbanese beliefs and practices. The veneration of snakes was undoubtedly important even before the colonial period. It has been reinterpreted into a specific series of beliefs about rajas in ways that are, I would argue, influenced by Javanese precedents, and then in turn by Dutch embellishments on Javanese notions of tradition.[8]

LIFE STORIES AND AN INDONESIAN HISTORICAL IMAGINATION

Horo's life story contrasts in interesting ways with the Sumatran memoirs of childhood translated and interpreted in Rodgers (1995) and Minang novels surveyed by Els Postel-Coster (1977). Both authors examine the ways in which the protagonists of early Indonesian writing saw themselves as "growing toward Indonesia" through an expanding awareness of personal responsibility and national destiny that defined the generation that brought independence to the archipelago. Their Sumatran subjects saw the main conflict of their childhood as one opposing tradition (*adat*) and modernity. Postel-Coster calls the central theme "the struggle of the individual to disengage himself from a number of traditional rules and norms imposed on him by his society" (1977: 136–37) without completely rejecting tradition. Rodgers analyzes how "regional patterns of telling history while telling lives" (1995: 71) can be observed in the tendency of these writers to refer to periods of their own biographies as corresponding to the colonial era, Japanese occupation, or period of early independence.

Rodgers in particular argues for a situated reading of Sumatran autobiography as the vehicle of a new form of historical imagination, made possible by the acquisition of literacy and intensified interethnic communication in the national language. Using McKinley's notion of "a very nimble present" that can "move quickly to recontact its past" (much as the thumb moves quickly to count out past ages on the fingers), she finds in these stories of boyhood conflicts the seeds of a new nationalist vision:

> These memoirs are records of individual passages toward states of consciousness in which people can question the ideological givens of village life, the received truths of organized religion, and village notions of time and society and then go on to "migrate toward" (a major image for Sumatran writers) the new imagined community of Indonesia, as a multiethnic nation created by the conscious cooperative work of patriots drawn from these two authors' own exact generation. (1995: 7)

More than simply resisting Dutch colonialism, these writers evoke a "revolution of the spirit, an invention of modern Indonesia" through new forms of political consciousness and awareness. Religious schools (Protestant for the Toba Batak, Islamic for the Minang) are the primary context of socialization and discipline, and each of the writers details conflicts between individual desires and the constraints of old-fashioned pedagogy and obligations to authorities within the kin group.

Although Horo's life reflects some of these themes, the tension between them is different. First, it is significant that he did not write an autobiography, a childhood memoir, or a novel, but instead a (much briefer) account of the origin of his ancestral power. It is the encounter with the snake that defined for him his right to assume a position as ruler, and his right to call his funeral shroud a "royal cloth." Born in the early years of this century, he belonged to roughly the same generation as these Sumatran writers, and shared with some of them an education in Protestant schools and a career in teaching and government administration. His ancestral legacy emerges, however, less as a constraint on individual freedom than as a basis for personal power—a basis built on and expanded through the institutions of the colonial and later independent national regimes.

Horo's own position was established partially through his appointment by Dutch administrators, and he never tired of expressing his affection for Western ideals of modernity and progress. He was a man who saw himself as Christian, but who had a troubled relationship with the church leadership. He was a man considered an authority on traditional custom (*petua adat*), who earned respect and even some income as a healer, but was a strong advocate of education and universalism.

Rodgers and Postel-Coster probe the subjective side of transformations in temporality and historical consciousness by examining accounts of conflicts between fathers and sons, young lovers and older family members. Problems of hierarchy surface in relation to autocratic schooling, and especially in decisions about marriage: Young men are frustrated at losing their sweethearts to older, economically more secure husbands, and they respond by choosing to leave their homelands and seek their fortunes elsewhere. The *rantau*, the escape from the homeland, did not have the same importance on Sumba or much of the rest of Eastern Indonesia. Partly, this was because communications were more difficult, but also because of cultural differences concerning the meaning of origins in a particular homeland. But Raja Horo's view of his world was deeply affected by his travels to Java and Makassar, and it could be argued that he preferred to look back at his own homeland with an outsider's eyes.

At the eve of independence, Horo was not so much "inventing Indonesia" as becoming fascinated by the final years of a colonial image of royalty. And although he was able to read and write in Indonesian, he was a man whose words of wisdom remained phrased in Kodi, his native language. Of all the people I have written about in this project on autobiography and objects, his life history is the one most closely tied to national history and thus most "Indonesian," but it is anchored in a different place from the written accounts of Sumatrans on the rantau. It remains still part of a world of ancestral verities, adapted and changed to suit external fashions, but rooted in an oral tradition of many generations.

The image of the snake, dangerous but regenerative, was the metaphor that Horo used to express his own sense of self. The snake's scales were imposed as a design upon a textile that wrapped the body in noble splendor, but that could also hide an ancestral treasure from its descendants and rightful inheritors. It is the ambivalence of this gesture, both giving and withholding, revealing and concealing, that brings us closer to understanding the ways objects are used to represent persons in this particular society.

The idea that a certain form of cloth could stand for royalty was not Horo's invention. The elaborate ritual verse of East Sumba often describes the "cloth of kings" as the *patola ratu*, the imported Indian cloths given to local leaders by the Dutch to signify their appointment as colonial rulers. The design of the *hanggi karaha kaboko* is a coarser, thick-textured version of this Gujerati silk, retaining many of its design elements but approaching a greater level of iconic representation. Using humbler motifs such as the "cassava vine" (*rou lugha*) border, "meat fork" (*hura*) and "vulva-shaped pendant" (*hamoli*), it provides a visual pattern that suggests agricultural fertility, wealth, and reproductive power. The overall image is linked to virility, physical strength, and regeneration.

The Kodi snake cloth is a local imitation of a pattern of power that came from Java and splendid kingdoms to the west. The Kodi notion of rulership had its origins in the same places. Imported notions of hierarchy seem to have played a more significant role in determining who a local raja was and what role he should play than did local notions of precedence. The narratives of origins and ritual order that were so important in the calendrical system (Hoskins 1993a: 80–117) were almost completely eclipsed by the weight that colonial authorities gave to education and wealth. Raja Horo was a member of a prominent family who enthusiastically embraced the world of the church and schoolroom, and through them came to try to imitate another world—that of princes and palaces. He worked out an original and, for a while, highly effective combination of traditional and external forms of rule, which has left a lasting impression on Kodi notions of political power.

Western researchers, traveling to other parts of the world in search of the same sorts of personal, introspective autobiographies that we know in our own literary traditions, are often disappointed. People in other societies may prefer to narrate themselves by narrating stories of their ancestors (Young 1983) or accounts of the exchange histories of possessions like net bags (MacKenzie 1991), betel pouches (Geirnaert-Martin 1992), gold jewelry (Keane 1988), or domestic animals (Hoskins 1996a). The object provides a miniaturized identity, like the biographer's representation, a sort of map to guide us or provide orientation in the unfamiliar territory of another's life.

I argue that in Kodi, a society still deeply focused on ancestors as well as rapid social change, biographical objects provide a point of orientation and an "anchor'" for storytelling that is really a form of autobiography, a reflection on the self deflected through the medium of the object. The object may provide a unity of self that is not given in the narrative, just as it may "stand in" for the person in ritual contexts when the person himself (or herself) cannot attend. Raja Horo's own snakeskin shroud was wrapped around him and buried deep in the stone vault of his megalithic tomb, but new shrouds of the same kind are now being woven for his descendants to wear and later be bound in for burial. In telling the story of his ancestor's encounter with the snake and his right to assume the rajaship, Raja Horo was turning the tissue of Kodi tradition into the uniform of a new form of state official.

NOTES

1. This account is based on many conversations held with Raja Horo during the six years (1979–1985) that I knew him, and his own manuscript describing his ancestor's encounter with a python, which was—he later said—the "basis of his position as raja." Although there was no single occasion where he provided a full narrative "life history," he did provide me with a few short manuscripts, access to government documents, and personal notes and journals. I have brought together notes from his own narrations of his life, and those of his wives and some older children, to tell a version of his experiences, drawing most heavily on his recollections during the last two years of his life, when I returned to the field three times and stayed as his houseguest for a total of six months.

2. This phrase is from the New Testament, and is part of the instructions Jesus

gave to his apostles, telling them they would need to be as "sneaky as snakes and as mild as doves" to carry out their evengelical work.

3. After Rato Hemba of Hali Kandangar, Reja Pote (also of Hali Kandangar) was appointed subraja, then Rangga Kura (the son of Rato Hemba), then Soleiman Tari Loghe of Rangga Baki (implicated in the theft of gold that also involved Maru Daku, he was imprisoned and died in prison), and Linge Kendu of Hali Kandangar.

4. Another interpretation of this name (which Joel Kuipers reminded me of in recent correspondence) was Negara Ikut Tuhan, which would translate as "the state that follows the [Christian] Lord," as opposed to a state made up mainly of Muslims serving Allah. A large number of Indonesia's Christians are concentrated in the eastern provinces of Nusa Tenggara Timur, Maluku, and Sulawesi Utara, which were once part of the Dutch loyalist state of Eastern Indonesia. The history of the conflicts of this period is detailed in Chauvel (1990).

5. Details of this dispute are treated at greater length in Hoskins 1993a: 131–34.

6. Alan Thomson noted this pattern in a study of conversion on Java (1993). Similar patterns have been documented by Rita Kipp among the Karo Batak of Sumatra (1995) and by Robert Hefner in East Java (1994).

7. The term *wola remba* or "woven like a net" is a euphemism used by women for the python cloth, which they hesitate to label explicitly as a snake, although they also know the term *karaha kaboko*. Geirnaert-Martin argues more generally that women are reluctant to provide exegesis of a cloth's sacred function, although they are aware of its uses and are the only weavers and dyers of cloth (1991: 36). I also found this true in Kodi.

8. A captivating, if perhaps overly totalizing, recent account of Dutch embellishments on Javanese notions of tradition may be found in John Pemberton's *On the Subject of "Java,"* which pays particular attention to the elaboration of ceremonies of royal installation.

5.

SPINDLES AND SPINSTERS

The Loss of Romantic Love

A young Kodi girl holding a spindle and pulling cotton thread to be spun by hand. (Photo A. Buhler, 1949. Used with the permission of the Museum für Volkerkunde, Basel, Switzerland)

When I played tapes of the long stories I collected from older people, my house was often filled with young listeners—adolescent girls and boys, friends of the girl who lived with me, who giggled together in the shadows. The reasons my house was such a popular gathering place were many: There were few places where young people could gather, and since I was a respected "foreigner visitor," I was allowed to serve as a chaperone. People were worried that I would be lonely, living so far from my family, and perhaps felt that my own activities should also be watched. Parents encouraged their children to visit me because they were themselves interested in

The author with three young Kodi girls who often visited her home.
(Photo S. Hoskins, 1980)

my project of collecting materials on Kodi custom, and worried that their sons and daughters were too exclusively interested in the modern world of schools, popular music, and Indonesian national culture.

One story that I was transcribing had a particular appeal for a young woman I will call Tila, who had recently passed her examinations to become an elementary-school teacher. It was an account of a magically made boy with lovely pale skin, "Kalanggu of the Sesame Stalk," who was chosen as a bridegroom by a princess who lived on the seventh level of the heavens. I collected two versions of the story, one from Wonda Kaleka of Wai Panda, the other from Pati Bani (Maru Daku's younger brother) of Wainjolo Wawa.

The story was quite long and interspersed with songs, told over a period of four or five hours—"a whole night," in Kodi practice, since storytelling did not usually begin until well after dinner and continued, with pauses to chew betel, until dawn. It had a complex narrative construction, moving abruptly from one set of characters on the seventh level of heaven to another set on the ground. It is not until the end that the connecting thread (to use the story's own metaphor) is revealed and the two sets of characters, including the pair of star-crossed lovers, are brought together. But the part that most fascinated Tila (and that she often asked to listen to again and again) was the passage about a spindle, in which the tool normally used for spinning thread was used instead to snare a husband. I will summarize large parts of the narrative, but quote the sections that Tila most liked to repeat.

The Spindle Story

The story begins in the middle of a drought, with the old Bitter Creeper woman (*warico lolo kapadu*), who was suffering from the famine. She cleaned her garden very carefully but had only bitter creepers to eat. She begged a wealthy man to give her a few corn seeds to plant, but he refused. "Well, then, I may just die of hunger," she thought.

Meanwhile, on the seventh level of heaven, a childless couple, Londongo Tana ("living on the ground") and his wife, Kahi Ali Pyrara ("golden rainbow"), were trying to arrange the marriage of his sister Nggyoro. Nggyoro was very beautiful, but there was no man that she liked. Then, one day a young man named Nggoto chased a runaway horse into Nggyoro's village and fell in love with her as soon as he saw her. She offered him water from a golden beaker, and he promised to return in a month. His father, Rato Nggengge (Lord Spider), saw his son was pining for Nggyoro and brought hundreds of horses and buffalo, as well as ten male slaves and ten female slaves. Nggyoro agreed to marry him, and in three months she was pregnant.

Much to everyone's surprise, Kahi Ali Pyrara, who was so old she had no more teeth, also became pregnant. After three months, Nggyoro had a miscarriage. She felt the labor pains coming, so she pulled back the boards of the bamboo veranda and sat down over the opening between the planks. When the fetus (*watu manoho*, literally the "aborted stone") began to slip out of her, all the levels of the heavens and earth began to shake, trembling and rumbling like thunder. Then, after a minute, they started to shake and tremble again. Seven times, the heavens and earth shook, until they shook open the rain clouds and a huge amount of water fell, along with the aborted fetus, into the garden of the Bitter Creeper woman. "This is certainly an unusual birth!" said Londongo Tana. Then he saw that his sister had lost the child.

His wife had a normal pregnancy and gave birth to a lovely girl named Kahi Lendu Awango ("Kahi who looks at the sky").

The Bitter Creeper woman began to weed and clean her garden as soon as the rains started, and in four days she found a sesame sprout. "What good fortune the spirits have brought me!" she said. "My garden has already produced a child." She tended the stalk very well, and after seven nights it was full of seeds. All the seeds fell off except one, which grew into a gigantic fruit, as big as a forearm and still growing.

Two wealthy girls, Kahi of the Ivory Bangles and Leba of the Round Bracelets, saw the fruit and asked the old woman to let them taste it. Although they tried to tempt her with fine foods for exchange, she refused, and so they beat her savagely. When the fruit was very large and full, the old woman carried it into her house, and the house instantly became large and beautiful, with a high thatched roof and many fine porcelain plates. That night, when the morning star appeared in the sky, the fruit turned into a handsome young man, with fine bracelets, an ivory knife, and a splendid loincloth and headcloth, sitting beside a one-stringed fiddle (*dungga*).

"Grandmother!" he called to the old woman when she awoke. "Do not be afraid. I am your white sesame fruit, who has come to be your kindred spirit and life companion (*ndewa tou, ura dadi*). My name in Kalanggu Langa Kaka, and I will provide for you from now on. But you must help me to find a wife."

The old woman went over to cradle the handsome young man on her lap, and wanted to cook and care for him. He agreed, but asked her to help him test the girls in the area. Covered with soot and ash, the old woman went to beg eggs from Kahi of the Ivory Bangles and Leba of the Round Bracelets, but they refused and beat her. Another girl, however, Randa Peda, was kind to the old woman, feeding her and bathing her, and sent her home with eight eggs and some pork. That night, they boiled the eggs, with the old woman eating the whites and Kalanggu Langa Kaka eating the yolks. The next morning, he went out to defecate, and twelve gold pendants (*hamoli*) came out of his anus. The old woman brought the pendants to Randa Peda's father in a betel bag (to propose marriage), and received a countergift of a man's cloth, a woman's sarung, and a pig speared and butchered for her to take home. The two wealthy girls who had abused the old woman followed Kalanggu Langa Kaka to his home, but were left outside to wail their apologies in the rain.

On the seventh level of heaven, Kahi Lendu Awango watched these events and prepared a signal to send to Kalanggu Langa Kaka, her cross-cousin, to let him know she was now old enough to be courted and married. When he came home, Kalanggu Langa Kaka saw a gold spindle hanging from a slender thread at the peak of his high thatched roof.

The spindle had been prepared carefully by Kahi Lendu Awango, sitting beside her seven baskets of raw cotton. The cotton had already been beaten and carded and cleaned of its seeds, so she sat on the lower veranda of her house, patiently winding and spinning enough thread each day to empty one basket. Once she had finished one basket she would take up another, and go on with her work. Her mother and father saw her sitting there spinning thread, but they did not ask why she spent all day winding it so carefully. "It is best if our daughter knows how to do such things," they said to each other.

Kahi Lendu Awango took the gold spindle and put it inside a coconut shell, and twirled it until it was full of twisted cotton. She went back to the veranda and pulled back a few of the bamboo floor planks to open a space for the spindle and the coconut shell. Then she took one basketful of the cotton yarn and let the spindle drop between the floorboards and down, down, down until it had pierced one layer of the heavens and one layer of the earth. Then she brought it up again, took up another basket of carded cotton, and wound it onto the spindle, and sent it down, down, down until it had pierced through a second level of the sky. She went on like this, spinning and winding the thread from each of the seven baskets, until she had pierced through all seven levels of the heavens and six levels of earth, and arrived at Kalanggu Langa Kaka's house, just above his bed.

The one-stringed fiddle saw the spindle hanging from its thread and called out: "It's here! It has already come, younger brother! We must get ready to travel upwards to find your wife from the seventh level of heaven and the sixth level of earth, the kingdom of Rato Nggengge!"

Kalanggu Langa Kaka asked the two wealthy girls to prove themselves worthy by caring for his old grandmother. Then he picked seven areca nuts to plant, wrapping them in the folds of his waistband, and mounted the gold spindle as he would mount a horse. "Go ahead, fiddle!" he called, and the fiddle sang a song that made the spindle rise and pierce through the levels of heaven and earth like a rocket.[1]

Ngge . . . ngge . . . ngge	Where . . . where . . . where . . .
Pa kalete baka pongga	Ride astride it like a pillar
Ba kinje wu malandi	The spindle of the pinang fruit
Ta duki wandi nyono	So it will take us to
La inya wulu hungga	Mother who bound the forelock
La bapi rawi lindu	Father who smelted the crown
Pitu ndani awango	Through seven levels of heavens
Nomo ndani cana	Through six levels of earth
La ambu Rato Nggengge	To Grandfather Spider[2]
Na wangero kere ghuro nggama	Who heats his pots to greet us
Na wei katopo tandi nggama	When we seek the value of the knife
Na marawako koba mata nggama	Whose forehead runs with sweat
Na wei kahudi ryoro nggama	When we ask the value of our sword

The spindle arrived at the first level of heaven and earth, which was so hot it was impossible to plant the pinang seed. They continued on to the second level, which was inhabited by spotted people, and planted a pinang seed there. Then they went to the third level, inhabited by long snakes (*wugha*) that are sometimes seen in the rainbow. They planted another seed and went to the fourth level, which was filled with white water fowl (*katura kuka kaka*). They planted another seed, and came to the fifth level, where Byokokoro Kori Lyoko lived, a great hare-lipped ogre who guarded the gates of the rains. There, Kalanggu Langa Kaka negotiated the exchange of tools to make fire with the ritual objects needed to ask for water.[3]

On the sixth level, they came to the kingdom of the Father Who Can Judge and Mother Who Reaches the Ends (Bapa Pende Punge, Inya Loho Lombo), and Kalangga Langa Kaka sought to marry their daughter Ratu Hawulla Ndoka. This awakened the jealousy of a hairy giant (in one version it is a fierce "wild man," Maghu Rumba, "the shadow in the grass," and in another a one-breasted woman, Kali Nggaka, reminiscent of the Hindu demon goddess) who stabbed Kalanggu Langa Kaka to death. The ruler of the upperworld, Rato Nggengge (Lord Spider) heard the fiddle's funeral lament and realized the young man was his grandson. So he asked for the help of the python, the cockatow, the hawk, and the eagle, all of whom slithered and swooped around his body until they fanned the life back into him. Kalanggu Langa Kaka left his new bride behind and went alone up to the last level of heaven and earth, as the fiddle sang:

Ngge . . . ngge . . . ngge	Where . . . where . . . where . . .
Pa kalete baka pongga	Ride astride it like a pillar
Ba kinje wu malandi	The spindle of pinang seed
Ta leta duki nyono	So we can quickly arrive at the
La Ngyorro-Nggyto	Home of Ngorro and Nyotto
Loka Londgono Tana	My mother's brother Londongo Tana
Inya Kyahi Paryra	My aunt Kyani Paryara
Lete wu hamburungo	The steps I came down
La pandou kalele longge nggu	The home of my first hair swirls
Binye wu paloho	The door that I came out
La pandou haluru lyawo nggu!	The home of the heirloom sarung

The spindle took Kalanggu Langa Kaka directly to the lower veranda in front of Kahi Lendu Awango's house. The two of them looked at each other with smiles and happy hearts, but said nothing. Londongo Tana came to see who was this handsome young man sitting silently beside his daughter as if he had known her all his life. The young man did not know that she had called him with her spindle from the earth seven levels below.

Londongo Tana called together all the wise men and knowledgeable elders to advise him on where this young man came from, since Kalanggu Langa Kaka would not talk. Londongo Tana told them the story of his wife's mysterious pregnancy so late in life, which coincided with the pregnancy of his sister, Nggyoro, who miscarried during a huge rainstorm. Finally Kalanggu Langa Kaka spoke. "I am the child of that fallen stone (fetus), which fell into a sesame plant and was raised by a poor old woman," he said. "I was born without ever knowing my mother's breast or my father's lap. But when the spindle came, the fiddle told me it was time to travel home to seek a wife."

Then Nggyoro and Nggoto realized who he was and came to embrace their son, who had come to see them from the world below. Londongo Tana and Kahi Pyrara welcomed their nephew, who could marry his cross-cousin with their blessing. Using a magic ring he had received from Father Who Can Judge and Mother Who Reaches the Ends, Kalanggu Langa Kaka paid an impressive bride-price and prepared to return home.

He mounted the spindle with his new bride, and the fiddle sang again to descend each level of heaven and earth. At the fifth level, they met an angry Byokokoro Kori Lyoko, whose house had burned down because he was clumsy with the fire-making tools. But they made peace with him, and proceeded downward, seeing at each stage of their journey how the pinang seeds planted had grown into saplings. When he arrived home, he found his old grandmother poor and all alone because the wealthy girls had neglected her. They still wanted to marry him, but he refused, and they turned into vengeful forest nymphs (*lemba karingge*) who tempt men in wild places and drive them crazy. Kalanggu Langa Kaka founded the village of Waindimu and took up residence there with his two wives: Kahi Lendu Awango from the seventh level of heaven and Randa Peda from the earth below.

COMMENTARY: THE SPINDLE'S APPEAL TO TILA

Kalanggu Langa Kaka is presented as an idealization of the masculine partner, created from both an old woman's longing for a son and young woman's
longing for a bridegroom. Kalanggu Langa Kaka is so attractive that women
quite literally want to eat him up. Their longing for him is what brings him
into the world, nurtures him, and draws him up into the heavens. The
detailed description of how Kahi Lendu Awango went about her spinning
work, and the careful, deliberate manner in which she set out to snare her
bridegroom is intriguing. It both describes a technical process in a vaguely
didactic way and shows the bridegroom as in some way the product of these
carefully spun-out threads of desire.

But if Kalanggu Langa Kaka embodies female fantasies of masculine
beauty, he is hardly monogamous. He seeks to marry as many good women
as he can find. While he eventually rejects the wealthy girls, he proposes
readily to Ratu Hawulla Ndoka ("Princess of the Gold Moon") and to
Randa Peda. His match with Kahi Lendu Awango, while quite literally
"written in the stars," would never have come about without her actions.
Like the spindle, which must be carefully balanced and turned so that its
threads descend properly, the idealized partner must be managed and
manipulated to carry out his proper role in this narrative of romance.

The appeal of the story of the spindle to Tila was that it showed a
woman choosing her own husband and bringing him up to meet her. At the
same time, however, the spindle is associated with a traditional and now
somewhat antiquated model of feminine labor. A girl's skill with a spindle is
supposed to help her to attract a husband and keep him. Tila, like almost all
Kodi girls, had been taught to spin and weave as she approached puberty.
These "womanly arts" should ideally be mastered before any suitors can
come to ask for their hands in marriage. There is a certain coquetry to the
way a girl may spin, appearing industrious in order to catch a male eye and
show her skills as a future wife.

The action of spinning is time-consuming but graceful, and seen as quin-
tessentially feminine. It is no accident that one of the most popular dances
performed by young girls is the "spinning dance" (*nenggo pa hijolo*), in which
the hands are held gently off to the side and the fingers gently pull down
invisible threads as the body sways delicately above shifting feet. Tila learned
this dance as a little girl and first performed it in public when a feast was
held to consecrate the large stone dragged for her grandfather's tomb. At
that time, she was only about eight years old, the youngest of the girls officially presented to the ancestors by the payment of a small number of coins
to signal that she was now ready to "step into the ceremonial dance ground"
(*ndali nataro*).

When she returned from the feast, she was old enough to help her
mother set up the threads on the loom. Weaving is done with the weaver
seated against a carved yoke on a backtension loom, her legs alternately

stretched and bent against a foot brace to increase and decrease the tension on the warp yams as the shuttle sword is inserted into the shed and the weft is added. The new weft is beaten into place with the wooden sword, and the sound of wood banging against wood resonates throughout the house. The motions of weaving are said to help a woman conceive and bear children (Geinaert-Martin 1992a: 98), and the sounds of her industrious activity are reassuring to male visitors, who like to see a "woman who loves to work."

Tila, like many girls of her generation, had no patience for spinning, although she did try it for several months to keep an elderly aunt company. She told me the yarn that she spun was so bumpy and uneven that it had to be thrown out. With the increasing availability of supplies in stores, since the 1970s most Kodi cloths have been woven with commercial thread. The clothes have traditional designs, however, and perhaps a third are dyed with vegetable dyes.

Though young girls may spin and weave, the more demanding tasks of tying in the resist patterns of ikat designs (*wolo*) and dyeing the bound threads are reserved for mature women. The indigo bath cannot be prepared by any woman who is pregnant or menstruating, and cannot come into contact with blood (Hoskins 1989b). Meat and fish are taboo at the dyeing site, and no men are allowed to approach the special dyeing hut where the pot is prepared. Tila had sometimes accompanied her mother to an isolated hamlet near their ancestral village, where they brought thread to be dyed. She remembered the strong, almost putrid smell of the dye pot and the sight of many long skeins of yarn hanging, still only pale green, to dry and oxidize into darker colors in the sun.

By the time she was sixteen, Tila was ready to weave her first cloth—a simple sarung using the cheaper, store-bought threads. She struggled to keep the warp yams evenly spaced over the shed sticks, and had trouble managing the tension between the cross sticks. She complained of back-aches and took more than two months to finish the task, which some women can do in a month. Her mother laughed and said, "If you can't sit still long enough for spinning or weaving, you'll have to go to school. You'll need a schoolteacher's salary to buy store thread and store cloth."

Tila was happy with that because she had always wanted to continue her education. Her father was a schoolteacher, and she had a brother who had been sent to high school in the regency capital. But many families did not feel that educating their daughters was as important as educating their sons. She was sent first to a middle school near the Catholic mission. The mission had developed a "housekeeping school" where girls were taught to cook in Western style and to sew on a machine. Tila, however, was more ambitious. She hoped that her grades would be good enough to escape this school of "domestic arts" and go to the teachers training school in Anakalang, a district then several days' travel away.

In the story of the spindle, Kahi Lendu Awango acts without the knowledge of her parents and sends a signal to a suitor. This struck a responsive chord for Tila because she also had tried to take the initiative to find a husband, resisting her parents' dictates. Her father had supported her wish for further education, but he believed that he should take responsibility for arranging her marriage.

When she was a pupil at the middle school in Homba Karipit, a schoolteacher ten years older than she approached her parents about a possible engagement. Tila told me:

> My parents thought he would be a good son-in-law, since he already had a job and was educated. I didn't really know what to think. He used to wait for me when I came out of class, and we would talk as I walked home. I was glad that an older man took such an interest in me, and I laughed at the stories he told me. When he said he would go to meet my parents with a horse, I felt embarrassed. I wasn't old enough to be a wife! But he told me he would wait for me to grow up. I could even go to teachers' training school. He wanted an educated wife, and we would not have to live together until I was ready.

Her initial willingness, however, diminished over the years she spent in boarding school in Anakalang, as she became exposed to Indonesian national adolescent culture and romance novels. Popular images of girls who chose their own lovers and arranged their own marriages presented a window onto a more modern, individualistic set of moral guidelines.

The exchange of love letters was a game that everyone at the school played. Since their parents were often not literate, theirs was the first generation to enjoy the thrills of communicating private thoughts in secret envelopes. A great romance with the written word accompanied the subversive discovery that it could be used for purposes other than the official ones of school and work.

During her period at the teachers' training school, Tila had several correspondents, who may not have realized she was officially betrothed to someone back in Kodi. She sent playful little notes to them but did not encourage any of her schoolmates to get serious. She said she was always secretly in love with a neighbor, the elder brother of her best friend in Kodi. One day, she took the rather forward step of sending him a letter at his boarding school in the regency capital. She was delighted when he responded, and began an intense correspondence carried out in hand-carried notes stuffed into the notebooks and jackets of her friends.

After some time, Tila's father began to complain that Tila had not gone to visit her betrothed in Homba Karipit. "The issue is not the horse that he brought four years ago," he said. "The issue is your future. You will need a good husband, but you do nothing to please the man who has already asked for your hand. Tell me if there is someone else who would dare to come meet with me. If you don't decide on someone soon," he exclaimed, "you'll be buried with your spindle instead of with your husband!"

He was referring to a ritual practice of placing a substitute for the husband inside the grave. A spindle is most often chosen both because the girl herself may have used it and because its rather phallic appearance "completes" the missing organs in tombs which normally house a married couple.

The girl wrote to her boyfriend in town asking if he would go to meet her father. He answered that he had just finished high school, and needed awhile to look for a job. She urged him to apply to the civil service so that he would be in a position to propose. He hesitated, as many young men do, wanting to prolong the carefree days of bachelorhood before taking on a wife and office job. Tila finished her teaching credential and came home, since she still needed to prepare for national teachers examinations. She and her boyfriend met regularly for some time in Kodi, often at my house because her best female friend was living with me, and it was considered normal for her brother to come to visit.

Later she told me, "I remember those days so well, sitting in your living room and listening to songs, stories, tapes of all kinds of rituals. We felt free then, able to laugh at anything. Our parents wanted us to know these things, Kodi customs, how the words are said in other villages. And we did learn something, I suppose, but it was wonderful simply to be able to meet. And we both loved the story of the spindle."

When I left Kodi in 1981, the situation was unresolved. Tila was stalling her father, her boyfriend was delaying looking for employment, and her mother, probably suspecting what was going on, told me at my departure, "The young people in Bondokodi will miss you because your home was always a place of such friendly gatherings." When I returned in 1984 and asked about Tila, I was surprised to hear a story of violence and rape.

Fenina, the second girl who lived with me and Tila's best friend, told me the story with great dramatic flair: "Tila paid for her romantic dreams. She is in the regency capital now, crying for my brother. They came to take her away, tying her up just like a pig. We all heard her screams, we knew what was going to happen to her. They came on a horse and carried her off. My brother was sick for months afterward."

"Who is this 'they'? Who has the right to carry off a girl just like that?" I asked, not understanding the situation.

"Oh, they had the right. They said according to our custom she was already theirs. She had been theirs for five years already. So they just came and tied her up."

"But who did this?"

"Her husband. The schoolteacher. He went to her father and brought five more head of livestock, two horses, and three buffalo. They were received, although Tila did not want to even see him. She sat in the back of the house and would not come out to greet them. Her father was furious. He said his daughter should not carry on with someone behind his back. He said if her suitor would not come in the front door, he would not listen to him.

"Then, three days later, the schoolteacher sent three friends, and they followed Tila when she was walking back from the river with the laundry. They said they would take her to her new home. She swore she would never go, so they tied her up like a pig. She had no clothes, none of her things, she simply screamed and kicked as they hauled her onto the horse and took her away."

"And what did they do to her there?"

"The schoolteacher was waiting. He said, 'I have loved you for five years. You have been mine for five years. I brought you here to make you my wife.' He took her into the bedroom. People say she screamed there too, but to no use. Her father knew what they were doing. He had given his consent."

I was astonished. I had taken notes on "marriage by capture" as a custom and knew the different schedule of bridewealth payments it involved. I had even heard folktales about warriors from the past who had captured their wives or eloped with their sweethearts. But I did not expect the sweet, low-voiced Tila to become a victim of this form of male violence.

"What happened then?"

"She stayed there, of course. That evening she was already broken, so there was no point in coming back."

BROKEN WOMEN, BROKEN SPINDLES: CONTEXTUALIZING RAPE AND VIRGINITY

Virginity is an issue in contemporary sexual politics that seems to have been less marked in the past. Severing a girl's hymen is now called "breaking" (*paruha*) her, borrowed from the Indonesian term *rusak*. But the indigenous term is more neutral, speaking only of a "mixing" of the bride and groom (*hambola*), which may occur on the day they take up residence in his village but often precedes that time by several years.

A number of contexts where premarital "mixing" was tolerated and even encouraged have now been toned down because of the influence of Christian moral teachings. Cross-cousins (a mother's brothers' daughters and their sisters' sons) address each other as *anguleba*, a term that can almost be translated as "sweetheart" because it encodes a relationship where sexual contact is encouraged. The nights before sea worms are collected in late February or early March are devoted to *kawoking*, where groups of young people wander along the beach singing bawdy songs and coupling off in the sand. A retired Protestant minister told me he remembered those days with great nostalgia: "Now I have to teach my sons and especially daughters to be more careful, to remember the Bible's teachings, but those evenings used to be so sweet!"

Most commonly, once a suitor was accepted by a girl's parents and some horses and buffalo had been delivered to their corral, he would be allowed to "visit" and have access to his future bride. When five horses and five buffalo had been given, he was officially said to be "staying with his affines" (*londo la ghera*, in Indonesian *kawin masuk*), but even before then sexual contact often occurred, as long as the parents had accepted the boy.

Many brides came to marriage negotiations with swelled bellies, and families were prepared to be tolerant of young people who "couldn't be expected to wait" through the many months and even years that it might take for intermediaries to set up an alliance and arrange for the full sequence of payments. But while sexual relations were tolerated before marriage, rules of exogamy and the requirement of parental consent were strictly enforced.

Forced sexual relations that had been preceded by the proper exchanges were locally not considered rape, but the imposition of a husband's rights on an unwilling wife. Tila's parents were Christian, but they did not have the resources for a church wedding. In giving their consent to the "traditional resolution" of their daughter's romantic problems, they thought they were doing what was best for her.

Two months after these events, Tila received a mournful letter from her former lover in town. "Why are our parents the slaves of the possessions they must have?" it said. "Why are objects more important than persons and their feelings ? I would have found a job, but your father could not wait."

She did not answer his letter. To do so would probably have been considered grounds for a charge of adultery. But she did send to him, through a friend, a small gift that was charged with significance for both of them: an old spindle, broken in two.

OBJECTS AS PERSONAL MESSAGES: THE SILENT LETTER

The gift is evidence of the imaginative power invested in objects in this society. As an imagined husband, or an idealized image of romantic love in opposition to social pressures to exchange in economically beneficial ways, the spindle and its story stood for her own loss of freedom and self-determination. The husband she had wanted to bring to her with letters and messages was no more, and so her fantasy of choice was finished.

Two years later, she explained the gift to me: "It was broken, like I was broken. That was how I felt at first, torn in two by this man who had once seemed gentle and patient. But he became a good husband. Men are like that, you know. Sometimes they cannot wait."

Her comment echoes a certain ambivalence, acknowledging both the violence and the passion that lay under it, and expressing a certain awareness of the number of local stories that circulated about her abduction. The marriage, as it turned out, was not an unhappy one, and when I visited Tila five years later, she was not as critical of her father's actions as I had expected.

Using the same idiom that he had used, she told me, "Sometimes I wonder if I would have been happier embracing the spindle in the grave, but I think not. My father took the spear and the knife (the customary seal for the conclusion of traditional marriage exchanges) so I had to go along, giving them the value of their livestock." She indicated her young children playing at our feet, who would become the descendants of their father's line.

It is the idiom of these comments that interests me most here: Personal relations were discussed in a language of objects, through a mapping of the movements of possessions. The official social status of persons was negotiated through ceremonial exchange, so the location of objects could designate quite exactly the legal rights of actors. When Tila was carried off with screams of protest, neighbors commented: "But she is already his wife. His animals are standing in her father's corral." When, years later, she and her children met her former lover at a feast, he told her, "Your spindle may have been broken, but you have woven many fine cloths since then."

In Kodi society, the sexual politics of persons becomes the sexual politics of things. The exchange of gendered objects expresses relationships and provides the terms in which they are renegotiated. This is a far more pervasive process than simply the metaphoric extensions of conventional, figurative language. It is a complex, culturally specific imagery for masking emotional disclosures and making them socially acceptable.

The forms that the identification between person and object takes in these stories and others in my corpus can be described as either the surrogate or double, a direct substitute for the self, or the idealized companion, who completes the person's own identity through contrast—usually a contrast in gender. Tila used the image of the spindle to represent her attachment to an idealized romantic partner. When her ties to him were broken, she was herself broken, and so was the vehicle of her romantic dreams.

The unspoken imagery that she used in her communications with her boyfriend were modeled on the forms of gender dualism and complementarity eliminated in her favorite narrative. In the story of Kalanggu Langa Kaka, the feminine fiddle guides the hero in his quest for a wife (in fact, several wives) who will complete his identity as a man. Only once he is married and has established his own household can he also establish a village and descent line.

Tila was not the narrator of the story of the spindle, and it was not a fable of protest in the same way that Ra Mete's stories of buffalo, hens, and cats were stories of abused women. But Tila did love the image of a girl who could send a message to her future husband and have him journey upward to come marry her. In her parting gift to her lover, she appropriated the spindle and its story and made it a part of her own biography.

An appropriated object may seem less compelling than one fully fashioned by the subject's own narrative skills. But young women were not generally supposed to display their rhetorical abilities publicly. Tila was a poised and articulate young woman who became a skillful teacher, and she could playfully repeat sections of the spindle story for me in my own home. It would not have been appropriate for her to do so before an audience. The private, sealed communications she sent in love notes contrasted strongly with the traditional forums for expressing romantic sentiments— ballads of protest and courtship banter, performed in public but interpreted in private.

ARTICULATIONS OF ROMANTIC LOVE OLD AND NEW

The teasing, familiar tones of the letters Tila sent to her friend were peculiarly modern but shaped by an emerging national culture. Following an etiquette common in other parts of Indonesia, she addressed her beloved as "elder brother" (*kakak*) and asked for "protection" and "guidance" as part of his gestures of affection.

Her idea of how a "modern" relationship might work was influenced by romance novels she had borrowed from friends in Anakalang, Indonesian films she had seen or heard about in the regency capital, and magazines aimed at teenagers that circulated, dog-eared, from one girl to another in the small community of young readers on the island. She and her friends spoke of wanting to find a husband from one of the families that "understood" about young people's desires, and they juxtaposed this to a view of earlier generations as forced into a lockstep imposed by tradition.

The most consistent criticism Tila and others leveled at their parents' generation was that "they thought more of their buffalo corral than of their daughters." They chose important men as sons-in-law, men who would be good exchange partners but not necessarily those who most appealed to their daughters. The reference to the new bride as *wei haranga*, literally "what was received for the livestock," was cited as particularly offensive. "Fathers who really love their daughters would not sell them to fill their pastures," they argued. "They would wait to see how the young man is, and let them get used to each other, instead of just looking at the buffalo in his corral."

But traditional genres also contain expressions of youthful longings and a desire for choosing one's own partner. Declarations of personal sentiments in more traditional genres, such as song, were often in opposition to parental control. One of the best-known Kodi folk songs is a protest by a young girl against a forced marriage. She argues that she is simply too young, but that is what girls always say until they find a suitor who pleases them.

Nja ku wawa bapa	I don't want to be sent away, father
Pa heka wali byaba bapa	Separated from the paternal lap
Nja ku wawa inya	I don't want to be sent away, mother
Pa heka wali hyuhu inya	Separated from the maternal breast
Na kaka pango a wungnandu nggu	My teeth are still a youthful white
Na moro pango a longge nggu	My hair is still a girl's blue-black

Tila's fondness for the story of the spindle is consistent with her aspirations to become a "modern" woman who would still have the feminine, nurturing qualities of Kodi tradition. She wrote her script for marriage in love letters, but it has resonances with older versions of romantic interchanges, such as the harvest dialogue I witnessed in 1980.

"CAPTURING A MAN WITH WORDS": THE SEXUAL CONTRACT

Women who speak their minds and persuade men to do things they may not originally have intended to do are certainly no recent development. The following exchange, taken from a staged ritual dialogue at a harvest gathering, presents a model of courtship banter in a traditional mold. It shows the more formal paired discourse of public performance, where familiar idioms are reworked by a pair of speakers to suggest the tensions of early courtship.

This is a performance piece, designed to entertain but also to edify, where the "typical" attitudes of the boy and girl are somewhat caricatured, so that the ironies involved in each side's self-presentation will emerge more clearly. Both men and women enjoyed watching this piece, laughing at the somewhat clichéd versions of their own sentiments, but they also judged the portrayals to be accurate.

The piece is staged by a boy and girl sitting at opposite ends of a veranda and playing the parts of lovers at odds with each other. The boy is accused of seducing the girl without approaching her parents first to become accepted as a suitor. He begins with a denial:

Wuku danggu yayo	Why am I accused?
Maka a wokico pa dimya nggu	She lifted up and tossed this at me
A taki a ngara ngila nggu	Saying my name falsely
Kari dangga yayo	Why should I suffer?
Maka a rabikyo padala ngga	She drew me into her net
A numa ngara ngongo nggu	Giving me a bad reputation
Ba di yayo mono nja kundoku	As for me I didn't even
Mbaha mata nggu ela pyahero kaleku	Wash my face by her betel pouch
Nja ku ndanga lomo witti nggu	I didn't try to rest my feet
Ela tanjolo wulu witti	Beside the decorated calves of her legs
Londongo ha wu koro	Sharing a single room
Njama lodongo ha wu koro	We didn't share a single room
Napingo hawaka nopo	Lying together on one mat
Njama napingo hawaka nopo	We didn't lie on one mat
Londo monanikya a ura nggu	But my forelock sits still
Dulango paneghe	Surrounded by malicious speech
Ndende monaniya a ndewa nggu	But my spirit still stands
Ela pandango patera	In the center of this talk

He objects to being made the subject of gossip by her accusations, which he says are unfounded.

She counters by asking if he denies that he made any advances:

Pena ba indi ngandi utta	Didn't you bring me sirih pipers
La kandaghu wulla taru?	In the forest under the full moon?
Pena ba inde ngandi labba	Didn't you bring me areca nut
La kapandu pohi myalo?	In the darkness of the evening?

The boy replies that he may have been misinterpreted:

Inja utta lembero pa duki	It was not the sirih of a formal visit
Inja labba palako hamamaya	It was not the areca you chew in public
Inja lembero kandangi nggumi	Not the visit to exchange tubers
Inja loduro mandara nggumi	Not the trip to seek more food

He presents his "gifts" (whatever they were) as informal, not as part of the established sequence of courtship, where a boy goes looking for "grains of rice" that will grow in his new home.

His female companion responds that he misled her with flattery and temptation:

Uru paneghe moka	Because the words were
Na kari witti ghyoghi	Used like bait to catch crabs
Na mingyaka ela ghoba	Delicious in the mouth
Ura patera moka	Because your talk was
Na pane kere ghele	Luring the snail shells
Na langgihyo la lama	Sweet on the tongue
Na hale pimoka la ndara ndelo kaka	You lifted me up on your white horse
Pei kinggaka kere	Then pushed me off the backside
Ma woti pyaka la tena mbolo rongo	You carried me off in the round canoe
Ha bale kinggaka mata	Then turned your eyes away
Kama kimongo nggaka lawaro	Tasting me like coconut milk
Menge pika ba ghughundi	After holding in your hands
Huhu tobo reda	Breasts round like gourd plates
Otu ngguka la kandaghu danga yora	You ran off to the forest full of nymphs
Kami kimungoka mburato	Sampling the flavored rice mound
Menge pika ba napindi	After resting with your legs
Ha kahenga kuku wewe	On the thighs of bright butterflies
Otu ngguka la marada danga pongo	You ran off to the fields full of bad spirits

The metaphors used by each side here deserve some analysis. When the girl accuses the boy of seducing her, she uses images of illicit eating (tasting her milk, holding her breasts like plates), but once he proposes to make her his wife, the feeding idiom is reversed: She will become his wife because instead of his eating her, she will prepare food for him and his domestic animals. Her message to him is, essentially, "You have already eaten me, now let me feed you."

She stresses that what she fed on herself was not her husband but his speech, the "sweet talk" he used to coax her out to meet him and the promises he baited her with. He placed her behind him on his horse (as a man rides with his wife or sweetheart), then pushed her off carelessly. He proposed to carry her away in a canoe, then looked the other direction. The temptations of other women (wood nymphs or bad spirits) distracted him from the delicious things he had already tasted with her and deprived her of the chance to feed him again, but within the legitimate category of marriage.

She accuses him here of enjoying her favors and then deserting her, going to pursue other women in unsafe places. This was the passage where she confessed most openly to feeling seduced and abandoned, but it was also the one where listeners most admired her verbal skills, saying that she persuasively demonstrated her ability to "capture a husband with words."

And, in effect, the speech reached its goal, as it was followed by a grudging but nevertheless clear proposal to make her his wife:

Ta ku hake bongoka!	Let me swear to you then!
Ba tane ngghuku manu	If I tempted you like a chicken
Mono ba leko ngguka kura	And if I baited you like a shrimp
Kete we binggaka kamba	Then come spin thread for me
Maghana wa binggaka nopo	Come weave some mats for me
Pane we binggaka manu	Scatter seeds for my chickens
Pagha wa binggaka wawi	Pour gruel out for my pigs
Ba hei wainggu	So I have come to ask you to be
Koba tanggu wete nggu wenggo	My own coconut shell, I ask you
Kalogho ndamo uma unggu wenggo	The banana in my home, I beg you[4]
Ku ole londongo ha wu koro	I will sit in a single room with you
Ku ole napingo ha wala nopo	I will lie on a single mat with you

Having extracted a proposal, the girl then turns back to him to try to secure a promise of fidelity:

Yayo danggu mono	As for myself now
Ba koba tanggu wete mu	If you do want me to be your coconut shell
Mono ba kalogho ndomo uma mu	And the banana in your home
Ambu otu wali nggaka	Do not go off again

La kandaghu danga yora	Into the forest full of nymphs
Nggeho wabingoka koki	Chasing after them like monkeys
Ambu otu wabingoka	Do not go off again
La marada danga pogho	Into the fields full of bad spirits
Kalola wabingoka wawi	Hunting them like pigs

She then asks that he take an oath that he will not pursue other women or take another wife:

Kira doru longge	Promise with a lock of hair
Haka teba tana	Swear with sliced earth
Tana na hablingoka kapa hamama	Let this betel quid be transformed
Ba inde patera hei pinya doyo	If you do not tell the truth
Tengge watu kaka mono	Into the cough of white stones
Wiria wei kalogho	And the mucus of the north
Nja ku mbeingo	I do not want to be like the
Pa katonda legho wataro na	Corn hung up with other cobs
Nja ku mbuhango	I do not care to be on the
Wunango kadungo dungo deke	Shuttle that pulls two threads at once

Nja ku mbeingo	I do not want to be
Kanenggelo kahumbu	Cooked with other rice packets
Nja ku mbuhango	I do not care to join the
Ombolo katalu talo ngale	Shed stick that holds up three in a line

Here, she reverses the meanings of all the homely domestic images that her prospective husband has summoned up for her, taking up his idea of a dutiful wife who spins thread and prepares food to argue that she does not want to share her household with another woman. She turns to the idiom of weaving to note that she does not want to be pulled into place like the threads on a shuttle, or held there with others by the shed stick.

These metaphors of homespun domesticity are those turned around to challenge male domination and secure a binding promise of sexual exclusivity. If her prospective husband agrees to the oath, marking his assent by exchanging locks of hair and burying a piece of the hair in the ground, then the betel quid that he receives from another woman can turn into poison in his mouth, giving him the symptoms of tuberculosis (a cough of white stones and northern mucus).

Performances like this one of "courtship couplets" (Ind. *pantun*) are widely described in Indonesian ethnography, from the ceremonies involved in greeting sea worms (Ecklund 1977, Hoskins 1993a: 147–53) to ritual sequences that precede marriage (Rodgers 1979), or are part of the rites of the harvest (George 1996). It is widely recognized that certain jocular forms of sexual antagonism are part of the process of courtship, and watching this exchange provides an occasion for men and women to laugh at themselves.

The women readily admit that they seek fidelity and commitment, while men insist on their freedom and deny that their advances should be taken seriously. Comments that I heard on this piece were delivered in sexually segregated groups, as people relaxed afterward to eat a meal and chew betel.

"That woman was very clever," a male spectator acknowledged, "but her lips must remain true to her words. I think she was a bit too eager to receive him. A dutiful wife is more than a mouth. She must also know when to hold her tongue, when to be quiet."

A young mother saw things differently, "Men are always doing things and then not wanting to be responsible for them. The girl was right to push him, to force him to own up to his own acts. All those denials! Often they deny it right up to the moment that the girl's stomach swells up."

Said a male schoolteacher from the district capital: "Young people today are rarely as articulate as those two. They know the words of tradition, they could make us laugh even as we recognized ourselves in what they said. Only in these more isolated hamlets in Balaghar do they still know these things."

"Ooooh, they don't want us to know these things any more," added an older woman caustically. "We used to have many girls like that, girls who could talk back, taking their own words and turning them around. Now, parents only want their daughters to learn Indonesian, to say the proper phrases for school and receiving guests."

Their perspectives suggest a generational difference in the weapons used in the conflicts between the sexes and a change in both orientation and modes of discourse. Later, in my home, I played the tape of this performance for Tila, Ria, and a number of girls their age. They saw the debate about polygyny as one that had consumed their parents, but as no longer the central conflict in their lives.

"Our fathers and grandfather felt that to be a great man you had to have many wives and many children," one said. "But now people see that it is better to have just one wife and send your children to school. Then they can be something, have government jobs. Then you have more than a garden and a few animals in the back."

Another added, "This is the modern age. People want to be Christian, to follow the ways of the church and the state, both of which recognize only one wife. But we still have the problem of boys who do not want to admit what they are doing when they visit a girl, when they offer her betel. We also have a lot of problems with who decides who she will marry, and when."

The coming of Christianity introduced the ideal of a virgin bride, dressed in white for her church wedding, but the form that it took in Kodi was heavily idealized. Most families were too poor to afford such a celebration at the same time that they were marshaling scarce resources for bridewealth. So the church wedding occurred as part of a "feast to improve the marriage" (*pesta memperbaiki perkawinan*), which was held in church sometimes a decade or two after the bride and groom had begun living together. It was more like an anniversary, a celebration attended by their children to show what they had accomplished through their union. Older converts to Christianity could also decide, at whatever age, to marry in the church, so often grandchildren and even great-grandchildren attended the weddings of their elders.

When Christians came to meet at marriage negotiations, sometimes there were references to the bride's virginity through new couplets, which spoke of "fresh grains of paddy" and "seeds that have never been sown." These may emerge from the most common Indonesian way of referring to pre-marital sexual relations in love letters—"The rice has already turned into porridge" (*nasi sudah jadi bubur*). The "cooking" had already gone on for too long, and the image of a gluey sludge left in the pot suggested early pregnancy.

OFFICIAL AND UNOFFICIAL DISCOURSE

The lines of verse from this traditional performance suggest that a youthful longing for autonomy and greater sexual freedom is nothing particularly new. Taking an object like a spindle, however—associated with virtuous female industriousness—and using it to represent a greater assertiveness on the part of the woman, and a calculated series of actions to realize her own fantasies, is somewhat subversive.

This raises the question so fittingly presented by Abu-Lughod (1986) of the different discourses of sentiment in each society, and the problem of which sorts of messages are appropriately expressed in each discourse. Among the Awlad 'Ali Bedouin, women and young men revealed in elliptical short verses feelings of attachment that they denied in everyday conversation, dominated by the discourse of honor and autonomy. The artfully improvised performances of this short lyrics or *ghinnawas* resemble in some ways the longer exchange of paired couplets I just cited, and the songs of laments that dwell on romantic disappointment. They provide a cultural space in which feelings of dependency, emotional vulnerability, and personal longing can be expressed, even if they are publicly denied.

Poetry in Bedouin society constitutes a "dissident or subversive discourse" most closely associated with "disadvantaged dependents who least embody the ideals of Bedouin society and have least to gain in the system as structured. . . . Poetry is the discourse of opposition to the system and of defiance of those who represent it" (1986: 251). Yet at the same time, poetry is powerful precisely because it is not a spontaneous outpouring of feeling. It is formulaic, disguising the identities of the speaker and the person addressed so that messages that are counter to official ideals are carried subtly in an elaborate and culturally admired code. The verbal genres favored by women and youths allow them to refuse to be dominated (displaying a culturally valued autonomy) while at the same cloaking their defiance in words, which are fleeting and ambiguous.

In Kodi, there are many forms of oral poetry, which can be manipulated in different ways by men and women. Ritual speech is used primarily by men for formal negotiations and statements that have a quasi-legal status—announcing the transfer of land, women, rights to ritual office, and so on. However, the couplets also surface in more private contexts, in love songs and mourning songs, which are among the genres favored by women. Paired ritual couplets make up a form of discourse that gains its authority by reference to tradition, and its place is most clearly expressed by the general reference to this as the "words of the ancestors." In the mouth of a skilled female speaker, however, even these words can be turned in a different direction and can be used to offer coded criticisms of male dominance. There is, as Gal notes, "a paradoxical intertwining of official and dissident discourse" in the clothing of subversion and defiance in carefully crafted metaphors (1991: 194).

Tila also admired the performance piece that caricatured male denials and female strategies to force them into admitting illicit sexual activity. She would not, however, have been able to perform those ritual couplets herself. When young people today want to deviate from the ancestral path, they do not speak the local language but Indonesian, whose source of authority is distant (the public culture of Java and Indonesian national media) but important to them precisely because it is opposed to the world of their parents.

The wordless "language of things," communication based on the exchange of objects, is also used in both official and unofficial ways. But one thing I hope to show is how objects and their symbolism can become weapons on the battleground of sexual politics, invested with different tactical meanings.

THE PERSONAL SYMBOL VS. THE PUBLIC STATEMENT

Since Tila was not a storyteller or a ritual specialist, not a high government official or the widow of an important man, the intimate details of her biographical investment in the spindle appear "personal" rather than "public"—and my writing about them challenges the boundaries of an ethnographer's discretion in ways that earlier chapters have not. The identities of my earlier subjects could not be disguised by a pseudonym, but Tila's story is not widely known to those outside her circle of friends, so I have not used her real name. Though she will recognize herself in these pages, her husband's family may not. I acknowledge my inconsistency in naming some subjects and not others, but feel nevertheless that my method is appropriate for the rather different kinds of revelations I am publishing about each one.

The theoretical argument that I am trying to develop about biographical objects is based on the personal significance of the possession rather than its public recognition. In several contexts, Tila chose to weave the significance of the spindle into her own personal story, but this representation was not played out on a ritual stage before a wide audience. She articulated it in a private narrative of confidences and in a wordless gift to an old friend. The more public identification that the old Raja had with his snake cloth or the storyteller with his betel bag were based on narrated events of personal significance and also a tie to ancestors. Women, including not only Tila but also Ra Mete, Daku Maru, and Ria (whose story I tell in the final chapter), form their ties less through ancestry than through experience: the experience of being exchanged, of being neglected or discarded, of losing an idealized partner, or of falling and breaking into many pieces on the road.

The objects that women tie to their own biographical narratives are not ancestral heirlooms or ritual intermediaries, but more homely domestic possessions (a sarung, a cooking vessel, a backyard animal), which express their feelings of being moved away and separated. The spindle is the consolation of the spinster, who clings to a substitute for an idealized husband instead of accepting the real one chosen by her parents. Tila did not become a spinster, but in breaking the spindle, she performed a small sacrificial act to show the loss of her own romantic dreams.

NOTES

1. The reference to rockets is part of the Kodi tale. One of the commentators added that the different levels of heaven and earth in this story could be translated as "planets" visited in a story of travel through space. Traditional ideas of cosmology have obviously already incorporated some more recent information about interplanetary communication. This account of the quest for a wife from the heavens could now be seen as a Kodi science fiction adventure.

2. "Ngge" has the literal meaning of "where" in Kodi, but it also designates the kingdom of the upperworld, ruled by a spider (nggengge) whose name could be translated Lord Wherewhere, a sort of Kodi never-never land. Ngge is a refrain used in all traveling songs, such as those sung to accompany the dragging of tombstones or house pillars (Hoskins 1986). It signals that one is headed somewhere, and the destination is then elaborated in the rest of the verse.

3. The incident repeats a narrative told about the culture hero Lete Watu that I have written about before (Hoskins 1993a: 72–74) It occurs in very similar form in both versions of the Kalanggu Langa Kaka story I collected.

4. The couplet "koba tanggu wete, kalogho ndamu uma" refers to an official wife who has become a "possession" of her husband's house. Note that contrary to vulgar Freudianism, Kodi thought had no problem with seeing a small sweet banana as a very feminine object.

6.

THE DRUM AND MASCULINITY

A Healer's Story

Markos Rangga Ende posing with his drum at a nightlong healing ceremony (*yaigho*). The gongs lie in front of him on the mat, as well as a plate with betel nut and money in it. (Photo J. Hoskins, 1980)

I first met Markos Rangga Ende, the singer, and his drum on September 29, 1979. It was the first month of my fieldwork in Kodi, and I had received news that a singing ceremony or *yaigho* would be held in the remote coastal hamlet of Waikahaka. The rite would be attended by the older woman I lived with, Gheru Wallu, and two of her children, and we prepared to go there in the late afternoon. As the sun cooled and the shadows lengthened, we packed up our contributions of ground coffee, sugar, and tea, and placed them on the back of a small horse ridden by her youngest son. Then Gheru Wallu, her older son, and I walked for two hours to reach the coast.

In the first few moments that I saw Markos, he sat down behind the drum, raised a stick to strike it, and began to sing in a full rich baritone. The words that I taped then, initially without understanding them at all, were a long invocation to the drum. They told the story of the origins of the drum, its sufferings and travails, and its eventual transformation into a healing cavity, a place where troubles could be placed and carried up to the upperworld to seek help. The story of the drum was also, I came to realize, a distorted version of Markos's autobiography, a reference to his own troubles and to the trauma that made him into a healer.

All singers open with an invocation of the drum, and with a payment of betel nut placed on top of its buffalo-hide cover. But they do not sing the same words, and although they all must respect the canons of parallel ritual speech, they mold the narrative line to suit their own personalities and past experiences. The song that Markos sang at the beginning of each rite was a personal song, one that he had crafted and refined over years of practice, and one that he claimed was uniquely effective because of his own biographical investment. "The story of the drum is also my story," he said.

Although the story of the drum was told in a personal style, it had to wed individual idiosyncrasies to a cultural paradigm. The origin narrative of the drum is generalized for all drums that have been properly carved and consecrated with sacrifices for use in curing and singing ceremonies. It must be recognized by the orators, other ritual specialists whose dialogue with the singer establishes the causes of the affliction and seeks a way to appease the angry spirits. This narrative was, in its overall form, passed on to Markos by his grandfather, who was also a singer.

What the story of the drum defines, I would argue, is something of the "vocation" that a singer feels when he takes up the profession of ritual healing. It is also a reflection on his own experiences of pain and suffering, which the patient can identify with and use as a guide to relieve symptoms through the dissolution of this suffering into music. The singing ritual does not always result in a "cure" (Hoskins 1996c). Often, its goal can be more realistically defined as a response to illness that expresses the concern of family members. The ceremony provides a temporary respite from discomfort so the patient can put his or her social affairs in order in an effort to remove the cause of ancestral displeasure that brought on the symptoms.

The drum is carved in a curved, hourglass shape that is said to recall the female body, with its "rounded full chest" and "slender waist" (*tamboro kuru, taranda kenda*). Externally seductive and curvaceous, it is internally hollow and receptive to the voice of the singer and orators, who pierce it with their words. The physical form, and particularly its description in ritual speech, emphasizes the drum's role as the counterpart of the male singer, the companion of his voice as it travels to the upperworld.

THE INVOCATION TO THE DRUM AS SUNG BY MARKOS

The singer opens with a call to the drum's cavity—"Magho Bela! Magho Bela!" meaning "the shade (beneath) the spotted hide." The hollow center is addressed as the baton begins to beat above it, telling the story of how the first drum came to be made. A piece of wood came down from a "corral on a steep hill, a corral in the distant heavens," and fell into the sea. Carried off in the surf, it was tossed by the waves and drifted all the way to the furthest western tip of Sumba, Cape Karosso. There it was found by two children playing in the sand. They were the children of "Nggudi who knew how to carve, and Lando who knew how to sculpt" (*Nggudi peghe tepe, Lando peghe hono*), the ancestors who first gave it shape.

A lara la pa lini mono	The path that it followed and
A annu li hamane	The way that it traveled was
Ba wale di koghu ela mbanu nale	From being tossed in the sea worm waves
Ba wale di konggolo ela wangu loro	From being turned in the flooding sea
Duki nono ela lete la karoho	Until it came to the cliff at Karosso
Toma nono ela mbali la kawana	Until it arrived at the right side
Kede mata wei pa toboko dani	That was the source where they met
Kede lolo ghai pa rangga dani	Those were the crossed tree vines where they found it

They took the piece of driftwood into their hamlet and carved it into a Kodi ritual object. But since the clans of Nggudi and Lando are not identified, the drum is not placed in a specific descent line. This is important for its transcendence of partisan divisions between clans, as its history binds it to cosmic forces but does not anchor it in existing social tensions.

The two children took the driftwood to the back door of their house, where they set it aside. They left it in a pig's trough there, in the area where domestic animals were fed (*pandou keka manu, karaba wawi*), not realizing how important it was. Then they heard a strange shaking sound near the coconut shell that had been put out to feed the chickens. They recognized that the driftwood must be animated in some way, and they stripped off its bark and scored it with vertical designs.

Then Nggudi and Lando carried it off to a secret place, an abandoned ancestral village ("the land stepped on by many feet, the stones sat on by many buttocks"), where they sat by the trunk of a sacred kandelu tree. There, they began to carve the drum into its present shape and fill it with magical objects:

Magho bela, maghu bela	The spotted hide, spotted hide
Na ngandi ghumi la kandelu biha	They brought you to a sacred tree
Maka na hona pa kaleka nggumi limya	And carved until his hand was bent
Lando peghe hono	Lando who knew how to carve
Di runggo ghai ka pioto	In the tangled limestone bushes
Na ngandi di ghumi di punge kambala hari	They brought you to the barkcloth trunk

Maka taipa pa kambidi ghumi mata	And decorated you till the eyes squinted
Nggudi peghe taipa	Nggudi who knew how to decorate
Di tara ghai karahi	Among the twisting thorns

A brace formed in the shape of the moon and a bow formed in the shape of the sun (*wunda mata wulla, pana mata lodo*) were inserted into the cavity to help it resonate. The wunda is a tool used to clean and soften cotton, to prepare it for spinning. Inside the drum, it is placed underneath the bow to create a sharper, clearer tone when struck with the baton.

The objects recall the story of the beginning of months and the phases of the moon. A man from the village of Toda shot off a piece of the moon and brought it home in his hunting net. Intermediaries were sent from the ceremonial center to negotiate for its release, and Toda was promised the privilege of receiving the first fruits of the harvest in return for releasing the moon back into the sea. This exchange was one of several primordial ones (see Hoskins 1993a: 60–76) that marked the beginning of ritual trans-actions between the human world and the spirit world. Their initial unity was followed by separation, creating the possibility for exchange and communication.

It is appropriate that the drum as an intermediary between the human community and the spirits bear the emblem of these primordial acts, and that the moon brace and sun bow create musical sounds that carry messages back and forth. The other objects contained in the cavity of the drum are emblems of sacrifices made to cement these exchanges: Three bundles of tail feathers represent the roosters killed to ascertain the willingness of the ancestors to listen to the drum's song (*talo tonggolo wulu ghailo*). Seven bundles of candlenut wrapped in sirih leaves with a chip of silver in each leaf (*pitu lighito wu kawallu*) represent offerings to the spirit inside the drum which must be replicated at the beginning of each ceremony. The number seven is significant because the Kodi world consists of six levels of earth and seven levels of heavens (*nomo ndani cana, pitu ndani awango*), and the drum must travel upward, piercing through each of the these levels (like the spin-dle) to reach the upperworld of the deities.

The slender female "waist" of the drum was carved and decorated with wood chips, tied to it with vines, "like a belt." The anthropomorphic aspects of the drum's shape are made clear in the verses addressed to it:

Yo na katiku liyo	You of the sharply resonant voice
Yo na malenggaroka ghoba	You of the wide open mouth
Ghilyo tadu kuha	The small bundles at the knees
Babaro likye bengge	The chips rising up to the waist
Yo na tamboro kuru	You of the rounded full chest
Yo na taranda kenda	You of the delicate slender waist

Nggudi and Lando then began to search for the proper material to cover the drum. First, they wrapped it in "keladi leaves from the cave tops, and wide green leaves from the forest" (*towako tadu liongo, mbulango bei kandaghu*). But this weak layer of vegetation was immediately broken by the drumsticks. So a series of animals were sacrificed to find the right one. First, they tried the hide of a mature buffalo from the sawah fields (*kari maninggu la pamba*), but it was too tough. Then they took the skin of a spotted python (*kaboko manggiko la patola*), but it was too slippery. Finally, they settled on the hide of a young buffalo calf with white markings on its head (*kabondi bela di togho*) for the upright drum and a young bay colt (*kamboka ndara rara*) for the horizontal drum (*diliro*). The youth of these animals recalls a rule for sacrifices to the highest deities: They must be yearlings "with black eyes," not the more expensive and impressive long-horned animals used for prestige feasting.

The drums are still addressed with the names of the animals sacrificed for their coverings, as their spirits are said to still inhabit the drum's cavity. The animals who gave their lives to make musical communication possible must be recited first, then the singer can call out:

Ho maka di taki la ngguniya	Now we have pronounced them already
La ngara ndi wawi mu	The names of the pigs
Maka disena la numandi nggumi	Now we have said them in front of you
La ngara igha mu disena	The names of the fishes

Their sacrifice has been recognized, so now the instruments can be called with their ritual names and assume their roles.

In Hangga Koki, a particularly sacred drum is found that was said once to have been covered with human skin. The victim was a young girl, a war captive whose tender skin made her appropriate to empower the most important musical intermediary. The drum once covered with human skin is still said to have a higher, purer voice because of the human life it once claimed. But the young girl's skin was not durable, so even there they now re-cover it with a calf hide.[1]

Whenever a new drum is made, the animal whose hide is to be used must be specially dedicated to that purpose and told why it is going to die. Its meat is butchered and divided among the members of the ritual house that stores musical instruments (Uma Dungga Poghi, literally House of the Fiddle and Flute) and has the exclusive right to consecrate new ones. This house must also be invoked at each ceremony, called:

Pandouna a kere bendu	The home of the base of the drum
Pandouna a pude tala	The home of the navel of the gong
Pandouna a dungga ndaha liyo	The home of the fiddle with a fine voice
Pandouna a poghi ndaha halio	The home of the flute with the fine frets

When the drum is covered and dedicated by sacrifices, it can be taken out onto the ritual stage and placed near the trunk of the hamlet deity (*Mori Cana*, literally "The Lord of the Land"), which takes the form of a large leafy tree in the center of each garden settlement.

The singer sits in front of the drum and begins to strike it with a padded stick. As he starts to sing, his voice is said to pierce into its cavity and animate it so that it can travel to the upperworld:

Pa toghi kyaka marou ngandu	Pierced by the cockatoo of the long beak
Ha bola pero manumba ghoba	Bored by the parrot with the large mouth
Yo dikya a kahikya pa ha puningo	You are the bird we set singing
Yo dikya a kapudu pa pa lerango	You are the butterfly we send flying

The sexual symbolism here seems obvious, as we note the penetration of the male voice into the female cavity. But it should be noted that the drum is not spiritually efficacious until both elements are present: The singer's words cannot "fly" without the hollow drum as their vehicle, and the bird or butterfly does not come alive until it is pierced by the ringing voice.

Complementarity and mutuality are continually stressed in the long narrative sections of verse that follow. The drum is supposed to travel on a healing journey to help the patient escape from the constricting forces of illness. A metaphor detailing the driftwood's descent from the heavenly kingdom specifically describes this process:

Yo na mburu la kandula kondoko mayako	You are the one who came down from darkening skies above
Yo na mburu la karamba rara tena	You are the one who sailed downriver in a red canoe
Ba kodi kendu pala	Leaping out quickly from
La kandaghu daiyaro koti lighya	The forest of high ginger vines
Bu watu lande lolo	Slipping like a stone
La kalembu lekero wini coro	From the tangled roots of tomato plants

The coupling of the singer and the drum is associated with a similar coupling between the patient and the healer, who travel together in spirit as companions seeking a common destination, the land of cooling waters and restored health. The singer says, with some ambiguity:

Enge pa onggle lolo wunato nda	We are bound together like the roots of a banyan tree
Enge pa diri la cokalo kaboka nda	We are wound together like the coils of a giant python
Pa kalete ha wu ndara	Riding together on one horse
Pa halako hawuna lara	Walking together on one path

Here, he asserts both his unity of purpose with the drum and with the patient, who will accompany him in his imagination to seek the source of his illness.

Once the singer has finished telling the story of the drum, he calls on the orator (*tou ta liyo*) to join him in the task of unraveling the mystery of this affliction:

Maka ta ndende ndicako waingo	Let us stand firmly in front of
A papa ndende kundo	The pair of opposing knees
Maka ta mangga di rema waingo	Let us wait patiently for
A nggaba horo longge	The counterpart with parted hair
Mai pa toboko la lara donggandi	Who comes to meet us on the path
Pa maghana nopo luna	To plait a mat to pillow the head
Mai pa londo taloro wu mandattu	Who comes to sit in the dancing ground
Pa oro manerio mango dalo	To make a mark in the garden's growth

The orator will join with him in a dialogue, a form of ritual work compared with working the fields or plaiting a mat. Each suggestion that they make for the cause of the spirit's anger is called "making a scratch on the kandelu bark, cutting a line in the kambala wood" (*pa oro kandelu, pa lara kambala*), as they trace the history of the patient's village and garden and look for errors or omissions in the rites performed that might have provoked the disapproval of the *marapu*.

COMMENTARY ON THE DRUM SONG

The biography of the drum is the story of its release from constrictions and its formation into an instrument of communication.

This symbolic linking of the drum to an escape from constricting forces explains why the first identification established in Kodi curing links the patient to the drum. Its story loosens the tangle of social relations that trap the patient inside the mystery of his illness, and allows him or her a certain conceptual distance from these relations. It also retraces experiences of illness and hardship that the healer had, and helps him to draw on these experiences to help the patient.

The mediation of objects in Kodi healing changes the dynamic of ritual efficacy. In an earlier analysis, I interpreted this process as one whereby the drum became the shaman, taking on a role given to a human being in many other societies (Hoskins 1988: 819–28). Now I would describe the process a bit differently, since I have come to see how, in a sense, "the shaman was always there in the drum," because the story of the drum as it is sung by the singer is the story of his own shamanic calling. The object is important only because of the importance given it by the healer, and this verbal portrait is what the patient is expected to respond to.

My first interpretation associated its narrative of dislocation and dissociation with the experience of illness, and interpreted the account of its gradually taking shape as a way to lead a patient out of pain and suffering and into more ordered understanding of the connection of events. After more extended conversations with Markos Rangga Ende in 1988, however, I also came to see another role given to the object: It paralleled his own personal experience of loss of family and of the search for a wife, a ritual counterpart who would allow him to assume a position of social adulthood. Only because he had also been tossed and turned by "the waves of outrageous fortune" (as Hamlet, another son of a murdered father and unfaithful mother, had put it) was he able to work as a healer and lead others out of confusion into dialogue with the invisible forces that control their lives.

BECOMING A RATO MARAPU

Markos Rangga Ende explained his calling to become a priest and singer as a combination of a heritage from his grandfather and the experience of hardship as a child. Born during the Japanese occupation, he was a weak and sickly boy. There was very little food or clothing for anyone at the time, and he reports that he had no clothing at all until he started school.

His mother, a beauty famous for her pale skin and elaborately tattooed thighs, was abducted by another man when Markos was barely weaned. He never saw her again, and his father tried to pursue the man to at least recover some of the brideprice paid. A hardworking peasant with few other resources, he left the boy with his own parents. Some years later, Markos's father was killed in a confrontation with one of the relatives of his wife's lover. His son was raised as an orphan, knowing neither mother nor father and without any brothers or sisters. The one person who paid attention to him when he was a child was his grandfather, Kailo Mboro, a well-known singer and healer. He traveled all over Kodi performing at ceremonies and was accompanied by Markos as soon as he was old enough to help carry the sacrificial meat given to the ritual performers as payment.

Listening to his grandfather's singing was the great joy of Markos's childhood, and he also loved the life of almost constant travel from one hamlet to another, with little time to rest in any one place. As his grandfather's assistant, he would set up the small set of musical instruments used at each rite: The main, upright drum (*bendu*), which was beaten by the singer with a baton and addressed in the first offerings, the horizontal drum (*diliro*) beaten with the hands, and the five gongs hung from a frame and struck with padded sticks.

He started playing the gongs and the horizontal drum when he was five or six, along with other young boys who kept rhythm with the singer during each rite. By the time he was ten, he was directing the others and setting the tempo for the whole group. Sometimes, he told me, when his grandfather wasn't looking, he would pick up the baton used to strike the upright drum and play on his own, singing to himself.

One day, his grandfather came back and found him playing the drum and imitating the songs of ritual. "You can't do that, you know," he told him with a mixture of pride and anger. "These drums are sacred. You can't strike them just for your own amusement. The marapu will come down and ask why you are calling them."

But at the same time, he realized that this fooling around with the drum was a sign that Markos was feeling his own vocation as a singer. "He knew I dared to break a taboo because of my descent line, because his blood was in my veins and his words were echoing through my mind," explained Rangga Ende. "He decided to help me become a real singer."

The house where the drums and gongs were stored in their ancestral village was called Uma Tedda, and anyone wanting to train to be a singer had to bring a chicken to be sacrificed in that house to tell the marapu. No one could play the musical instruments without the permission of their invisible owners, and so Markos's boyish experiments had to be defined as a form of apprenticeship.

Once they had checked that the chicken entrails were positive, Kailo Mboro began to let his grandson strike the upright drum in public rituals. He let him sing the opening phrases, and then Kailo Mboro would join in a dialogue with him as the orator, the "giver of the voice" (*ta liyo*), giving him directions and suggesting new phrases to him all night long. The techniques and couplets that Rangga Ende would need were taught to him in the context of public performance, in front of an audience of both human listeners and invisible spirits.

Before he could work on his own as a singer, he had to go through a purification rite. First Markos went to the house of his mother's brother to ask for a cleansing. He brought a horse as a sign of his respect for the authority of his mother's village. His mother's brother speared a pig, and presented him with a man's cloth. Then he gave him a bath with water and coconut milk, and he rubbed grated coconut on Markos's hair and body. The bath was to remove any traces of sin or contamination from him, and the exchange of gifts was to offer him protection in his newly chosen vocation.

Then the members of his immediate family, his mother's brother's family, and several traditional priests came together to pray to the clan spirit (*Marapu Matuyo*) and the spirit of the drum (*Marapu Dungga Poghe*, "Spirit of the Fiddle and Flute," the protector of all the musical instruments).

A diviner from another clan was invited to carry out an egg purification: A chicken's egg was placed on a plate, with instructions that it should clean out the contents of his stomach. A consecrated singer or *tou yaigho* must be very careful about what he eats. The stomach cavity, like the cavity of the drum, must be kept pure and uncontaminated. He cannot eat forbidden foods or stolen meat, or anything that was specifically excluded by his ancestors. Water is placed in a coconut shell and examined carefully, to see if it becomes clouded or obscured while the diviner is speaking. Then the egg is boiled with rice and peeled to check whether it contains any imperfections.

Four chickens were dedicated to specific spirits by scattering raw rice over them. The first was to the spirit of musical instruments (*Marapu Dungga Poghe*), the second to the spirit of Markos's grandfather, the third to the elder spirit of his clan (*Marapu Matuyo*), and the fourth to the local lord of the land (*Mori Cana*) in the garden hamlet. Each chicken's entrails were examined to be sure there were no objections to Markos's pursuing his profession.

But Markos could not be fully consecrated as a *rato marapu* until he was married. He needed a female counterpart as a lifetime companion and a ritual adjunct. A man without a wife could not be an effective healer and could not complete the full cycle of purifications needed to act as a priest.

THE SINGER AS INCOMPLETE: THE SEARCH FOR A COUNTERPART

Markos had difficulty marrying because he had no parents, brothers, or married sisters to help him pay the brideprice. As a young boy, he had been engaged to a cross-cousin, but she was carried off by another man before the marriage could be consummated.

It was his voice and his skill at singing that finally allowed him to marry. Although he had no livestock, a lovely and talented dancer who had admired his performances agreed to elope with him. Although her family was opposed to the match, she defied them to live a life of travel and ritual involvement.

Pati Rangga was seen as the ideal complement to Rangga Ende because she balanced out aspects of his appearance and public persona that struck others as strange. She was tall, dark-skinned, and dignified, with a strong constitution and a desire to leave the isolated hamlet where she grew up. Markos, in contrast, had his mother's light skin and very pale, greenish eyes. To many people on Sumba, his appearance was slightly unnerving. They said his eyes looked like "cat's eyes'" (*mata wodo*), and he was "almost like a white foreigner" (*dawa kaka*) in appearance. Some of the more Westernized girls in Bondo Kodi even told me they were afraid of him: "He has the skin and face of a European," they said, "but the dark betel-stained teeth of a village Sumbanese."

In marrying Pati Rangga, Markos acquired a public respectability and a family of affines who could substitute for the family of his birth, which he hardly knew. It took him many years to gather the requisite ten head of livestock (five horses, five buffalo) to make the marriage official, but during that time he was allowed to live with her, and they had children.

His wife also had to return to her natal village to cleanse herself. Just as she had accompanied him to his mother's brother's village, so he had to accompany her and bring a horse to the home of his in-laws, where they were received by the sacrifice of a pig and a gift of a sarung. Another egg was boiled and peeled and set beside a handful of rice and half a coconut shell filled with water, to cleanse the throat and the belly so only pure food could go down. A portion of the rice and half the egg were placed in each of their mouths, but they could not swallow them. They had to rinse them around their teeth, then spit them out again. Then their mouths were rinsed again with water, so that anything soiled or unclean would come out with this water.

The spitting rite is performed so that the mouths that speak or sing the words of ritual will not be unclean. Contact with invisible forces is seen as dangerous, so any singer who does not observe food taboos or proper procedure may have his life shortened. "The marapu will spit on you" (*a pa tirughu marapu*) if you do not obey their rules, and the first of these rules is always purity in the mouth.

Markos explained further that simplicity is required of all ritual specialists. They must be paid for their work at each rite with a spear, a bush knife, and a man's cloth. The best man's cloth to receive is an unpatterned one (the indigo "plaid" called *hanggi gundul* is usually preferred). Many colors or designs (like the "spots" on the snake cloth) would increase the commercial value of the cloth but make it inappropriate for a ritual specialist. The spots might imply that "his liver was spotted as well" and not clear and unblemished. The spear and bush knife, likewise, cannot be decorated or carved. They also cannot be cracked or scratched. Their ritual names stress their protective purpose:

Kada ngdini lyodo	The umbrella to shield the sun
Magho ngindi ura	The cover to shut out the rain
Katopo njanga joda	The bush knife to cut out a path
Nambu nangga dahi	The spear to protect on the way

If a feast sponsor thoughtlessly offers a torn piece of cloth or a damaged knife or spear, then the singer or orator can refuse the gift, saying, "How can I be shielded from the sun or protected from the rain with this gift?" A new one would then have to be provided with another sacrifice to ask forgiveness.

Although the first stages of his several-year apprenticeship were done under his grandfather's guidance, Markos and his wife did not finish the process until two years after his grandfather had died.

Ritual vocations are more often passed from grandfather to grandson than from father to son, although both are possible. Markos explained this by saying that the spiritual contact between the very old and the very young is usually more intense than that between father and son. A grandson can be the namesake (*tamo*) of his grandfather, and the role of "replacing the name" is often seen as almost a form of reincarnation, even when the grandfather is still alive. Markos himself said that his grandfather's soul "lived in his forehead where bundles were bound, and rested on his shoulders where wood was lifted" (*ndo ela togho wu pa todo, ndo mbale holo ghaiyo*). He heard the echoes of his grandfather's voice whenever he himself sang.

MARAPU RITUAL AND THE CATHOLIC CHURCH

Markos had had more schooling than most members of his generation in Bukambero. He had attended a Catholic primary school and the first two years of the secondary school in Waitabula. He was therefore able to read and to write with a clear, fluent hand. During the period of time that he lived near the mission station in Waitabula, he became the assistant of one of the German Catholic priests. He was the altar boy who helped to set out the ritual vestments and the chalice for the votive wine. Markos was fond of the priest, and described himself as the priest's favorite among the school-children (Ind. *anak emas*, literally "the golden child"). He remembered many small gifts of clothing, sweets, pencils, and notebooks, and even a small book about the lives of the saints. When the priest reached retirement age and was sent back to Europe, he cried and stroked Markos's head, telling him he should never forget the love that the Catholic Church had for orphans and abandoned children.

Though he did not forget the church, Markos chose to carry out his own spiritual vocation in the marapu tradition. He remained ambivalent about stating his loyalties too strongly, however. As an infant, he had been baptized in the Catholic Church. He received lessons in religion in school, and at one point was encouraged to think about continuing on to the Catholic seminary in Flores, where a new generation of Indonesian priests were to be trained. However, he did not complete his religious training in Waikabubak because he began the apprenticeship to his grandfather. Traveling from village to village carrying the meat and the drum, he had no time for lessons.

When asked for official purposes if he was Catholic, however, he would generally reply that he was a member of the Catholic community, in the wider sense. When he began to practice as a singer, he was invited to sing at large Catholic feasts on Christmas and Easter. The European-born priests were very interested in using local forms of music and dance to carry their message, and they were curious about local forms of healing and ritual. They hired him to perform at the public celebrations held when new churches opened or new schools were built.

I never heard Markos explicitly reject the Catholic Church, although he did not participate formally in its rituals. Like various other people with a foot in both worlds, he presented his position as embracing all religions, not limited to any single one. Steedly (1993: 208) tells the story of a medicine peddlar among the Karo Batak who had "five religions but no ID card," and Tsing provides an engrossing account of a female shaman among the Mera-tus of Kalimantan who blended elements of Islam, millennarianism, Indone-sian bureacratic ritual, and indigenous spirit worship to produce her own religious visions (1993: 253–83). Markos's articulation was less outlandish, but equally noncommittal:

> I like to talk to the invisible ones, but I am not limited to one religion. If they ask if I am Catholic, yes, I say I am, because as a boy I was well treated by the church. If they ask if I am a Protestant, I say, "It is one Lord that we all pray to," and I have no quarrels with them. If they ask me if I am a *rato marapu*, I say yes, since I sing to the drum. Even the Muslims from the port come to hear me when I sing, and no one sends them away. I do only what I was trained to do, following the rules as they were laid out on our island by our people.

They showed us one way to speak to *marapu*, but the Europeans have other ways. I do not say one is bad and one is good. I sing, I strike the drum. It is the way that I have learned.

The apparent modesty of this statement should be understood in the delicate political context of a spiritual leader whose command over local knowledge has recently been eroded by pressure from the state to convert. Markos was committed to the ways of his ancestors, but he was also a performer who was always seeking newer and wider audiences. He clearly loved the ritual stage and loved the attention that it brought him. As long as he could attract people to come and hear his songs (whatever their formal religious affiliations), he saw himself as successful.

Because he craved listeners, he was also in many respects an ideal informant. Although his busy ritual schedule made our meetings sometimes difficult to arrange, whenever he came to see me he was willing to talk all night. He insisted on noting minute details of ritual procedure, and would check my notebooks to see that I had written them down properly. He would help me to transcribe all the ceremonies that he performed in, providing Indonesian translations of couplets and careful exegesis of their figurative meanings. He was self-centered enough, however, not to want to work on other people's materials:

> When I sing, I have to take my words from what the orators say, to reconcile their different arguments and present a full account to the *marapu*. I take their speech and set it to the rhythm of the drums and gongs. But I always do it my way, the Bukambero way. I can perform in Kodi, but I do not want to try to interpret the way they speak. We each have our own way of doing things, and I can teach you my way, but not that of the others.

Markos's comment has to be understood in the context of the special marginality of the people of Bukambero, his own homeland and a territory with a somewhat anomalous history on the island. Though many people saw no problems with my taking lessons from Maru Daku or Raja Horo, they were suspicious of what someone from Bukambero might say about Kodi. Markos showed himself to be less of an intellectual then Maru Daku but a more skillful local politican by his refusal to meddle in the ritual affairs of the Kodi core villages.

SORCERORS AT THE MARGINS: BUKAMBERO AND KODI

The 8,000 people of Bukambero were often said to be witches and sorcerers. Officially a part of the district of Kodi, they spoke their own language, *paneghe bukambero*, which was closer to the languages of Laura and Weyewa. The area was famous for harboring danger and disease, because it was far from fresh water and said to be full of poisons.

A popular guidebook to the more out-of-the-way parts of the archipelago,

Bill Dalton's *Indonesia*, referred to Bukambero in all of its editions published in the 1980s as containing "an isolated and very traditional population." But the people of Bukambero, despite this forbidding reputation, are not really an Eastern Indonesian equivalent of the famous Badui of West Java. They are instead mainly people who have moved from Kodi to make their gardens there because of population pressures.

The famous sorcerors of Bukambero are associated with its oldest ancestral village, Wai Walla, the location of ancient and powerful ways of knowledge. Shortly after my arrival, many people advised me not to go there, and especially not to accept any food that might be given to me there. I was too intrigued to respect these warnings, and I am glad I did not.

Wai Walla was a forlorn and rather ramshackle collection of older high-towered homes, arranged near a spring plagued with large numbers of mosquitoes. The mosquitoes alone could explain much of the village's history of disease, especially malarial fevers. (One person, perhaps mixing mission hygiene lessons with indigenous narratives, told me, "It is not really the people in Wai Walla who have witchcraft in them but the mosquitoes.")

The people of Wai Walla have been slowly dying out for the past three generations, and they see these illnesses as signs of some sort of ancestral curse. One older man told me that the village site was "too sacred" to support new inhabitants, and the marapu there now were angry that many of their cult houses had not been rebuilt. Others said that the poison of Wai Walla had turned on its own masters because they had sold or given away too many of their heirlooms. The theme of punishment for recent misdeeds, which they stressed, contrasted with the interpretations of people from other areas that emphasized a sinister side to the village's origins.

Wai Walla means "flowering waters," but the dense tangle of vines that now clogs the area near the springs has few flowers. Walla has the additional meaning of matriline in Kodi: It is the "flowering" of female blood to produce children in other houses, who will not carry on the ancestral seed as lineage descendants. Matriclans are also deeply immersed in witchcraft. Two in particular (Walla Kyula and Walla Ngedo) are associated with the origins of death in the call of a small black bird with red eyes called the Kyula (Hoskins 1990: 292, 1993a: 62). Other matrilines were said to be formed as the result of a scandal, such as sexual relations with an animal (for Walla Gawi, a goat, for Walla Mandaho, a swordfish), which caused a woman to be excluded from her natal home.

The witchcraft of certain matrilines is an inherited, physical characteristic, which can be glimpsed in slightly red, shifty eyes or a navel opening that allows the soul to wander during sleep. Witches here, as in many parts of the world, are supposed to wander about at night, sometimes taking the form of birds or mice or small darting lights. They feed nocturnally on the inner organs of their victims, eventually sapping their strength completely. The first witches were said to be the original inhabitants of the island, who ate their food raw and were skilled at preparing herbs and medicines. They made peace with later immigrants to the region, but were still suspected of sometimes craving human flesh. Many men are reluctant to marry a woman from the village of Wai Walla for these reasons.

The founder of Bukambero, Lendu Myamba, brought the sea worms from overseas, but then passed them on to Mangilo and Pokilo in Tossi (Hoskins 1993a: 88–92). He also brought honey, wild tubers, caterpillars, and the megapode bird, whose large mud incubators for her eggs provided the inspiration for Sumba's high-towered houses. His descendants, in the lineage of Pati Merapati, are now those most often associated with the occult arts—and especially the deliberate use of malicious charms and poisons (*pawunu*), which anthropologists since Evans-Pritchard have called sorcery rather than witchcraft.

The poison found in Bukambero was said to be an invisible substance, which could be blown, spat, or breathed onto a potential victim. It was sometimes suggested that the poison had a will of its own and would ask to be placed on someone's food. I also often heard that its owners had to "let it run into someone's plate" or else it would turn on them and consume them instead. Tuberculosis, the "deep cough" (*tengge mandattu*) of someone who has swallowed something reluctantly, was often linked to the use of this poison, and was in fact particularly common in Bukambero.

During the many months that I collected stories of sorcery and poisoning in Bukambero, no one ever denied that these practices existed, but each person argued that they were restricted to a very small group of the original inhabitants, which did not include the speaker. Sometimes the sorcery and poisonings were attributed to members of the Wai Walla patriclan but not its matriclan; sometimes to the descendants of one house founded by Pati Merapati but not another. Carrying the aura of sorcery could be useful, since it encouraged people to be generous and cooperative out of fear of retribution. The advice I was given when other people realized I would travel to the witchcraft villages was inevitably to appease them and then move on. "Be careful when you talk to witches! Do not offend them, but do not spend much time with them. Give them what they want and send them on their way!" No one ever admitted that he used supernatural powers for nefarious purposes.

Markos Rangga Ende was a member of the Bondo Maliti village, more recently founded and genealogically separate from Wai Walla. As a ritual specialist, he had had often had to consult elders from the origin villages, especially Temba Palako of Pati Merapati (who narrated the account published in Hoskins 1993a). As someone guiding me in Bulambero, he did not hesitate to visit the witchcraft villages that others were afraid of. However, his unusual appearance and fondness for arcane details made many people in Kodi suspect him of sorcery.

He denied, of course, that he had any personal experience of sorcery. But he admitted to having various kinds of occult knowledge that were unusual among men. He could deliver children by massaging the belly of a woman in labor, and delivered more than half of his ten children with Pati Rangga. As a *tou pa tunda* ("person who pushes") he had also intervened in difficult births in several other hamlets. He knew certain herbal preparations that could stanch bleeding or relieve pain. Such knowledge was normally kept within a closed world of women's secrets. Most midwives were women, and they were very critical of the intervention of a man from outside the house. Although people turned to Markos in moments of need, they wondered how he had managed to cross gender boundaries to learn such things. Similarly, though they knew he came from a more recent patriline, they said he seemed too fearless among the famous sorcerors of Bukambero, and concluded that he was secretly related to them in ways that he was not willing to divulge.

Healers and ritual specialists are often suspected of "mixing the ways of the left hand with those of the right." They deal with dangerous forces that can be turned to their advantage or used to attack their enemies. Hidden inside the cavity of the drum were secrets of murder and powers to heal. The ambivalence that people felt about Markos may have enhanced his reputation as a singer and performer, but it did not make his life in the arena of local politics any easier.

THE SINGER AS CITIZEN: POLITICS AND GOVERNMENT SERVICE

In the 1950s, Markos Rangga Ende was a pupil in Catholic schools. In the 1960s, he finished his apprenticeship to his grandfather, beat the drum on his own at ceremonies, and married. In the 1970s, he became involved in local government in Bukambero. In the 1980s, he was elected the head of the whole ward (*kepala desa*) and then thrown out of the office by a team of outside investigators. Each of these developments was both part of his own biography and part of Indonesia's wider transitions in the early years of nationhood.

After Indonesian independence, there was an expansion of education and of interest in ideological struggle. Though the Catholic schools of Waitabula would seem a strange place to hear about Marxist ideas, it was in remembering his school days that Markos first spoke to me about different theories of value.

> There was someone I knew in school who told me about another way of thinking about work and value. The value of something you make comes from your own sweat, your own aching muscles, the time that you spend working on it. It does not come as a blessing from heaven, the way the priests say, or a return gift from the ancestors for what we have offered them.
>
> The person who is paid for something should be the one who produces it, not the Chinese storekeeper who buys it for less than half of what he will sell it for somewhere else. Horses that we raise, pigs that we tend, all of them are produced by our own sweat. The rich man has many people herding his

animals, so he does not sweat for them. But when he sells them in town, does he give that price back to the herders? No! He turns it into gold, a stone house, money to send his sons to school. The sweat is what should be paid for, not the name of the owner.

These ideas, overheard in youth and presented to me and others as a "sweat theory of value," were obviously influenced by the climate of revolutionary reform and leftist idealism of the Sukarno era.

The Indonesian Communist Party, once the largest voluntary communist organization in the world, never had many members on Sumba. Because the area had a very low level of political consciousness throughout the early 1960s, it largely escaped the mass killings that followed the attempted coup of 1965. A few people were executed in the regency capital of Waikabubak, and a great many were questioned. Students at schools that had once had a leftist reputation decided abruptly to study for the Christian ministry.

But Sukarno's mystical populism was well known to members of Partindo and later the Indonesian Democratic Party (PDI). Markos did not formally join either political party. But he was far from indifferent to the huge social dislocation of those events, or the problems of inequality and injustice that they reflected.

Rangga Ende's memory of the debates about value he took part in with schoolmates was reflected in a social conscience that was part of his vocation as a singer. He wanted to travel from hamlet to hamlet helping people, listening to their misfortunes and calling on invisible spirits who could come to their aid. He saw himself as a Sumbanese "barefoot doctor" (without ever hearing of Mao's village medical program with that name) and a populist practitioner.

In the 1970s, he was invited to join Golkar, the official government party. They asked him to sing at rallies during the 1977 and 1987 electoral campaigns, and to compose couplets that could announce their promises of development and solar-powered water pumps to the local population. He went on an extensive tour of hamlets in Bukambero, telling them of the "cool waters" that government funds would bring, "since independence came to the land, and campaigns arrived on the stones" (*ba duki a tana merdeka, ba toma a watu kampanye*). Never someone to turn down a chance to be in the spotlight, he proved to be a tireless and enthusiastic political campaigner.

At the elections, Golkar got a full 100 percent of the votes in Bukambero. Markos was encouraged to seek election to the position of ward head (*kepala desa*). Although his schooling had been cut short, he was still substantially more literate than most Sumbanese villagers. For ten years (1975–85), he served as the ward clerk (*panitera desa*), keeping books and records for the district office. When I met him in town, he was dressed in a civil servant's uniform and a baseball cap, and he seemed the antithesis of the traditional priest. I soon found that the two costumes—the traditional loincloth and headpiece and the bureaucratic uniform—were donned and exchanged regularly in his life.

When he traveled with me to rituals, he would also sometimes have *desa* business to take care of. Notebooks to collect statistics, or information on new cropping techniques and soil conservation, would be carried in his betel bag or hoisted onto a horse's back along with the sacrificial meat. His humble house, bamboo and thatch on high piles, was decorated with posters about family planning and village development. But his life as a public servant was soon endangered by strains in his domestic situation.

While he served as the ward clerk, Markos took a second wife, in Kodi, and then a third, in Bukambero. The second wife had been a widow, whose house proved a convenient overnight stop on his many travels. Her brideprice was low, and there were no children. Since she did not have to meet her or mix with her at all, his first wife bore the news with stoic acceptance.

The third wife, however, was much younger, and already pregnant when Markos decided to make the union official. The brideprice would be substantial, at a time when the family economy was strained. Other people were already saying that his meager salary should be invested in improving his home, raising it to the standards of other government officials, rather than wasting it on another woman. But Markos was totally devoted to his new love, showering her with gifts and bringing her with him on all his trips, just as he had once done with Pati Rangga.

During 1984, I received visits from both his first wife and his son to complain about this irresponsible behavior. His wife was worried about his support for the other children, and his son wanted to save livestock in the family corral for his own marriage. Knowing that polygamy was outlawed in America, each of them begged me to discourage Markos from this match. Embarrassed, I promised to tell him about their concerns, but noted that I had little control over the private life of this man who called himself my "brother."

Markos was elected to the position of ward headman at the time that his first wife and family were most alienated from him. Although the position came with a modest salary and some funds for entertaining government guests, little of that money found its way to the family home. Instead, he traveled with his new bride and introduced her to others as Ibu Desa (literally "mother of the ward," the respectful title given to the headman's wives who serve as official hostesses). He continued to perform as a *rato marapu*, fitting traditional rituals and government meetings into an increasingly crowded schedule.

I left the field in 1986 and did not return until 1988. I heard on my arrival that the child conceived with this youngest wife had been born and died, and six months later the girl ran off with someone else. Markos returned to the thatched house he shared with Pati Rangga and their children. He stopped visiting the home of his second wife in Kodi and reverted to monogamy.

In 1987 a task force from the provincial capital in Kupang was sent to carry out an extensive investigation of local government that aimed at increasing "efficiency" and eliminating corruption. Many headmen were removed from office because of suspicions that they had used government funds to improve their homes or fill their own pockets instead of helping the local population, Markos was one of the only ward headmen in the late 1980s who did not have a permanent house built of stone or at least bamboo woven walls with a roof of corrugated iron.

People complained that he was very hard to find and rarely came to the ward office. His domestic difficulties were well known, and others said that this very irregular life style of travel and ritual performances was not "suitable" for a government official. Since his family lived in a very modest home at considerable distance from the road, he was unable to host government visitors in the style that they expected.

Markos saw himself as a populist leader, someone who had come up "from the most isolated villages" and knew the people well because he had so often helped to heal them. His victory in the 1985 elections confirmed that he had popular support, but many people in the district office were unhappy with him, saying he could never be reached when needed. The outside task force was supposed to rationalize and modernize traditional forms of leadership, and they did not think a marapu priest was an appropriate role model for the younger generation. At the end of their investigation, they removed him from office and replaced him with the younger ward clerk, who had a secondary education and a more modern home.

Markos Rangga Ende was deeply disappointed at what he saw as a great injustice. He asked me to contribute to a new home, to be built of stone, which would convince others that he could be the leader of Bukambero. I did give him money for that purpose in 1988 and again in 1992 (when another researcher visited Kodi). But when I last heard from him, the house had still not been built. Illnesses in the family, bridewealth for his sons, and traditional exchange obligations had taken it all up, he wrote, and he hoped that I would come back to Sumba to help him again.

THE SINGER AS A PERFORMER OF MASCULINITY

The symbolic power of the drum that Markos played on (in all senses of the word) was articulated through an image of gender fusion and empowerment. "A man's voice, singing alone, would not be heard by the *marapu*," he explained, "but, combined with the sound of the drum beats resonating from his padded stick, his speech can travel up to the upperworld."

A single man, without a wife, is not an adult in Kodi society. He needs a woman to become a head of household, and he needs children to become someone whose name will be remembered in the cult of the ancestors. Masculine power is incomplete if it is not supported by feminine cooperation. When I asked what formal roles women played at brideprice negotiations, there seemed to be none. They sat, usually silently, at the sidelines, chewing betel and talking with other women. But if the father or a prospective bride or groom ever came to a negotiation without his wife, people knew immediately that the negotiations would fail. "His wife has not come because she does not agree," they whispered. "Nothing can happen now."

The drum could summon the power to heal and to communicate because of its symbolically female characteristics. Markos was able to elicit its power through an exaggerated display of his own virility. The combination of womanly receptiveness and manly aggression, the female cavity and the loud male voice, was what created an efficacious performance in Kodi. Much of his public behavior might be interpreted in another context as macho swaggering: He attracted his audience by singing loudly, traveling extensively, and showing off each new wife as widely as possible.

His eloquence was appreciated and seen as distinctively male. Women had to be wooed with graceful rhetoric and pleasing tones. They could be moved by an arresting image, a convincing turn of phrase, a song that echoed through the memory. Women themselves were not expected to be eloquent but receptive, good listeners who would know when a man sang the verses of the *marapu* properly, and who would appreciate a strong melodic performance.

Ritual healing performances take the form of a dialogue between men, in front of an audience of men, women, and children. The spirits themselves are addressed as parents, with respectful decorum, but the strutting and shouting of male orators has an undoubted element of courtship and male display.

Male restlessness and wandering are part of the pattern of masculine performances. From my perspective, much of Markos's narrative related suffering and betrayal caused by wounds that were self-inflicted. His song about the drum tells a tale of loneliness and isolation finally relieved by the companionship of a good wife. But although he often praised Pati Rangga for dancing well, bearing ten children, and receiving guests graciously, he was too restless to stay with her consistently. His need to keep moving, to seek new things and new people, meant that he was not true to the ideal of conjugal fidelity that he sang about in his performances.

The view of Kodi sexual politics that emerges from these lives makes it clear that few men who had the opportunity to marry more often resisted it. Kodi masculinity needs to be constantly reasserted and demonstrated, and its very inconstancy is praised. Men are volatile, quick tempered, potentially explosive, and all of these things are appreciated as signs of their full manhood.

Using the imagery of the drum companion, Markos pointed out to me that the spotted hide had to be changed every few years, as it wore out under the constant assault of the drumstick. "I beat this drum like a real man, and I sing with a loud voice. How could the hide resist? I am not like one of those weak men who simply taps gently onto the surface."

The need for a new hide to cover the drum was, metaphorically, the need for a new woman, a new muse to inspire his verses, a new cavity to receive his voice. *The ritual discourse of manhood focuses on the problem of renewing the counterpart.* In ritual performances, the manhood of the singers and orators is put into action and on display. Singing to the drum in a courtship mode, inviting the drum to travel with the singer's words on a journey to another world, also traces the path of other invitations to living women and other roads taken in biographical experience.

Although Markos renewed his commitment to Pati Rangga in 1988, his commitment may only be provisional. But since social hierarchies predicated on seniority and gender are linked, he seemed to be at somewhat of a turning point in his life. Now a grandfather, his social role began to shift into that of a senior adviser. His interest in novelty was diminishing as he strove to hold onto qualities that might endure. Pati Rangga's patience and devotion may finally pay off.

In a similar vein, many of his disappointments may also have come from attempting to do too much, to move between very different worlds as if they were compatible.

The story of the drum, like his own story, was one of hardship, neglect, and sacrifice followed by his great achievement in attracting and drawing a female audience. The stages of the ritual invocations addressed to the drum later replicate stages of Markos Rangga Ende's own emergence on the ritual stage and his efforts to be taken seriously as a public figure.

AN AMBIVALENT PARTNERSHIP:
MY "BROTHER" AND HIS RELUCTANT SISTER

The reader may sense here some of the complicated feelings I had toward this man, whose culturally appropriate performances of masculinity were grating on a Western feminist sensibility. Since he was only about ten years older than me, his working relationship with me could not be so easily neutralized through generational distance. I could not call him "father," and he could not call me "daughter." The other metaphors we used, the fictive kinship of being "brother" and "sister," was also more heavily charged with sexual tensions.

Part of Markos's sexual posturing was his eagerness to deny—in the loudest voice possible—that he could have thought of having a sexual relationship with this "foreign lady" who, as part of her research, followed him from village to village, sleeping on the veranda while he sang throughout the night and often giving him a lift on the back of her motorcycle to make a dramatic entrance. He would do so by elaborating what was involved in the central Sumbanese concept of coupling—*panggapango*, the term which also designates the coupling of metaphoric images in ritual speech.

> "What do you think is going on here?" he would ask, gesturing toward me sitting beside him. "Don't you realize this is my sister, my sister in our work together? What do you mean by asking me if we have been coupling?

"The coupling that is going on here is not the coupling of a man and a woman, not two bodies that are joined together. No, this is someone who traveled across the seas to seek knowledge, not to seek a husband!

"What is being coupled here is not two people but two languages: the Kodi language and the English language. I give her words which she records, which go into that little box and those little cassettes. Later, I write these words down, and we go over them at her house. The Kodi words are followed on the next line by the English words. Sometimes she doesn't even write the Indonesian. The Kodi and the English, they are directly coupled, they meet together just like this."

Then he would pause to hold forward both his hands, clasped together so that the fingers were interlocked. Then he would loosen his hands and hold them at slight distance from each other, dancing in front of each other, until first the fingertips touched, then the palms, then the fingers would slip in between each other and finally they would be held together so firmly the skin would turn white with pressure.

"This is how they fit together. Very closely, very firmly . . . but it is only words, only speech, never the bodies themselves."

This graphic public display of verbal coupling usually provoked nervous giggles and appreciative laughter from his audience, but it made me squirm with discomfort.

If Sumbanese masculinity is, in part, the search for an audience and for a female counterpart who can be renewed and replaced, finding a foreign researcher willing to serve as that audience was certainly a major coup. Older men like Maru Daku and Raja Horo may also have enjoyed being sought out for interviews, but I did not follow either of them on long ritual itineraries as I did Markos. Although each of them had a young wife less than my own age, they were refined leaders who would not speak so openly about rumors of closer contact, or enjoy denying them so publicly.

THE DRUM OF SUFFERING AND HEALING

My discomfort at a certain macho posturing only underlined Markos's presentation of self as a great healer because of his inexhaustible virility. His suffering had made him stronger, toughening his hide like the buffalo hide on the drum, and marking him as male in contrast to the more tender skin of the original female victim. The woman's skin was pierced and penetrated by the drumsticks. The male singer showed himself as a conqueror of adversity who could go on to lead others to health and recovery in the same way.

The story he sang told a tale of sexual difference and the combination of male and female, which was locally seen as necessary to success. The desire for power is often eroticized, and it seems clear that Markos's reputation as a healer was based in part on his hypermasculine performance style. His somewhat shakier success in seeking public office foundered partly because his private life appeared "messy," and he had neither the economic resources nor the "modern" trappings (education, stone houses) of a new generation of leaders. However, his struggle to rise from adversity to a position from which he could be heard is admirable. I grew up with two sisters but no brother, and although I felt a deep ambivalence about the claims of fictive kinship that this "Sumbanese brother" made on me, on one level I did appreciate our strangely manufactured siblingship: His aggressive masculinity was supposed to fill the holes in my listening femininity. Our transcriptions would be able to be complete only because they had elements of the two halves of the universe, a native "voice" and a foreigner's pen (or cassette tape), a ritual actor who could translate and explain his own words and an appreciative audience willing to record them.

NOTE

1. The narrative told about the drum in Hangga Koki says it was carved by Ngawi and Nende, and brought down from the heavens by an ancestor named Mada Wolo Woli, with the assistance of a wild spirit who took the form of a maghogha bird. The orphaned first son of a wealthy man, he was killed by his jealous half-brothers, and then brought to the heavens by the bird, who revived him at a magical source and found him a bride. After paying a brideprice of gold, horses, and buffalo provided by magic ring, Mada Wolo Woli asked for the drum made from human skin as a countergift. The whole village of Hangga Koki was created by the bird to store it, and a large feast was held to celebrate. At the end of the feast, when the skin ripped open, the new village inhabitants agreed to replace it with a buffalo hide.

7.

GREEN BOTTLES AND GREEN DEATH

Modernity and the Ephemeral

Ria Rihi doing needlepoint in her room at the author's house. (Photo J. Hoskins, 1980)

Not every biographical object is chosen by its subject. An object can at times be imposed or attributed, linked to someone who did not consciously choose it as a vehicle for her own identity.

The unintended association of a person and a thing that was inscribed most deeply on my own memory took the form of the tragic accidental death of Maria Rihi, the first girl who lived with me in my house in Bondokodi. Just nineteen years old, with large dark eyes and a wide, friendly smile, "Ria" was one of the loveliest young girls in the community. Her death at the middle of my fieldwork deprived me of the person who had been my closest daily companion in a strange land.

Because of the circumstances involved, however, her death also came to assume a particular position in Kodi notions of modernity: It was the first traffic fatality in the district capital, and so the first "modern" form of accidental death—a new form of commodity killing, in which a person was crushed by a machine and not a wild animal or human enemy. In the traditional ritual system, it was the kind of death that required elaborate ritual mediation. But because Ria's family were Christians, it was a death that would remain unmediated—unfinished, untransformed, the beginning of a new regime identified with disposable objects rather than ones that could be recycled.

Kodi ritual verse expressed the new attributes of a traffic fatality by labeling it with the metaphor of a green bottle. A sudden death was traditionally called "green" (*mate moro*) because it cut down someone like a young plant while still young, a sprout not yet golden on the stalk. It was seen as a "raw" death, since *moro* has the additional meaning of uncooked, incompletely processed. Ria's death was "green" because it was not only premature but also violent. Her life was cut short in an unexpected way, with no warning, by a form of sharpness (another term for the category is *mate pa lakiyo*, "death by piercing") that occurs outside the protective walls of the house. Although children may die of illness, slowly wasting away, their energy is lost slowly, rather than being consumed whole by a moment of violence.

The metaphor of the green bottle associated a new form of mechanical violence with the absolute destructiveness of Western consumer objects. If an earthen dish broke, it could be reassembled and rebaked. If a gourd plate shattered, it could be buried, and from its soil new gourds would grow. But there is no way to reuse the shattered pieces of a porcelain dish or green bottle.

The young girl struck by the truck was the first Kodi victim of an outside force that does not allow regeneration or reassemblage from previous materials. Like the disposable items of consumer production, she fell beside the road, and her soul was sent off to wander through the skies. In this way, a single metaphor sheds light on the arresting similarity between the wastefulness of a world of easily separable objects, and the directionless separation of the souls of those dying violent deaths.

The green bottle is an unconventional, attributed biographical object that provides us with Kodi reflections on the changing meaning of objects in their world, and the influence of mass production and commodification as it enters a village society. Along the road that links Bondokodi to the mission station at Weetabula and the regency capital of Waikabubak, new things travel the trajectories of capitalist penetration of a noncapitalist economy, and new dangers come to threaten young lives. Ria was not conscious of the dangers that come along with many new forms of technology, and (like many others in her generation) she was attracted to trucks and recorded music and new machines. But her death caused many others to pause and think again about the disjunctions created by rapid social change, and for that reason it has come to assume a wider symbolic importance in an ambivalent reaction to modernity.

I must write about Ria in two ways; as a person who shared time with me and touched me directly in many ways, and also as an icon of the darker side of progress, the losses suffered along with the hoped-for transformations of development. I cannot allow the meaning her death has taken in the decade after her passing to totally eclipse my memories of her as a person, but I cannot disregard this meaning either, as it gives her personal tragedy a much wider significance.

RIA AS A PERSON

Ria was the daughter of a local schoolteacher, but she had not continued her own schooling. She was living at home, helping to raise her younger siblings, and awaiting marriage when I moved to Bondokodi. With the help of an older woman who was my neighbor, I sought a companion who would help out in the household like the "younger sister" I could not bring along: preparing food, receiving guests, walking with me down to the river to bathe and do laundry, and getting water and firewood for the kitchen. I offered a salary, but Kodi people are too proud to work as servants. The position had to be defined through a form of fictive kinship for it to be acceptable.

Ria was adventuresome enough to be willing to live with a strange Western woman, six years older than herself, who wanted to learn the language and collect materials for a book on Kodi custom. She was fluent in Kodi and had lived there all her life, but her parents were originally from Savu, so she was also a bit of an outsider. We spoke Kodi at home, and she would giggle and correct my mistakes, but she was never a "teacher."

Older men—Markos, Maru Daku, and Raja Horo—"instructed" me in a formal manner in highly valued forms of ritual knowledge. Conversations I had with Ria and her friends were relaxed and full of gossip. The confidences we shared were whispered in conspiratorial tones between two young women, not dutifully transcribed and translated in the field journals. She told me about boyfriends, longings for travel, and family dramas that she did not see as part of local "custom." It was only after her death that I struggled to write what I remembered of Ria. She did not become an object of study until she had lost her own voice and been the object of violence.

A MEMORY OF RIA'S DEATH

Ria was a cheerful and industrious girl who had just discovered that she was very attractive to men. With this discovery came certain dangers. Schoolboys sent love letters, young civil servants sent gifts of clothing and jewelry, van drivers offered her free rides. Some thought she accepted the admiring attentions of her suitors a bit too readily. Perhaps the problem lay mainly in the warm, enthusiastic smile she gave to everyone, even when politely demurring.

The man in the minivan that killed her was also an admirer—a policeman who had repeatedly invited her to come to visit him at his rooms in the police barracks. She declined, but asked to borrow his policeman's hat, which she played with at home and wore when posing for a picture for me. One night, he came by and asked her repeatedly to come see him. She shook her head, giggled, and enjoyed the scene that others were witnessing, but left him with a simple "You'll see later on!"

That evening she sat up with me, doing needlepoint while I typed my fieldnotes. Near midnight, the small community of Bondokodi was rocked by the sound of a gunshot, coming from the police barracks. The next day we heard that the policeman had been punished for shooting off his gun for no reason. "It was you who drove me to this!" he told Ria later. "I was waiting for you, and you didn't come!"

Policemen were generally considered good husbands by the local girls, since they had a salary and could travel. Ria's older sister was romantically linked to another policeman, but the family was adamantly opposed to the match, because her intended was Muslim. They also did not like the young man interested in Ria, even though he was a Christian. "Policeman are often rough with their wives," her mother warned. "They are too used to beating people." They saw this young man as hot headed and irresponsible, and did not encourage him to visit at their home.

Ria flirted with the policeman, but many others also had her eye. One afternoon, I found her laboring to answer love notes, which she carefully read and then copied back onto new pages in reply. "She just sent our own words back to us," one young man who had written to her later complained. "I know she didn't have a lot of schooling, but she should have written something new." He, like many others, remembered declarations of affection and interest, but was never sure how exclusive they were.

For many young men of that generation, Ria emerged after her death as a figure of idealized desire. She was the girl they all wanted but could not have, a representation of the promise of beauty that was never fully possessed. Envy and competition among the eligible bachelors of the area no doubt played a role in the vehemence of their hatred for the policeman, who was universally held responsible for her death.

The night that Ria died, she spent dressing up in my house. Her family had invited her to come over to join them in frying shrimp crackers, but she wanted to wear an elegant long dress that a neighbor had given her. She powdered her face and put on makeup, admiring her image in my small mirror. She wore around her neck a star-patterned pendant, set with torquoise, that I had given her. On her feet were high heels, a bit unsteady, on which she tottered over to her parents' house, holding the hand of her younger sister.

I remained behind to work on fieldnotes. An hour later, I heard screaming and a great commotion coming from the road behind our house. Traffic noises were unusual in the evenings, since the two or three minivans that drove to Bondokodi each day from town usually returned by dusk, and no vehicles drove through after dark.

But that night, one van had arrived late and had to spend the night. Its driver was a friend of the policeman and had invited him to take it for a spin. The unlighted dirt roads were usually deserted, but that night Ria, her sister, and a friend were walking along, bringing a basket of krupuk for me to taste as she returned to my house. They heard the policeman's voice calling out a greeting from the dark cab of the minivan. They ignored him and stayed by the side of the road. The van drove closer, meaning probably just to scare them, and the policeman recognized Ria and called out her name.

The driver lost control of the van at the muddy edge of a ditch by the side of the road. The van tipped over, and Ria was caught underneath, still alive and asking for help. When I arrived at the scene, her best friend ran up to me and shouted, "Ria! Ria is under that van!" The van lay on its side, its headlights shining out across the grass, the cab door open and empty. The policeman and the driver were gone, taking the keys with them.

Women and children stood by the van and wailed in the highly stylized, traditional tones of a funeral lament. Ria's parents, her sisters, and neighbors were all there, but paralyzed by their grief. No one seemed to be doing anything to help the girl whose voice could still be heard, crying from underneath the van.

There are moments when cultural relativity falls completely flat. I was furious at the passivity of their reaction, which was—in its cultural context— the appropriate way for women to show their emotional distress. But in my own culture the time for mourning should come not when the victim is still alive, but only once the possibility of saving her is gone. This was a time when I did not respect proper gender boundaries, and my rage moved me immediately from the circle of screaming women to the group of men who were leaning against the side of the van and trying to lift it up from her body.

One neighbor had the sense to fetch a coconut trunk and wedge it under the edge of the van so it could be lifted. It took six or seven of us, pulling together, to raise the van high enough to push the trunk underneath. Then one man crawled under the van and was able to bring Ria out in his arms. She was still warm and breathing when four of us carried her, apparently unharmed, to the small clinic near our home. The nurse had been summoned, and placed her on a cot where she could receive liquids intravenously. But when she moved to take her pulse, the blood had already stopped moving through her body. She had died in our arms in the time it took to move her to the clinic.

There were no marks on her body, but the weight of the van had done the fatal damage. Her face, still bearing traces of makeup, was unblemished, and her long dress had only a few grass stains. There were no last words or glances, only a warm body that gradually cooled down and became firmer and that we had to move away from to leave room for her mother and sisters who came to stroke it again as a corpse.

After we knew she was dead, I went home alone to cry. I did not share in the collective expressions of grief around her body or stay behind to keen throughout the night. I wanted privacy, quiet, some time to sort out my own emotions. I did not conform to Kodi expectations of sorrow, publicly displayed, which would validate their questions about whether Westerners experience emotions in the same ways that they did. I could hear the people gathered at the clinic, but I did not want to stay there.

I was still angry at people who left a girl crushed underneath a van while they showed culturally appropriate signs of distress. My rage mixed with feelings of loss, of bewilderment, and of fury at the absent drivers of the van. For several hours, I wanted no more part of fieldwork, of living in a strange place where my closest companion had just died, of pretending to be "just like them" when moments like this made me feel incredibly alien. I wanted out, a different kind of out from the one Ria had just taken, but out nevertheless.

The next day I was able to go to visit her family's home, where the body had been taken and a wake had been organized. Ria's body was placed in an open casket in the front room, and I joined many others in bringing the appropriate mourning gift: a sarung to be unfolded on top of her body. The house was full of visitors, as houses of the dead are supposed to be, and coffee and tea were being served, food was being prepared, and the bereaved were being shielded from the loneliness that would affect them later by filling the home with noisy activity.

I was able to play a socially appropriate role at that time, to shed a few public tears by the casket, and speak with her family and friends. The people closest to me did not doubt the sincerity of my emotions, but I was struck at the tactless probing of others.

I went to the market two days after her death, buying my own vegetables. An older woman sitting in front of batches of sirih pipers called out to me, "Where is your little sister? What has happened to her?"

Given the speed that bad news travels, there could be no doubt that she had heard. "I think you know already," I answered dully.

"Did you cry?" she continued, pressing me. "Do foreign people cry when these things happen?"

"Yes," I said, "they cry." I felt furious at this woman's adoption of the role of the ethnographer, wondering at my humanity and questioning my emotional responses. I also felt my eyes getting damper that very minute, as much from rage at her questions as the memory of my sorrow.

"They cry only after," I heard her explain to another woman sitting beside her. "I heard from people who saw her by the van that she didn't shed a tear when the accident happened."

I felt violated, misjudged, my own grief invalidated by its being subjected to her unsympathetic scrutiny. And I felt no doubt some of the same things that many Kodi had felt when I attended earlier funerals, where I had not known the people involved to any extent, and I spent my time taking photographs and filling my notebooks with ritual procedures.

Death may provide lessons to us all, but the lessons change as time passes. I first published a song sung for Ria's funeral in 1987, as part of a highly abstract analysis of the relationship of gender and agency in Kodi mortuary ceremonies (Hoskins 1987b). The details of Ria's own biography are recorded faithfully there, but not her relationship to me, or the conflicts that I felt while sorting out my own emotional responses. It has taken me much longer to confront them, and even longer still to be willing to admit to them in print.

RIA REMEMBERED IN A FUNERAL LAMENT

The transformation of Ria's death from a matter of personal grief into a vehicle for reflections on the dangers of modernity began with the metaphor of the green bottle. As with much in oral tradition, this metaphor had no clearly established author. The old woman whose singing I recorded and transcribed did not claim originality in using the series of couplets that develop this metaphor. It was "something people were saying" after Ria's death, a refrain, we might even (in our culture) call it a cliché—a set of images repeated and shared by one mouth after another in response to a tragedy that needed to be understood in some new way, by a new set of words.

But her song develops the metaphor by setting it poignantly within a lament that addresses the supreme deity (whether Christian or marapu), and evoking Ria's own characteristics. The singing of funeral laments may seem to intensify the experience of loss. It articulates the emotional trauma of death, but does not praise the dead so much as describe the pain involved in separating from them. The focus is on the sufferings of the errant soul, and of the survivors who feel confused and lost because they are bereaved.

The song begins by representing Ria through the image of her clothes and jewelry fallen by the road:

Pemuni a hengeti lawo harinya	Alas the fated falling of the sarung
Myori mandi lama	The Lord whose tongue is true
Pemuni a oro bei marakana	Alas the traces of the gold earrings
Myori bihya wiwi	The Lord of the sacred lips
Njaingoka na pei byohongo ngorana	There is no way to turn one's nose aside
Ha wu ndara dola kokona	The horse must stretch its neck willingly
Njaingoka na warahongo kikuna	There is no shaking the tail in refusal
Ha wu karimbyo manunduka	The buffalo must follow along

The obedience of domestic animals is forced upon human beings as well, who must submit to mortality even though their hearts push them to rise against it.

The song then shifts to adopt a mother's perspective in mourning the loss of a child. The mother is said to feel a visceral sort of sadness, located in the womb where the child was once carried, and suggesting that she now experiences the dissolution of her daughter's body as if it were the dissolution of her own insides:

Wuu! Tanekya liku njamo	Wuu! The twisted entrails are now gone
Nona Ria na heda la kambu tilu lara	Nona Ria dead like cotton blossoms on the road
Wuu! Hambule pare mboghi	Wuu! The stomach filled with rotting rice
Nona Ria na mate la mata wei maradaby	Nona Ria deceased in the meadow the source
Wuuu! Ana timbu nini	Wuu! Child formed straight as river reeds
Nona Ria nopongo kadoki loko tana	Nona Ria rests by the banyan tree near the river
Wuu! Ana kapuda hapadi	Wuu! Child carved like a spear handle
Nona Ria na lunango kalimbyo lali myone	Nona Ria pillows her head on the raised earth

Dying outside the protective walls of the house, on the road, meadow, or riverside, is particularly disturbing in Kodi, as the person has slipped out of the circle of ancestral protection and fallen victim to unknown forces.

The singer continues with an account of Ria's youth, which follows the earlier couplets that referred to her beauty ("straight as river reeds / carved like a spear handle"):

Wuu! Ana nona Ria na mate moro longge	Wuu! Our child Ria died with blue-black hair
Nona Ria na heda kaka ngandu	Nona Ria deceased with still white teeth
Mate inde kodelo la ando	Dead before she had a betel post to cling to
Heda inde tonggolo kapaka	Deceased before she reached the top of a kalumpang tree

The absence of a husband is lamented in the last couplet. Traditionally, an unmarried girl would receive a male "companion" in her grave to make up for her loneliness—most commonly a spindle (hence its earlier possibility of representing the idealized but incorporal husband), placed in a betel bag. For Ria, no substitute male object was used. This was one reason several of her suitors maintained that her image continued to haunt them.

The next lines articulate the green bottle metaphor as a reflection on perishability without renewal.

Mbera ghuro tana pighu	If you had broken like an earthen dish
Ku konda helu pepe	I would dig you up again and bake you
Mbera toba lolo pighu	If you had shattered like a gourd plate
Ku tondo helu pupu	I could plant you again and pick your fruit
Pemuni a mbera pengga kaka	Alas you broke like a porcelain dish
Nja pa helu buri	Cannot be stuck together again
Pemuni a mbera nggori myoro	Alas you shattered like a green bottle
Njapa helu lala	Cannot be formed anew

Then the singer turns to a description of the shock of hearing about the traffic accident, in terms that directly mirror my own experience.

Yingga tiku njana wena	I was staying quietly alone
Ku kandoko wudi ryongo	When I heard the commotion in the kapok tree
Nonikya a ana timbu nini	My child formed straight as river reeds
Na katongango a tana mete	Was resting on the black earth
Yingga baha njana wena	I was not making any noise
Na kabanda wudi jeta	When I was startled by the clamor at the top of the tree
Nonikya a ana kapuda hapadimu	My child carved like the spear handle
Na nopongo a rumba rara	Was lying on a mat of yellow grass
Ku kambura lednu ngamba	I ran blindly to the cliff's edge
Ku dukinya a ana ngguna hario	I came upon the child whose games used to lift our hearts
Na mate oro motoro manamalo	Dead because of the motor going too fast
Ku palaiyo karodo rame	I rushed into the wild branches
Ku toma nikya a ana ghanggu lelu	I arrived at the child of the cotton playthings
Na heda oro bemo bali mema	Deceased because of the returning truck

The physical violence of Ria's death is here contrasted with the emotional violence that the sudden news inflicted on her survivors—the screams heard in the darkness, the child lying on the ground as confusion and panic spread, the inexplicable loss of someone healthy and full of life just seconds before.

It is common in Indonesia to try to soften the blow of the news of death by presenting it initially as simply a serious illness: The next of kin are informed and rush home, fearing the worst, but their fears are not confirmed until they have had a few days to contemplate the possibility of a more permanent loss. Receiving this news so suddenly is believed to cause such severe disorientation it can become a form of mental illness. I was already deeply affected after knowing Ria for only a year. Her father, an intense and volatile man even before, did in fact lose his mind for some time after her death. He wandered the road at night with a spear, saying he was waiting for the policeman to return to the scene, and his family had to restrain him from traveling into town to pursue a more personal form of vengeance.

The funeral lament finishes with a prayer for Ria's errant soul:

A ndewa toumu, ta na nomi la turu ndende	Your personal fate, let it stand by the upright post
A ura dadimu, ta na noni la nggallu kole	Your birth crown, let it return to the enclosed corral
Ba na hamangggango la lete pamba uma	As you wait beside the ceiling drain in front of the house
Ba na engana la wanggeho kawendo	As you linger beside the roof thatch
Tana bali wani la rengge rou karudi	So you will come back from the fringe of lontar leaves
Ela Tila horo lodo	Of Tila who rides astride the sun
Tana mbiku wani la ngape ngandu wulla	So you will be released from the teeth of the moon
Ela Pati njera wulla	Of Pati who clasps the moon
Ela lombo alipo rara	From the end of the yellow rainbow
Ela kere awango hada	From the edge of the colorful sky

The soul of someone who dies a violent death remains a prisoner of the spirits of the heavens, Tila and Pati, who will not release her until the proper ceremonies have been performed. She cannot come into the house to be addressed as an ancestor, or to give her blessings to descendants.

Ria's parents also prayed for the safety of her soul, but as Christians, they would not sponsor rituals dedicated to the marapu. They were, however, also distressed by the form of her death, and planned eventually to give her another funeral, some years later, when her bones would be dug up and taken to the Savunese Christian burial grounds in Melolo. "That is is our ancestral village," they explained to Kodi funeral guests, "and that is where her soul can find a final rest."

THE GHOST OF DESIRE: INJUSTICE AND EROTIC LONGING

The uncertainty of her fate contributed to a pervasive feeling that haunted many of the young men who had known her, and who came to remember her as beautiful and now forever inaccessible, the ghost of desire.

Their regrets mixed with the unfortunate details of the police investigation into the accident. Although witnesses had heard the policeman's voice and believed that he was the driver (since he had been seen driving the vehicle earlier), the official testimony in court was that the driver's assistant or *konjak* was at the wheel when the accident occurred. The policeman would have lost his job with a reckless driving conviction, but the assistant (who may have been paid off) was willing to take the blame. He was given a short sentence and later left the island to seek work elsewhere.

The policeman was reassigned to another district, far from Kodi, where he was reported to be morose and alcoholic. The green bottle, presented as a metaphor for Ria's death, was also his undoing: He spent many hours downing green bottles of beer and reflecting on a death he had not intended to cause. Though he never confessed or took responsibility for the events, people said that he too was haunted by the ghost of his desire. A young man in town told me that after these events, the policeman had visions of *pontianak*, an Indonesian term for erotic female spirits that take their revenge on men by driving them crazy with desire. In Kodi, pontianak are spotted near the river, where they appear to men and invite them to wander after them. Either the men never find them, or they find that even if they do, their desires cannot be satiated, so eventually they lose their minds.[1]

The belief that Ria's soul was uneasy stemmed from feelings that no justice had yet come from the investigations. Her loveliness was mythologized, and her death became part of a darkly romantic youth culture of longing and regret. The associations with the changes of modernity—the building of new roads, the expanded number of motor vehicles that traveled them—were part of the ambivalence that these transformations in the local landscape provoked in all Kodi residents.

For myself, and for Maru Daku, the storyteller who was my "teacher," this haunting took the specific form of rumors about our own deaths, and suggestions that the dangers that had caused Ria to fall under the van would also visit her close acquaintances.

THE ETHNOGRAPHER'S BLACK MAGIC: DANGERS TO MARU DAKU

A year after Ria's death, as I prepared for my return to the United States, Maru Daku fell seriously ill. Thinking that his fever and chills were due to malaria, I sent supplies of chloroquine to his village with his sons, but after ten days he was still no better. Despite my plans to go visit him, I could find no one who would agree to ford the river with me, and I hesitated to undertake the rather dangerous journey on my own. When, on the twelfth day of his illness, Maru Daku's frail and wasted body was brought to my house on horseback, he seemed very close to death.

He was put to bed in my spare room, which had been where Ria had slept, and immediately asked me to bring my tape recorder. In the presence of his sons, he recited the verses that I have earlier cited in my account of his own life (see chapter 2). He also added a reflection on Ria's death that is relevant here.

Maka ma londo pa kadungo dengeni	The one who lived as a twosome with you
Maka ma ndende pa katalongo	The one who stood as a third with us
Na paghili nggama a ngagha hamu	Who prepared the rice to eat
Na pandende nggama a wei pa inu	Who boiled the water to drink
Dela njana delako a tana natu	The rising sun had not yet risen on the land
Na tomaka a wawi hyayo	When a pig came to block the way
Na malo njana malongo lodo	The evening sun had not set on the day
Na dukikya a ghai mbyapa	When a log fell to close the path
A nona Ria mbungaka	The young girl named Ria disappeared
Dikya pa ndende paktaku dengema	Who stood as a third with us
A mburu lodo meme yaka mate	The day grew obscure with her death
A luna nanikya kandoki loko tana	Pillowing her head on a riverbed
A pa katonga nikya tana	Lying on a platform of open land
Oro motoro rou manamalo	Because of the motors traveling too fast
A ana nona Ria na mbapa	The child named Ria vanished
A rewa rou kahumbu yaka mbunga	Disappearing with the funeral rice packets
A pa luna kalimbu lale tana	Resting her head on the bare earth
A pa nopo nikya rumba	Lying on a mat of wild grass
Oro bemo bali mema	Because of the truck returning at night

Ria's death is presented here as an obstacle that came to block our path, a tragedy that afflicted our work together but was eventually overcome.

But this account of her death was also designed to answer rumors that Maru Daku's illness, like Ria's death, had come about because of his association with me. I heard from Fenina, the second girl who lived with me, that people at the market had asked her whether she was afraid to stay at my house, since "the spirit of the white woman may not be good for you" (*ndewana a waricoyo dawa njana ndaha*). Dangers that are associated with violating ritual procedures or revealing ancestral secrets were said to congregate around my house, contaminating those who came in contact with them.

Maru Daku heard those rumors as well, so his testament in verse turns to address them directly:

No wadi yinggama la mbumbilo haghogha	We were also there when she breathed her last
Ela eliro kawuku	At the stroking of the bound hair
Mai pa dorini wei myata boghi	Coming to shed tears on the corpse
No wadi nggma ela eta loha luna mate	We were also there when she rested on the pillow of death

La ghodoho karaha	At the caressing of the ribs
La panamango wei wiri njamo	The flowing of tears and mucus on the body
Inde kandaghu helu bali ngguni	But I shall not re-enter the forest
A mate nona Ria	Where young Ria died
A nona timbu nini	Girl lovely as a river reed
Inde marada helu duni ngguni	But I shall not go back into the fields
A hedana nona Ria	Where young Ria disappeared
A nona kapuda hapadi	Girl finely carved as a spear handle
Oro nonaikya ku toma pika	Since now I am penetrated by the
La redaho marere	Trembling and glazed eyes
Oro nonaikya ku duki pika	Since now I am overwhelmed by
La kapilye rengge manu	Feathers ruffled with disease

He acknowledged his physical weakness, but denied that it came from the same source as Ria's death. Then he reported the findings of a diviner who was called to find the reasons for his sickness and who told him that someone had used poison or bad magic against him out of envy, so that he would not be alive and well to bid me goodbye.

Nengyo toyo na pugha hepu laramu	There is a person who trapped the quail on your path
Nengyo toyo na malagho tati annumu	There is a person who tracked the mouse on the trail
Na wolo limya kambu tapi	Gesturing with his hand under a winnow
Na rawi hirio bali ryamba	Tying a net beneath the cloth
Tana ambu tomani binjalongo lango da	To prevent a peaceful parting of words
Yoyo dungga ana mu	Between you and your daughter
Tana ambu na dukingo a begha limya ndende	To avoid a peaceful separation of hands
Yoyo dungga ana mu	Between you and your daughter

Maru Daku refused to see Ria's death as a premonition of his own, despite the rumors that circulated about threats to the lives of those associated with me. This passage states clearly that her death came from the outside (the forest and the fields, by implication, the policeman's frustrated desire) and was not related to his own gradual weakening through fevers and chills. He blamed his own illness on others who harbored resentments against him and might try to bewitch him with traditional potions or magical gestures. In coming to my house, however, he placed himself again under my protection and asked me for new medicines.

He was wise to do so. The choloroquine I sent had had no effect because his fevers and coughing came from pneumonia, not malaria. The nurse in

Bondokodi prescribed antibiotics and bedrest, and after several uncertain days Maru Daku made a slow but sure recovery. He was still weak when I left, but well enough to see me off in good spirits. A year later, however, when the dampness of the rainy season brought on a second attack of pneumonia, he did not try to travel to the clinic. I received news that he had died at home, and would be buried in the traditional fashion.

THE GREEN BOTTLE TURNS AROUND:
I BECOME A GHOST AS WELL

When I received a letter from Raja Horo telling me of Maru Daku's death, I sent a large embroidered white cloth as a *ghabuho*, or funeral gift, a tangible expression of my grief and a contribution to the funeral shroud. The cloth was sent in a package to the home of the former raja, with a note asking his family to be sure that it found its way to the house in Balaghar where Maru Daku's widows lived.

By a strange sort of twisted logic, the presence of a funeral cloth sent from the United States seems to have sparked a series of rumors concerning my own death. I heard of these stories from two researchers from Holland, Professor A. A. Gerbrands and Danielle Geirnaert-Martin, who visited Kodi in the autumn of 1982. As Geirnaert-Martin reports in her later monograph dealing with the neighboring region of Laboya (1992: xxiii):

> Our first talks with the Kodinese informed us of the alleged death of J. Hoskins for whom they said they had already performed the traditional funerary rites. Fortunately, this tragic piece of news appeared to be totally unfounded. At the beginning of 1983, in answer to my inquiries I received a letter from J. Hoskins. . . . Understandably startled by this erroneous information on her fate, she wrote me a humorous letter telling me she was alive and well.

The situation is ghoulishly comic in retrospect, but also disturbing. I was summoned to the office of my department chairman at Harvard to respond to a request sent to get copies of my fieldnotes, dictionary, and tapes so that another researcher could make use of them after my own unfortunate demise. My first reaction was to wonder, in no uncertain terms, who in Kodi might wish me dead and thus have started such a rumor.

I wrote letters to several people I knew there to assure them that I was alive, and I sent recent photographs. These were studied by several "experts," only some of whom, apparently, were convinced. When I did return in the flesh in early 1984, many people greeted me as a ghost. Some turned pale, some exclaimed in terror, others tried tentatively to touch my flesh to be certain that it was still warm. If it had been troubling to be linked to other people's deaths, it was at least equally unsettling to have to explain the many stories focused on my own.

The only pattern I could discern, which I am now convinced is of a piece with the mythologization of Ria's death, is that I was supposed to have died in a very "modern" way. I quote from a section of my field journals:

> I have just heard several more accounts of "my" death. The people in Wora Homba heard that I had died in a railway accident, where a train struck a car. I was traveling with my family to a celebration of my engagement. The people at Wikico said they heard that I had gotten married and was about to leave on my honeymoon when the plane that I was to fly off in crashed into a house. In Balaghar, they thought it was a bus which collided with a motorcycle bearing my sweetheart, who was just coming to the wedding ceremony.

People who knew me well tried to put on a show of loyalty with statements that asserted that despite the rumors they did not believe I had died: "The members of this family did not join them in beating the gongs for you. We knew we should wait for more news before we began mourning."

A consistent theme of all the erroneous reports was that they involved frustrated attempts at matrimony, and final violence, of a rather complex, technologically sophisticated kind. In searching for a "reason" for these stories, I cannot help coming back to the way my story was tied to Ria's, and our fates were symbolically linked. People were concerned about my marriage prospects, since coming to the field as a twenty-five-year-old single woman signaled an already excessive delaying of marriage. I heard many verses about the problems that old maids experienced, and received a lot of advice about not being too picky. When I returned in 1984 and attended the wedding of Ria's younger sister, Naomi, I was constantly told, "Had she lived, Ria would certainly be married by now." My own, still-unattached status was becoming a problem.

Ria's death was provoked, even caused, by a surfeit of suitors. She was the victim of modern technology slipping out of control, and confused by frustrated erotic longings. My imagined death brought me close to the fulfillment of "every girl's dream" of marriage, but then cut me off before it was achieved. The logic seemed to be that if Ria did not live to marry, neither would I. If she died as the first casualty of higher technology in Kodi, her companion from overseas would have at least as dramatic an end in her own country. The connection to Maru Daku's death was the confusion over a gift sent to commiserate at a funeral and a gift sent to announce the death itself. (I did hear, in one story, that after I had died my lover had wrapped my body in a white cloth and declared he would carry it to Kodi so I could be buried there.)

The green bottle resurfaces in these fantastic imaginings of my own demise. I had told people in Kodi that modern life could be destructive and alienating, and that people in the United States did not always want to live right next to the road so they could watch the exciting spectacle of new motor vehicles driving by. I had tried to convey something of the confusion and aimlessness of modern cities, which had seemed to my listeners to be epitomized in the one moment when a young life had been claimed on the quiet dirt roads of Bondokodi.

My reading of songs about Ria's death and the rumors of my own is that both of them reflect an ambivalence about "development" even when it appears to be celebrated most enthusiastically. People in Kodi say they want more roads, more cars, and more economic activity so they too can be "modern" and live in a noisier, more animated world. But they realize there may be costs associated with these changes, and there may be ghosts from the past that are reluctant to see the landscape so thoroughly transformed. There is perhaps a foretaste of the alienated, Western notion of the self as a consumable, disposable object in the image of the shattered green bottle applied to Ria and, more indirectly, to me as well.

ANOTHER GREEN DEATH

In 1988, four years after my first return visit to Kodi as a pseudo-ghost, I spent six months on the island and introduced many of my Sumbanese friends to a new researcher from the Australian National University. Taro Goh was born in Japan and educated in Japan, the United States, and Australia. He came to the island at the age of twenty-nine to study the more hierarchical domains of East Sumba, where he wanted to focus on exchange, alliance, and precedence (Goh 1991). I had known Taro for four years when he began his project, and arranged to meet him in the provincial capital of Kupang in January, where both of us had to visit government offices before beginning research. He came to visit me in Kodi in February to see *pasola* jousting and ceremonial festivities (and the death rites described in Hoskins 1993a: 244–70), and I visited him in Kapunduk to witness a royal funeral in June. He learned a lot about East Sumba in the first six months, and we had long comparative discussions about regional differences. When I left him to return to the United States, I asked him to write to me about several specific ethnographic issues, and wished him good luck and a great time in the field.

Three months later I heard from friends that he had died. At first, I discounted the reports, which seemed of a cloth with the fantastic, grotesque accounts of my own demise. Had similarly wild stories circulated about Japanese trains and airplanes, interrupted weddings and engagements? But this death was no tropic play of mirrors. Taro had contracted cerebral malaria and been treated at the hospital in Waingapu. He entered with a high fever that resisted all available medication and was one of the new strains that could not be prevented with available prophylactics. Just a few days after his thirtieth birthday, he died another "green death"—he was cut down before reaching maturity, before marrying or having children, before becoming "golden on the stalk."

Taro is now buried in the Catholic cemetery in Waingapu, since his family in Japan was Catholic. He is the only foreigner to be buried there, as none of the members of the Japanese occupying force or the Dutch and German mission stayed on the island until their deaths. The Protestant linguist-missionary who lived for the longest period on Sumba, L. Onvlee, returned to the Netherlands to retire. Taro was the first foreign visitor to stay on the island until he died, although his sojourn turned out to be tragically brief. He was the first outsider to remain permanently part of the landscape, and not to leave it behind to return to his homeland.

The truck that killed Ria had been imported from Japan. None of the Sumbanese that I spoke to referred to this fact directly, but several of them expressed a parallelism between her death and Taro's. I quote here from a letter I received from one of Ria's sisters, in which she expressed her condolences and suggested a pattern behind the two tragedies:

> We were very sorry to hear of the death of Taro Goh, who had been our guest in Kodi at the time of the New Year festivities. Another young person, dead before he was golden on the stalk, another green bottle, shattered and never to be reformed. It makes us remember the time that you joined our family at Ria's funeral. The two of them will not easily escape from memory: One, the victim of a motorcar from overseas, resulted in the death of a Sumbanese on the road. The other, the victim of a Sumbanese sickness, resulted in death of a foreigner in the hospital. It is with great sorrow that we see that they had the same fate.

The letter establishes the opposition between a death in the house (note that hospital in Indonesian is *rumah sakit*, the "sick house") and one outside of the house, between someone from the island dying due to an outside force, and someone from the outside dying due to an inside disease. It suggests obliquely that Ria's death began a circle of changes that was only closed with Taro's death, as if the island had finally taken back the life that foreign instruments had once claimed.

While I find no consolation in the recasting of these tragedies into a dualistic scheme, I am intrigued that my Sumbanese correspondent would elaborate these contrasts and see them as important in the cultural "work of mourning" (to use Freud's term) that restores a dimension of meaning to the emotional world of the mourners. The juxtaposition and reordering of indigenous and foreign, inside and outside, and (implicitly) male and female shows how inversion and balance are complexly involved in efforts to readjust our view of the world after a traumatic loss.

Taro's death both defies and confirms the analysis that I have just presented of the imagined relations between Ria's real accident and my own imagined demise. Taro did not die in any of the spectacular ways they had thought I might go, but his death did invert many of the characteristics of Ria's death, and it, too, was given a mythological interpretation, fitted into an order of dualistic oppositions. Did it provide a retrospective sense that both of them were part of some larger project? I don't know, but it is intriguing that imported objects and imported persons were conjoined in this way, and that the metaphoric fragility of the green bottle was extended to a new victim.

OBJECTS, BIOGRAPHIES, AND MEMORY BOXES

Neither Ria nor Taro participated in forming the narratives that associated them with disposable objects, as the other people I discuss here did. Nevertheless, the manner of their deaths at a young age has given them a particular place in collective memory. If this writing is in some way a form of commemorating them, then it is also an effort to provide a context for understanding their loss.

Coming to the end of this volume, I realize that I, too, have a biographical object, and this object was also the source of the name that I was given in Kodi. One month after my arrival, an older woman in Bondo Kodi, Inya Feni, started teasing me about the notebooks I carried around with me. "What is really in those books?" she asked. "What are you really looking for? Can you ever write it it all down?"

Like many other anthropologists whose efforts to inscribe tradition are publicly witnessed (Traube 1986, Lavie 1990), I came to be defined by the magic of book and pen. People were intrigued by my scribblings, and often asked to read them over. Many argued that although a Dutch missionary-linguist had devised a transcription system for Sumbanese languages (Onvlee 1929, 1973), their language could never really be written down, since it could not be pronounced the way it was spelled. When they could recognize a few words, they still maintained that the "tune" of their own tongue, its special texture and resonances, could never be captured on the page.

My hours spend transcribing, translating, and interpreting texts were seen as somewhat futile efforts to "look for a book" that in fact "lived under the skin" of a few knowledgeable older men. In order to find the "Kodi book," I had to become a Kodi person myself, taking a local name that could be easily pronounced. Some people jokingly proposed that I call myself Mbiri Kyoni, after the famous priestess of the calendrical ceremony in Tossi. But hers was also the name of the rice maiden, killed and buried by her own father to create a life-sustaining crop, and I was hesitant to take on either the mantle of a great priestess or the name of a sacrificial victim.

Inya Feni proposed the name Tari Mbuku, which had belonged to several important ancestors, and was also the name of a number of other local women. "Tari" was one of the most common Kodi first names for either men or women, and "Mbuku" was a pleasingly feminine second name, associated with the affectionate nickname "bapi Lyeko."[2] The real reason it was chosen, however, was that Tari Mbuku, when pronounced in Indonesian (*cari baku*), meant "looking for a book," and that was what everyone could see that I was doing.

The "book" that should eventually emerge from all of this searching and notetaking thus became the "biographical object" around which my own identity in Kodi was formed. Just as my informants and friends chose to narrate aspects of their life stories around an object, a possession, which in some way reflected their central concerns, I have written an account here that includes snippets of my autobiographical experiences as they intersect with the lives of my "subjects."

But the book project, not my own narrative, takes center stage because it is the contrast between the way selves and objects are gendered in Kodi and the way they are gendered in other places that I wish to write about, not simply my own reactions or a "field memoir." Am I hiding behind the scholarly object of my own research? Yes, of course, just as my "subjects" also hide, or at least veil themselves to some degree, behind the objects that they use in narrating aspects of their lives.

Smadar Lavie tells us that the Mzeina Bedouin called her The One Who Writes Us, which Lavie describes as an "allegorical other," a role that makes her part of the "grotesque didactic tales emphasizing indigenous ethics and morality" that the Mzeina Bedouin enjoy (Lavie 1990: 307). She opposes this role to both components of her personal self (the anthropologist and Smadar the woman), which is composed of elements of being a woman, an Israeli with an Arab heritage on her mother's side and a European one on her father's side. In a similar fashion, Inya Cari Buku in the national Indonesian language translates as "Mother Looking for a Book," who is simultaneously an American researcher and a member of the local community, a foreigner and a fictive kinswoman, someone addressed as "daughter" (by older men) and "sister" or "mother" (by women and girls). She is often given the courtesy of being treated as an insider, but her appearance, her accent, all mark her as quite clearly an outsider.

She is also, I realize, a writer of obituaries, a recorder of those who have died and an inscriber of lost lives. Her book is a memory box, a container of souls and stories, which hopes to allow these narratives to travel overseas and reach a new audience.

MULTIPLE CULTURES, MULTIPLE SELVES?

The whole problem of how to render narrative experience is not an easy one. No account, not even the subject's own, is transparently "true." As Joan Scott has argued, "It is not individuals who have experience, but subjects who are constructed through experience" (Scott 1991: 779). The mechanisms and logics of difference must be understood as relationally constituted through a historical process. Linda Alcoff, wondering in a similar vein about "the problem of speaking for others," alerts us to the problems of representing other voices in our own theoretical languages.

What Clifford Geertz has called the "diary disease" (1988: 89–90) of autobiographical revelation is a trend for reflexivity that may conceal as much as it reveals. It also may call into question the relation between our own autobiographical representations and those of our subjects.

Critics of the old-fashioned anthropological construction of life histories have attacked from two sides. Some say that the unitary self, the single or plenary "I," should be problematized, for Western as well as non-Western subjects (Kondo 1985, Visweswaran 1994). They suggest that autobiography itself may operate as a form of colonial discourse, imposing a European idea of the unique and autonomous subject on a more varied reality (Kaplan 1992, Sommer 1988). Others note that when Boas's students collected the "lives" of Native Americans, the life history of an individual came to stand for the life history of a vanishing culture, so the subject shifted from a single person to a culturally constructed self (Krupat 1985, Lejeune 1988).

On the one hand, Western scholars are said to impose a unifying self. On the other hand, they are accused of conflating the individual with a cultural type, the person with the prototype. How can we maintain the individuality of our subjects while still granting them the capacity to be multiply defined and complexly constructed? Is a false wholeness suggested by the simple request to "tell me your story"?

Constructionist theories of the self tell us there may be no enduring, stable, and unitary self, but instead a self that is made rather than discovered, constructed through narrative or dialogue. The act of telling a story is itself an effort to construct narrative coherence, a way of asking oneself, "What kind of story am I in?" An assumption of more recent research in clinical psychology is that subjects may have no coherent personality apart from the stories that they tell (Polkinghorne 1988). They construct their own selves in narrative form, using an object-metaphor as a device for plotting out their own place in a given cultural context. This narration is done in front of an audience, in a sort of collaboration with their listeners, who may give them clues that tell them what about their narrative is most interesting, engrossing, or compelling. The life story can then be studied as a retrospective way of working toward narrative coherence, a plotting of one's own life for therapeutic purposes or simply to achieve a satisfying story, to tell about oneself in a way that brings pleasure to both the narrator and the listener.

My argument is that biographical objects provide an "anchor" for storytelling in Kodi, in which a reflection on the self is deflected through the medium of an object, a possession, a thing that stands for aspects of the person. The unity of the object may express a unity of the self that is not given or fully achieved in the narrative, but it expresses a determined working toward the goal of personal and narrative coherence, a striving to "make sense" to others as well as to oneself.

When—as in the case of Ria or Taro—someone close to us has died leaving their story unfinished, "green," and indigestible by our usual forms of narrative processing, then it is others who construct a biographical object retrospectively, who try to find the symmetries and the dualities within which a particular life can have its meaning. Every life, and every death, must be told to be understood, rendered if not whole by language at least more comprehensible. The debts left by these unfinished stories can be paid only by more storytelling.

NOTES

1. The Kodi pontianak, *minye lemba karingge*, are said to smile and dance in front of the men they tempt, then touch his body and tell him to go ahead of them on the path. As soon as he goes ahead, they vanish. They carry a small piece of wood at the back of their neck (*karingge*) that is covered with their long hair. The wood seems to cover a secret body orifice that cannot be opened. I was also told that these forest nymphs sometimes have their genitals on backward (the anus at the front and the vulva at the back) to confuse their prospective lovers and make it impossible to have intercourse with them. These nymphs never wear their hair in a bun, but always long and loose, and usually tempt men while they bathe.

2. The bapi nicknames are paired with particular first names to provide an indirect, and supposedly more refined, form of address. They seem related to the practice of teknonyms common in other parts of Sumba, since it is fairly common practice to give the bapi of one's own first name to a child, who will then repay the favor by naming his or her own child after the grandparent who gave him or her a bapi name. Bapis can be either directly reciprocal or part of a chain of related names and nicknames.

8.
CONCLUSIONS

Stories and Objects in Lived Dualities

In assembling these materials, I wanted to do more than simply bring together the remembered lives of six people and highlight their relations to objects. The format of these lives, narrated around an object and full of dualistic metaphors, challenges a universalist view of "life histories" as self-evident "documents" that one can simply find, record, and bring home from the field (Frank 1979, 1995). It also encourages us to go beyond a view that personal experience and "the ethnography of the particular" will only convince us of our own shared humanity. The lives of these men and women are full of recognizable conflicts over questions of identity and the relations between personal freedom and responsibility that may help to deconstruct regional stereotypes about matriliny, patriliny, or "the traffic in women." Though Lila Abu-Lughod sought to have her efforts to "write women's worlds" interpreted in the framework of a "tactical humanism" (1991, 1993) that would dissolve cultural difference, I prefer to lay the emphasis on the forms of difference that emerge in these biographical and autobiographical accounts.

My reading of these lives, once a number of scattered conversations have been gathered together and "entextualized" upon the page, sees them as expressing concerns that are quite alien to those of most Western biographies and autobiographies. Specifically, I argue that there is an effort to effect closure through the gendered union of opposing aspects within an object.

CLOSURE AND GENDER DUALITY: COMPLETION AS SEXUAL UNION

The pervasive dualistic form of much Kodi verbal expression, and especially its gendered divisions, provides a special cast to their interpretation of personal experience. The use of an object, a personal possession, as a metaphor for the self draws us into the complicated question of the relations of persons and things throughout the eastern archipelago (Howell 1989, McKinnon 1991, Keane 1997).

I argue that things are complexly gendered and may sometimes incorporate both gendered identities, providing a language for representing parts of the self. In an exchange-oriented society such as that of Sumba, objects both represent the sexual politics that involve women and men and seem to "participate" in constituting these relations. However, the object is given its significance by its placement within a human story, by the way it becomes part of a narrative of self-presentation.

Maru Daku used his betel bag as a "sack for souls and stories," which brought together in a simple object an image of double-gendered creation. The betel bag contains both the *ndewa* or ancestral soul (formed at the crown of the head by the Father Creator, Bapa Rawi Lindu) and the *hamaghu* or vital spirit (bound at the forelock by the Mother Creator, Inya Wolo Hungga). It was the memory box that held his grandfather's gift of the paired words of ritual, and also the empty container used to summon the errant soul of his burned younger brother. It represented a family tradition of respect for the ancestors and obedience to traditional law. When his son became rebellious, he was called back to the ancestral village and promised to serve as his father's "betel bag tucked in the armpit," a faithful companion and the inheritor of his verbal skills.

His wives, Daku Maru and Ra Mete, have a somewhat different perspective on the symbolism of the betel bag. The bag is usually filled with long, firm fingers of sirih pipers and areca nuts, which are cracked open and chewed for their juices. The combination of elements transparently evokes penises and vaginas, and a husband who "no longer gives us sirih" is immediately understood to be neglecting his wives sexually. Ra Mete told me a series of other stories of neglect, focusing on domestic animals, and her senior co-wife sang a long lament about her husband's infidelities. The good husband provides "a protective enclosure for my tobacco, a post for my ginger vine to creep up" (*nggalu mbaku haghu nggu, ando koti lighya nggu*), shielding his wife like the inner pouches of a betel bag (where the tobacco may be stored in a secret container). A bad husband wanders off to "gather areca nut scattered on the path," and treats his wives no better than domestic animals.

Raja Horo was also, in this respect, a man who created tensions in his domestic life. The wives who wove fine, indigo-dyed textiles for his funeral shroud and for ceremonial dress felt excluded from the splendid royal prerogatives he enjoyed during the last years of Dutch colonialism. He imagined the source of his own power as the snake depicted on the shroud—a snake that he saw not as a Freudian phallus but as an enticing bedmate and "spirit wife" (*ariwyei marapu*) who occasionally pushed aside his human wives. Local images of fertility and rainfall were wedded to imported ones of centralized power and divine kingship, creating this personal symbol as a hybrid form, an appropriate image for the biography of a man who represented Sumba on his travels overseas and brought this distant island into the new nation of Indonesia.

His granddaughter Tila was also transfixed by a combination of the traditional and the modern. She loved a folktale about a heroine from the upper-world who used a spindle, the emblem of virtuous femininity, to snare a husband of her own choice. Her affection for the story was shaped by new images of sexual freedom spread to adolescent girls allowed, for the first time, to leave their homes to attend school. But her family would not let her follow her romantic impulses. They held her to an engagement that gave her financial security but made her lose the idealized husband of her dreams. The spindle became an image of the love that was lost, the companion she could not have.

In a strangely similar way, Markos Rangga Ende also saw his singing to the drum as the evocation of a lost beloved. To demonstrate his efficacy as a healer, his masculinity had to be constantly performed and displayed. He had to attract new clients and new followers, much as he tried to attract new women—with the powerfulness of his singing voice and the force of his personality. Orphaned at a young age, without siblings or family support, he was a populist politician and a self-made man. The song that opened each ritual performance told the story of a search for the proper materials to build a drum—its hollow cavity carved from driftwood, its top covered with skin originally taken from a young girl. But no drum covering could resist the constant beating of the baton and (metaphorically) the penetration of his male voice. This is why the ritual discourse of manhood presents an image of a counterpart who must constantly be renewed. A new woman had to be found, just as new audiences had to be wooed and new voters had to be persuaded to support him in the electoral campaign. Tila remembered the adolescent sweetheart she lost as an idealized male companion, and Markos looked out at each new ritual performance at many potential female companions among his listeners.

Both Tila and Markos tell stories that show how they felt themselves to be "incomplete" without a companion of the opposite sex. Even after marriage and children, this longing continued, in transformed form, because it focused on an ideal mate rather than the real one. Since this is hardly an unusual feeling in our own society, this form of romantic longing may not seem very alien to the personal experience of many readers.

The difference, I would maintain, comes not in the feelings of erotic uneasiness that we may all recognize, but instead in the idea that *closure* is achieved through a balancing of gendered attributes. In the paired couplets of ritual speech, a metaphoric image is expressed twice, and its true meaning does not emerge until the second line of verse is also spoken. In a similar way, all parallel expressions involve saying something twice to convey subtle shadings of meaning. I think these stories told by women and men about their own possessions share a similar attribute: *The story is not finished until the counterpart is present.*

The messy world of real persons does not come neatly arranged in pairs of corresponding metaphors. What these people, as narrators of their own lives, had to do was to fashion for themselves an identity in dualistic terms. They sought to define their own relations to others through an object that shared in male and female elements—a betel bag for ancestral words or a shared chew between lovers, a shroud with the image of serpentine power, a spindle standing for an absent husband, a drum evoking female receptivity to a male voice.

My final chapter concerns an object that was not chosen by its subject to narrate her own life but that was imposed on her by others to explain her death. Ria's biography was seen as tragically incomplete because she did not live to marry and have children. The many strange stories that circulated about her death and my own, eventually including Taro Goh as well, were all efforts to "finish" her life, to "close" a circle of correspondences and find their hidden meaning through matching one term with its counterpart. When I disappeared from the island and was not heard from for more than a year, people imagined that I would serve as Ria's counterpart in death, by proposing a series of fantastic scenarios for my own death overseas. They did not come true (although the speed at which these accounts spread does seem to demonstrate their "narrative coherence" for many Sumbanese!). But eight years later, when a foreign researcher did die on the island, his fate seemed to them an even closer match: The neat inversions of the gender of the deceased (female into male), the circumstances of death (violent accident and fatal disease), and the location of the death (outside the house and inside the "sick house") all confirmed to them that this was finally the end to Ria's story.

In my earlier discussion of Western autobiography and memory, I noted Frank Kermode's remark that both the "search for truth" and the "search for closure" were almost irresistible in projects of self-narration. What I would argue here is that Kodi stories about biographical objects express the particular characteristics of gender dualism in their notions of what is "true" and which stories are "finished."

A "true" story in this society is one that successfully encompasses its narrator's gendered opposite in a dialectical process of tacking back and forth. A story is not "closed" until it has managed to include both its subject and a counterpart. Objects can serve as convenient metaphors for the self in part because they are already gendered in complex ways, both through formal prestations of "male gifts" and "female gifts" and through the processes of producing them.

When I first decided that I wanted to concentrate on the sexual politics of possessions, and told people I wanted to turn to my notes on men's and women's lives to do so, most people expected me to produce an object-centered vision of sexual antagonism: Male and female things lined up in opposing formations in a battle of the sexes, played out through exchange. But the objects I had to contend with were not simple stand-ins for men or women, and the sexual politics of Kodi objects is much less confrontational. On the contrary, many objects themselves contain both male and female elements, and the paramount concern seems be one of longing, envy, and desire—the move to union and combination rather than opposition and separation.

Nevertheless, the life stories that attach themselves to these objects are full of deception, infidelity, the neglect by one spouse, and the longing for another. Sumbanese storytellers may idealize sexual union, but they are not noticeably better at negotiating all of its complications than many of the rest of us. Where they do differ from many others, and reveal an ethnographic and regional particularity, is in their attitude toward the gendering of persons and objects in a dualistic fashion.

ANDROGYNY AND GENDER DUALISM: ARE THEY THE SAME?

Strathern (1988) revolutionized the study of exchange by focusing on its role in creating gender identity. She argues that "Melanesians" (a possibly problematic category) see the person as partible and constituted through the exchange of objects. Exchange can start with an initially androgynous person and make that person less complete (and more clearly male or female) by detaching aspects of identity and circulating them.

People in Eastern Indonesian societies, equally caught up in a world of exchange and thus in some ways "Melanesian," also circulate gendered objects and use them to define identities. The objects that circulate most widely travel the pathways that articulate the relations between social groups, while those that are hoarded and treasured become linked to their owners' biographies and may serve to index status and prestige, measure time, or express a commitment to an ancestral heritage or a longing for an idealized partner.

Marilyn Strathern summarizes the multiply gendered identities of persons and objects with the term "androgyny." Though I draw on her insights linking exchange and identity and her great insight into many aspects of sexual politics, I find this term does not fit my Sumbanese materials. Androgyny implies a confusion of male and female, an obscuring of gender in general, or an absence of identifiably gendered aspects. I would agree that some relatively unmarked and unimportant spiritual entities in Kodi could be called "androgynous" (such as the spirits of rice and corn). But all of the most powerful and important objects and anthropomorphized spirits are characterized by a surfeit, not an absence of gender. They are both female and male, both mother and father, and "overgendered" rather than "undergendered." In the past, I have described this as a "double-gendered" image of power (Hoskins 1990), which I linked to Kodi notions of double descent.

Rethinking these arguments now, I might loosen the ties to notions of descent, but I would emphasize even more strongly that what is usually called "dualistic symbolism" in Eastern Indonesia is a profoundly gendered vision of the world, where the *combination* of male and female—not their confusion or blending—is a characteristic of overarching power.

Strathern's analysis of exchange in Papua New Guinea has shown how social agents can be identified with objects, and how their identities can circulate through things. Building on these innovations but extending them in a different direction, I would suggest that Kodi "biographical objects" can themselves be gendered because of their significance to the narrative process of identity formation.

Strathern uses the notion of androgyny to highlight the potential for manifesting unified, cross-sex identity (male and female) as well as a differentiated (male or female) identity: "Social life consists in a constant movement from one state to another, from one type of sociality to another, from a unity ... to that unity split or paired with respect to another.... Gender is the principal form through which the alternation is conceptualized" (1988: 14).

Examining how Strathernian notions might apply to Eastern Indonesia, McKinnon looks at the process of unity and differentiation in the manufacture and circulation of Tanimbarese exchange valuables (1991). The "possibility of movement" from one gendered identity to another is analyzed with ideas of "extraction" and "recombination" in which single-sex identity is an incomplete version of an initially androgynous whole.

In a similar fashion, Howell describes how both women and men in Northern Lio, Flores, may assume "ritually male" or "ritually female" roles in ceremonial interactions, concluding: "Men and women, maleness and femaleness are not unambiguous categories or values. Rather, their meanings are derived relationally and, according to context, clusters of gender qualities are brought out which are variously anchored in, and expressed through, the bodies of men and women" (1996a: 265). Much as in Kodi, descent in Lio is traced along both the father's and mother's lines, with male relationality linked to houses and ancestral worship, while female relationality is tied to blood and the life cycle. But she argues that "such neat gender duality is overlain and destroyed by the androgynous character of the significant actors and objects. It is precisely the potential for activating opposite gender qualities within the person, building or objects which renders these powerful. It is this potential which allows significant situations to be constituted in either a male or female mode of sexuality regardless of the biological sex of the actors, and denies absolute gender attribution of the objects" (1996a: 267).

There is much that I admire in this nuanced and theoretically sophisticated account of Lio gendered values, but I do not find that the idea of androgyny is especially helpful. Howell uses it to describe the salience of the brother-sister idiom and the ritual importance of the mother's brother: "Androgyny is taken to mean that persons or objects inherently carry within them both male and female qualities which are variously brought to bear according to context" (1996a: 258). However, what she is really talking about is nearly always the *combination* of female and male in images of overarching power. The cross-sex sibling couple is seen as central to ritual practice not because of any oscillation or neutralization of gender attributes (which would make either member of the pair "androgynous") but rather because *both genders are present in partnership.*

Thus, although I agree with her analysis of the ethnography (and find many resonances with Kodi gendered values), I think it is misleading to assimilate Eastern Indonesian notions of gender dualism to Strathern's view of Melanesian "androgyny."

To do so is to fall into an essentialized view of the gift where questions of power (including male and female strategies of self-representation) are marginalized. *The Gender of the Gift* was a provocative and unsettling view of Melanesian sociality as characterized by a primordial and distinctive cultural logic—there was no concept of alienation and no institutionalized exploitation of women by men. The radical alterity between Melanesians and Westerners lifted one part of the world out of history and distanced it from notions of individual experience.

One thing that I have tried to do in this book is to place Kodi men and women in history and in the experiences that they construct as part of the process if narrating them around objects. Kodi double gendering of deities, spirits, governmental figures, ritual offices, and images of authority expresses not so much a movement from male to female, or vice versa, as a dynamic bringing together of sexually opposed entities. The great "Mother/Father" prayed to as the double-gendered Creator, or named in genealogies of village founders and ancestors, is an image of reproductive union, not gender uncertainty. The particular ways in which gendered values are expressed in a twofold form is a marked characteristic of the region.

The life experiences of men and women, and the ways they are narrated around possessions that embody them, reflect this pattern. The pervasive pairs of Kodi ritual discourse are neither signs of a supposedly universal binarism of thought (as an earlier "vulgar Levi-Straussianism" would have it) nor manifestations of androgynous exchange, but instead a culturally and historically specific ideology that gives primacy to the powerful combination of male and female. Sexual union, as a symbol of completeness and (potential) parenthood, comes to stand for the closure and coherence that each person strives for in telling the story of his or her life. When male narrators speak of their search for a counterpart, and female ones evoke an idealized husband, their search is also for a completed self, a balanced life, and a culturally satisfying narrative resolution.

If androgyny is equated simply with gender fluidity in the process of representation—the idea that many things become male or become female in particular contexts—it is unobjectionable, and certainly a characteristic of Eastern Indonesian symbolic forms. But even more characteristic of the forms of speech and narrative used in this region is a pervasive dualism and doubleness that goes well beyond what is found elsewhere.

Gender dualism could be defined for comparative purposes by the formal requirement that a female and a male component be included in each unifying, hierarchical entity. This is the idea that defines double-gendered deities, which are *both* mother and father, both wife and husband. It is the idea expressed in a the great many societies on Sumba, Timor, and Flores, where any overarching governmental power is called the *Ina Ama* or "Mother Father." My Sumbanese informants would find it profoundly offensive to refer to these spirits as of androgynous or uncertain gender: They are undoubtedly complete because they contain the union of a fully female component and a fully male one.

Parallelism, as it has been extensively discussed and documented in the region, is generally treated as a disease of language—the famous "speaking in pairs," where two images are summoned together to create a single meaning (Fox 1980, 1988). However, parallelism is also a trait of ritual, architecture, and gender constructs—and its implications for how people conceive their own lives in the more intimate, autobiographical narratives are the subject of this book.

Gender dualism is not necessarily a vision of gender equality, but it does highlight interdependence, complementarity, and what can only be called a vision of sexual union—the bringing together of male and female in an act of pleasure, release, and potential reproduction. The importance of opposite sex couples, portrayed as parents, siblings, or ancestors, in Eastern Indonesian social imagery is an index of the value given to heterosexual relations, not androgyny.

The particular features of Eastern Indonesian life narratives may also help to shed light on some of the unacknowledged particularities of our own society, with its marked gender battles and frantic consumerism. Certainly, Americans often express their identities through objects and may choose to tell their lives through the lens of certain possesions. In a purely speculative vein, then, I think it might prove interesting to wonder how the notion of biographical objects would travel back to my own home, and where there would be contrasts.

BIOGRAPHICAL OBJECTS: AN AREA FOR COMPARISON?

The objects imbued with particular personal significance in our own society are often more directly representational. Instead of a betel bag as a sign of the tie to the ancestors, we decorate our homes with portraits or photographs of our grandparents. Instead of a spindle as the idealized bridegroom, we may have a poster of a pop singer. Instead of a drum to receive the story of our sorrows, we go to visit a therapist or inscribe a chronicle of our agonies in a diary, a letter, or an autobiographical narrative. The trials and tribulations of modernity are etched on e-mail in cyberspace, rather than being contained in the image of a breakable green bottle.

But the use of an icon, a concrete vehicle for our thoughts, is of course common across the divide of cultural differences. The correspondences between the object and that represented is more often visual in the examples from Western contexts that come most readily to mind, while I would argue that it is established verbally (through both formal ritual couplets and more informal metaphors) in the materials I have been reviewing. It must first be constructed in words before it can be appreciated, even indirectly, as a personal symbol and significant personal possession.

Recent efforts to develop a comparative theory of the self set out a number of issues that we must consider if we want to interpret biographical objects as presenting a "metaphor of the self." The idea that the self is a cultural configuration, that the concept of the individual might be differently articulated in the indigenous psychologies of other groups, has been with us since Mauss's classic essay on "the notion of person." Mauss saw the idea of self as evolving historically and taking different forms at different periods, but he believed that the modern Western self had "become clearer and more specific, becoming identified with self-knowledge and psychological consciousnessness" (1985: 20) and was thus superior to earlier, less differentiated notions.

Other theorists have taken a less sanguine attitude toward the historical situation of the modern Western self. Anthropologists who have explored the process of "crafting selves" (Kondo 1990, McCracken 1988, Miller 1987) working in modern industrial societies do not find selfhood becomes more enduring, stable, or unitary, and stress instead its negotiated, unstable, and fragmented nature. Cushman traces the historical emergence of an idea of the "bounded, masterful self" as paralleling the rise of industrialism and reaching its culmination in the post–World War II period, when this form of self began to appear as empty and fragmented: "One of the disquieting results of this constructionist perspective is the realization that our current era has constructed a self that is, fundamentally, a disappointment to itself" (Cushman 1990: 608).

The modern self experiences an absence of community, tradition, and shared meaning, which is expressed as a lack of personal conviction and worth. Through consumerism and the search for therapy, "it embodies the absences as a chronic, undifferentiated emotional hunger," a yearning to buy things and for professional advice to take the place of what has been lost (1990: 600). People who go to shopping centers on weekends to "shop until you drop" are compulsive consumers, but they cannot really enjoy what they purchase (Willis 1991). Buying commercial products may soothe, but never competely satiate, this hunger for novelty and this need for "life-style changes" to revitalize the self with newly manufactured identities.

Such views of an alienated, fragmented self that depends on objects to supply identities contrasts in interesting ways with my efforts to understand how Sumbanese women and men articulate their identities in relation to objects. While Sumbanese are in no position to consume commercial products in the obsessive and excessive way that some Americans do, they can and do displace parts of their personhood on objects that circulate. They also actively craft certain objects (cloth, wooden tools and instruments, houses) that they use in their daily lives, investing both time and artistry in the production of things that may represent them.

Cushman argues that modern Americans try to buy new identities at shopping malls, desperately trying to fill an "empty self." I argue, in contrast, that Sumbanese construct a narrative self through the metaphoric language of objects, and they acknowledge the ways in which aspects of that self may be negotiated in exchange and intergenerational transmissions. These objects play roles in local sexual politics, but most often not as simple icons of maleness or femaleness but as representations of the urge to bring the two together. The spinster or the drum is an idealized companion of the opposite sex. The betel bag and the snakeskin shroud are both containers of an ancestral heritage that are crafted by women but serve as vehicles of male identity.

Differences between modern consumer objects and Kodi exchange objects, especially the most valued and "biographical" of these objects, can be summarized briefly as (1) investment in form, (2) investment in work, (3) novelty versus age, and (4) exchange histories and paths. Form is important because most Sumbanese possessions are locally crafted and are, if not directly produced by their owners, then at least produced in consultation with the prospective owner. The modern consumer exercises choice over a number of manufactured items. The Sumbanese owner chooses form and materials beforehand, and helps to constitute the object's shape and stylistic features. The work invested is paid with sacrifices and small gifts of coins or cloth.

The value of novelty versus age would seem to oppose the language of objects in societies such as Kodi to modern consumerism, as would the importance given to innovation rather than tradition. For Maru Daku, adopting a particular, simple style of betel bag is significant because it identifies him with his grandfather and with a storytelling line. For modern Westerners, a purse design may be valued more because it is the latest thing—although the fashionability of "classic" designs, and even the nostalgic appeal of "retro" (including the "primitive" and "exotic"), is also notable (Torgovnick 1990).

The most important difference emerges in the contrast between Kodi exchange histories and the depersonalized circulation of objects in modern industrial nations. We do not usually know where an object was made, what materials went into it, or the exact processes involved in the manufacture of substances such as plastic or glass. We are thus alienated from even the voyeuristic pleasures of participating in production and made to play the role of consumers whose only choices lie in supermarket aisles, not in the workshops of local manufacturers. Our exchange of objects is rarely carried out in face-to-face encounters or in direct contact with the producers.

The aggressive, somewhat desperate acquisitiveness of modern consumers is equated by Cushman with a need to "take in" and merge with a self-object celebrity, an ideology or a drug, to escape the danger of fragmenting into feelings of worthlessness and confusion: "By using the right toothpaste or identifying with the most reassuring or powerful politician, consumers are thus covertly promised a magically different, transformed self" (1990: 606). Psychologists, and particularly therapists, have contributed to this discourse because of their ahistorical insistence on a scientistic epistemology that does not recognize political causes of personal distress. "While psychologists have been treating the empty self, they have, of necessity, also been constructing it, profiting from it, and not challenging the social arrangements that created it" (1990: 609).

Interiorizing cultural absences, and perceiving them as located in the self, have led to a series of life-style therapies that Cushman sees as being fundamentally in bad faith. However, we can go too far in seeing the modern self as totally fragmented, tossed around in the currents of history and politics and completely without conscious agency, laid "out on the table with self-induced multiple personality disorder" (Haraway 1988: 578). Our own efforts at self-narration and self-justification in such genres as the confessional memoir or autobiography show that we still wish to be held responsible and accountable for our actions.

Roy Wagner proposes a different reading of the Western fashion for conceiving and reconceiving the self in rhetoric. He sees both consumerism and confessionalism as linked in the "acute vulnerability of solipsism":

> What I have called "the need for a need" [to consume the products of advertising] is personalized in the self-conception of someone who wants to believe that he or she has invented the world whole in the imagination, and so needs the affirmation and the language of others more desperately that those others need him or her. (Wagner 1995: 75)

The flaws that he sees in the culture of "gimme America" come from a lack of appreciation of precedent, tradition, and ancestral heritage, which manage nevertheless to shape our lives at a deep, although often unacknowledged, level. Advertising encourages us to imitate a life that, like that of the movies, is never lived, and provides the "surrogative narratives of the self" that are most familiar to our own society, attaching them to public commodities instead of biographical objects.

Anthropologists who have recently turned to analyzing forms of consumption in Western industrial society have noted that some older objects can acquire a certain biographical dimension. McCracken proposes the term "patina" to designate the property of goods by which their age becomes a key index to their status (1988). Only certain kinds of goods—old silver, well-polished wooden tables—can be said to acquire patina as "the gloss of age," instead of simple marks of wear and tear. They must not only be well maintained but also be displayed in the proper context: "The distinction between an heirloom and junk is not patina as such, but also the successful semiotic management of the social context" (Appadurai 1996: 76).

Our attachment to older furnishings has been linked to nostalgia for vanishing ways of life. Modern merchandisers even try to inculcate nostalgia by teaching consumers to miss things they have never lost (Halbwachs 1980), in which an imaginary past is vividly summoned up by objects that recall an aristocratic way of life that they might have wanted. Fredric Jameson even argues that there is a new "nostalgia for the present," which misrecognizes contemporary fashions by stylizing them and presenting them as already the object of an historical sensibility (1989). The sense that we are already mourning the loss of those very objects that we are now consuming evokes a more intense form of attachment, much as the awareness of our own mortality is said to intensify our wish to live. Both the nostalgic and the biographical elements of our own relationships to objects have strong echoes in these Sumbanese stories.

RETHINKING THE CATEGORY OF "POSSESSIONS"

Where we find a useful bridge between Sumbanese and American notions of things is in the category of possession. James Carrier notes that it can be used to designate all "objects that bear a personal identity" (1990: 693) and is thus perhaps a more useful category to oppose to the commodity than the usual one of the gift (Gregory 1982, Strathern 1988). Mauss's original evolutionary contrast between modern European societies dominated by the exchange of commodities and earlier societies dominated by the exchange of gifts can be rethought, along with his similar views on the evolution of the self, in a comparative framework that looks more closely at similarities than differences.

People in modern industrial societies convert commodities into possessions by endowing them with a personal identity (Csikszentmihalyi and Rochberg-Halton 1981), and it is through consumption that people are most likely to "buy" new identities through what is called a "refashioning of their own lifestyles." Miller (1988) studied how tenants in a North London council housing modified the kitchens of their apartments, in this way appropriating alien objects and giving them a more personal significance. Alienation is an "intrinsic condition" (354) of products in large industrial societies, but the need to endow particular things with a subjective meaning persists after purchase, and is evident in the self-presentation involved not only in home decoration but also in fashion. In his analysis of mail-order catalogs in the United States, Carrier argues that shopping and selling must be analyzed from a Maussian perspective as "key stages in the process by which objects move from the impersonal domain of commodity relations that dominate production to the domain of gift relations that dominate household transaction and consumption" (1990: 694).

The impersonal forces used in advertising, which Schudson calls the "capitalist realism" of abstract persons (1984: 211–12), have been analyzed in semiological terms as a kind of "identity kit" personality, selves constructed for consumption out of impersonal prefabricated elements. But this ignores the question of the personal relationship between owner and object, and also of the creative agency of the purchaser who may re-evaluate or even resist the way an object is presented by advertisers.

The decline in industrial employment in advanced capitalist societies has meant that an ever-smaller proportion of the population has any direct experience of making things, and there are few elaborate "biographies of objects" comparable to Markos's account of the making of his drum. But while "manufacture" is increasingly alien to people's direct experience, connoisseurship and consumer discrimination is not—especially, for instance, concerning such possessions as a high-quality musical instrument. The cultural meaning people attach to manufactured objects remains complex, and although it is susceptible to symbolic manipulation by advertisers, it can also be reinterpreted by purchasers in idiosyncratic ways. A possession can be seen as "an identity that is bought and sold" (Carrier 1990: 695), but what people are buying is not necessarily identical to what manufacturers think they are selling.

The use that Kodi storytellers make of objects as vehicles for their own lives and identity has parallels in other Pacific societies. MacKenzie formulates this contrast as based on different ways of constructing selves in relation to objects: "In our modern capitalist society the positive work of consumerism is the construction of self through consumer choice. In the pre-capitalist economy of the Telefol, the string bag is used both by the consumer and the producer to objectify their social persona" (1991: 149–50). This objectification is possible because the string bag is a gift, and an inalienable one.

Inalienability is a characteristic of any object that becomes steeped with biographic significance (A. Weiner 1992), and possessions that came into someone's hands as consumer commodities may then "deviate" from their expected trajectory and come to be invested with personal meaning. This process occurs, in its simplest form, whenever we become so attached to a hat, dress, or pair of shoes that they appear irreplaceable. In a wider sense, it can characterize the "biography" of any object associated with a life-transforming event, and thus filled with idiosyncratic meaning (Kopytoff 1986). The last shirt a man wore before his death, the plates used at a wedding dinner, the glass broken in response to shocking news—such events can attach themselves to ordinary objects and fix them in memory as markers of the extraordinary. Thus, it is not the physical characteristics of objects that make them biographical, but the meanings imputed to them as significant personal possessions.

However, there is also a more complex relationship between persons and possessions in a society like that of traditional Sumba, where the metonymic links between persons and things form what Onvlee has called the "spiritual underpinning" of an individual's personality: "Possessions do not exist on their own, nor can they be detached from their underpinning; a person's conduct is related to his possessions" (1980: 196). Keane describes the Anakalang notion of *dewa* or "spirit" as "a way of talking about the claims that persons (as possessors) have on things and that things (as prestations and ancestral valuables) have on persons" (1997: 207). The capacity of a person to act as a social subject is defined through his or her relation to the material world, and particularly to certain objects that represent him or her.

Recent work on Western consumerism has developed the notion of "appropriation" to give a more active, and resistant, cast to the thinking that people may have about their possessions. Miller (1988), influenced by Strathern's representation of the dialectic of gender in Melanesia, has interpreted council housing in London as a way of reconstituting gender as exchange. To escape the alienating consequences of commerce, people construct new personal relations with the objects that surround them most intimately.

The stories I heard people on Sumba tell about themselves through their possessions provide a vivid testimony to the ways in which objects are reimagined in terms of each person's subjective experience. While working against a background of conventional paired metaphors and ritual and mythological uses of these objects, each individual formulates his or her own version of what the object signifies. It is possible that similarly vivid, although quite different, stories might emerge from people in modern industrial societies (Dagognet 1996). But to assume that people in traditional societies have a view of objects that is restricted to conventional meanings, or that fantasy and imagination are not involved in their own practices of consumption, seems absurd.

Thus, the otherwise interesting speculations of Arjun Appadurai on the "newly significant role" played by the imagination in the postelectronic world due to such forces as migration and the mass media seem to deny that ordinary life and ordinary objects were endowed with much significance in "pre-electronic" societies—for instance Sumba of the 1980s:

> The imagination has broken out of the special expressive space of art, myth, and ritual and has now become a part of the quotidian mental work of ordinary people in many societies. It has entered the logic of ordinary life from which it had largely been successfully sequestered. Of course, this has precedents in great revolutions, cargo cults, and messianic movements of other times, in which forceful leaders implanted their vision into social life, thus creating powerful movements for social change. Now, however, it is no longer a matter of specially endowed (charismatic) individuals, injecting the imagination where it does not belong. Ordinary people have begun to deploy their imaginations in the practice of their everyday lives. (1996: 5)

It is not the case that people in other societies produce and consume objects as automatons, except for a few moments spent straying into the "special expressive space" of art, myth, and ritual. On the contrary, as I have tried to show, objects are used as vehicles for fantasy and imagination because they are saturated with both conventional and subjective meanings. These meanings borrow from but reinterpret views of these objects in songs, folktales and rites, and in places like Sumba they are suffused with the special tensions of a dualistic cosmology.

The imagination works on objects to turn commodities, gifts, or ordinary utilitarian tools into sometimes very significant possessions, which draw their power from biographical experiences and the stories told about these. Kopytoff (1986: 68) argued that one could speak of the "cultural biographies of things" because each object is a "culturally constructed entity endowed with culturally specific meanings and classified and reclassified into culturally constituted categories." Though the way possessions are imagined in modern capitalist societies is colored by the ubiquity of commodities, and on Sumba is colored instead by ideas of ceremonial exchange, the deployment of the imagination is equally important in each case.

DIFFERENT POSSESSIONS, DIFFERENT SELVES?

We can, therefore, go too far in setting up a non-Western self as the mirror image of modern or postmodern fragmentation: whole, grounded, nonacquisitive, and rooted in tradition rather than shifting fashions. My Sumbanese informants felt that their world had been turned almost inside out over the past century, and though they retained certain loyalties to the ancestors, they were also very conscious of changes in their circumstances that made these loyalties increasingly difficult to maintain. They used objects as signs of wealth, reputation, and renown as much as status-conscious yuppies do, although with a different symbolic language.

Do these stories reflect a different notion of the self from the modern one? In some ways, yes, since the people I knew in Kodi had been largely separated from most of the forces that supposedly helped to form the modern idea of the self: They were no more than partially literate, they had not been exposed to popularized psychology, and did not enjoy the measure of privacy that gives much time and space for introspection. On the other hand, they were also interested in how someone from far away might make sense of their lives, and when I asked more personal questions they often tried to direct my interpretations and guide me along the way.

It would be mistaken to argue that an individuated self exists only in the Western world and a relational self in the non-Western one, since (as others have pointed out, cf. Battaglia 1995) ideas of individuality and relationality coexist in both contexts. Certainly, I hope these chapters focused on particular persons and particular objects have shown how Kodi women and men strive for an individual vision of their relatedness and do not replicate the visions of others in a stereotypic fashion. Though their confessions are indirect and veiled (in contrast to the "tell it all" vogue of many Western autobiographers), they are also, in their own way, sincere efforts to narrate a life and arrive at a better understanding of their place in the world.

The stories here reflect some degree of self-reflexivity, and they certainly show the marks of a desire to construct a particular image of personal goals and autobiographic coherence. I would not claim that they represent an absolute sense of truth, but would argue (with Kermode) that no one would agree to tell her life without trying to understand it better herself in the process. "Closure" for my Kodi narrators would mean finding within their own lives the paired opposites that inhabit their ritual speech and their mythology. Introducing a sense of order by focusing on a quest for a missing counterpart, or honoring an ancestral mandate, is at the same time finding a meaning in a life that—to all of us—seems at times to resist being meaningful. This is, therefore, an alternate form of biography, narrated not in personal confessions but through the indirect medium of objects. It shows us also an alternative vision of gender difference, where dualism provides a sense of the balance each person aspires to, and where sexual union is the idealization of personal completeness.

I argue that the narrative construction of identity on Sumba is complexly entangled with personal possessions because of a general cultural preoccupation with the metaphoric properties of things and their use as surrogate companions. An object can thus become more than simply a "metaphor for the self." It becomes a pivot for reflexivity and introspection, a tool of autobiographic self-discovery, a way of knowing oneself through things.

REFERENCES

Abu-Lughod, Lila
   1986. *Veiled Sentiments: Honor and Poetry in a Bedouin Society*. Berkeley: University of California Press.
   1991. Writing Culture. In *Recapturing Anthropology: Working in the Present*, ed. Richard G. Fox. Santa Fe, NM: School of American Research Press.
   1993. *Writing Women's Worlds: Bedouin Stories*. Berkeley: University of California Press.
Adams, Marie Jeanne (Monni)
   1969. *System and Meaning in East Sumba Textile Design: A Study in Traditional Indonesian Art*. Yale Southeast Asia Studies Cultural Report 16. New Haven: Yale University Press.
Adriani, N.
   1894. Sangireesche teksten. Med vertaling en aanteekningen uitg. 2 *Bijdragen tot de taal-, land-, en volkenkunde van Nederlandsch-Indie* 5 (10): 1–168.
Alcoff, Linda
   1991. The Problem of Speaking for Others. *Cultural Critique* (Winter): 5–32.
Anderson, Benedict O.
   1972. The Idea of Power in Javanese Culture. In *Culture and Politics in Indonesia*, ed. C. Holt, B. Anderson, and J. Siegel. Ithaca, NY: Cornell University Press.
   1984. *Imagined Communities: Reflections on the Origin and Spread of Nationalism*. London: Verso.
Appadurai, Arjun
   1986. Introduction: Commodities and the Politics of Value. In *The Social Life of Things: Commodities in Cultural Perspective*. Cambridge, UK: Cambridge University Press.
   1996. *Modernity at Large: Cultural Dimensions of Globalization*. Minneapolis: University of Minnesota Press.
Atkinson, Jane
   1989. *The Art and Politics of Wana Shamanship*. Berkeley: University of California Press.
   1990. How Gender Makes a Difference in Wana Society. In *Power and Difference: Gender in Island Southeast Asia*. Stanford, CA: Stanford University Press.
Atkinson, Jane, and Shelly Errington, eds.
   1990. *Power and Difference: Gender in Island Southeast Asia*. Stanford, CA: Stanford University Press.

Battaglia, Deborah

1990. *On the Bones of the Serpent: Person, Memory and Mortality among Sabarl Islanders of Papua New Guinea.* Chicago: University of Chicago Press.

1995. Problematizing the Self: A Thematic Introduction. In *Rhetorics of Self-Making*, ed. D. Battaglia. Berkeley: University of California Press.

Behar, Ruth

1993. *Translated Woman: Crossing the Border with Esperanza's Story.* Boston: Beacon Press.

Behar, Ruth, and Deborah Gordon, eds.

1995. *Women Writing Culture.* Berkeley: University of California Press.

Benedict, Ruth

1931. "Folklore" and "Myth." In *Encyclopedia of the Social Sciences*, vol. 11: 288–93 and 178–81. New York: Macmillan and Company.

Benjamin, Walter

1969. *Illuminations.* New York: Schocken Books.

Bourdieu, Pierre

1986. L'illusion biographique. *Actes de la recherche dans les sciences sociales.* Juin 62/63: 69–72.

Bruner, E. M.

1984. The Opening Up of Anthropology. In *Text, Play and Story: The Construction and Reconstruction of Self and Society*, ed. E. M. Bruner. Prospect Heights, IL: Waveland.

Butler, Judith

1990. *Gender Trouble: Feminism and the Subversion of Identity.* New York: Routledge.

Carrier, James

1990. The Symbolism of Possession in Commodity Advertising. *Man*, n.s., 25: 693–706.

1994. *Gifts and Commodities: Exchange and Western Capitalism Since 1700.* London and New York: Routledge.

Carrithers, Micheal, Steven Collins, and Steven Lukes, eds.

1985. *The Category of the Person: Anthropology, Philosophy, History.* Cambridge: Cambridge University Press.

Chauvel, Richard

1990. *Nationalists, Soldiers and Separatists.* Leiden: KITLV Press.

Cox, Marian Roalfe

1893. *Cinderella.* London: David Nutt.

Csikszentmihalyi, M., and E. Rochberg-Halton

1981. *The Meaning of Things.* New York: Cambridge University Press.

Csordas, Thomas J.

1994. *Embodiment and Experience: The Existential Ground of Culture and Self.* Cambridge: Cambridge University Press.

Cushman, P.

1990. Why the Self is Empty: Toward a Historically Situated Psychology. *American Psychologist* 545: 599–611.

Dagognet, Francois

1996. *Les dieux sont dans la cuisine: Philosophie des objets et objets de la philosophie.* Collection Les Empecheurs de Penser en Rond. Paris: Synthelabo Groupe.

Dossa, Parin A.
1994. Critical Anthropology and Life Stories: Case Study of Elderly Ismaili Canadians. *Journal of Cross-Cultural Gerontology* 9: 335–54.

Dowling, Colette
1981. *The Cinderella Complex: Women's Hidden Fear of Independence.* New York: Summit Books.

Dundes, Alan, ed.
1982. *Cinderella: A Casebook.* Madison: University of Wisconsin Press.

Ecklund, Judith
1977. *Marriage, Seaworms and Song: The Sasak of Lombok.* Cornell University, unpublished Ph.D. dissertation.

Errington, Shelly
1990. Recasting Sex, Gender and Power: A Theoretical and Regional Overview. In *Power and Difference: Gender in Island Southeast Asia.* J. M. Atkinson and S. Errington, eds. Stanford, CA: Stanford University Press.

Forth, Gregory
1981. *Rindi: An Ethnographic Study of a Traditional Domain in Eastern Sumba.* The Hague: Martinus Nijhoff.

Fox, James J.
1980. *The Flow of Life: Essays on Eastern Indonesia.* Cambridge: Harvard University Press.
1988. *To Speak in Pairs: Essays on the Ritual Languages of Eastern Indonesia.* Cambridge: Cambridge University Press.
1991. Introduction. *Sumba: A Bibliography.* Compiled by Taro Goh. Canberra: Research School of Pacific Studies, Australian National University.

Frank, Gelya
1979. Finding the Common Denominator: A Phenomenological Critique of Life History Method. *Ethos* 7 (1): 68–94.
1980. Life Histories in Gerontology: The Subjective Side to Aging. In *New Methods for Old Age Research: Anthropological Alternatives*, eds. C. Fry and J. Keith. Chicago: Loyola University Center for Urban Policy.
1985. "Becoming the Other": Empathy and Biographical Interpretation. *Biography* 8: 189–210.
1995. Anthropology and Individual Lives: The Story of the Life History and the History of the Life Story. *American Anthropologist* 97: 145–48.

Frank, Gelya, and L. L. Langness
1981. *Lives: An Anthropological Approach to Biography.* Novato, CA: Chandler and Sharp.

Gal, Susan
1991. Between Speech and Silence: The Problematics of Research on Language and Gender. In *Gender at the Cross-Roads of Knowledge: Feminist Anthropology in the Postmodern Era*, ed. Micaela di Leonardo. Berkeley: University of California Press.

Geertz, Clifford
1973. *The Interpretation of Cultures.* New York: Basic Books.
1988. *Works and Lives.* Stanford, CA: Stanford University Press.

Geiger, Susan N.G.
1986. Women's Life Histories: Method and Context. *Signs* 11 (2): 334–51.

Geirnaert-Martin, Danielle
1989. Textiles of West Sumba: Lively Renaissance of an Old Tradition. In *To Speak with Cloth: Studies in Indonesian Textiles.* ed. Mattiebelle Gittinger. Los Angeles: Fowler Museum of Cultural History.
1991. The Snake's Skin: Traditional Ikat in Kodi. In *Indonesian Textiles. Symposium 1985*, ed. G. Volger and K. v. Welck. Ethnologica. Band 14. Cologne: Rautenstrauch-Joest Museum.
1992a. *The Woven Land of Laboya: Socio-Cosmic Ideas and Values in West Sumba, Eastern Indonesia.* Leiden: Centre of Non-Western Studies.
1992b. Purse-Proud: Betel and Areca Bags in West Sumba (East Indonesia). In *Dress and Gender: Making and Meaning*, ed. R. Barnes and J. B. Eicher. Oxford, UK: Berg.
George, Kenneth
1996. *Showing Signs of Violence: The Cultural Politics of a Twentieth-Century Headhunting Ritual.* Berkeley: University of California Press.
Gereja Kristen Sumba
1974. *Masalah Poligami dalam Gereja Kristen Sumba*, ed. M. Jiwa. Typescript from Sinode 27.
Goh, Taro
1991. *Sumba: A Bibliography* (published posthumously, with an introduction by J. J. Fox). Canberra: Research School of Pacific Studies, Australian National University, occasional papers series.
Greenblatt, Stephen
1991. *Marvelous Possessions.* Berkeley and London: University of California Press.
Gregory, Christopher
1982. *Gifts and Commodities.* New York: Academic Press.
Grimm, The Brothers
1982. Cinderella. In 1982 *Cinderella: A Casebook*, ed. Alan Dundes. Madison: University of Wisconsin Press.
Grosz, Elizabeth
1994. *Volatile Bodies: Toward a Corporeal Feminism.* St. Leonards, NSW: Allen and Unwin.
Gullestad, Marianne
1996. Why Study Autobiographies? In *Everyday Life Philosophers: Modernity, Morality and Autobiography in Norway.* Oslo: Scandinavian University Press.
Halbwachs, M.
1980. *The Collective Memory.* New York: Harper and Row.
Haraway, Donna
1988. Situated Knowledges: The Science Question in Feminism and the Privilege of the Partial Perspective. *Feminist Studies* 14 (3): 575–600.
Haviland, John
1991. "That was the Last Time I Seen Them, and No More": Voices Through Time in Australian Aboriginal Autobiography. *American Ethnologist* 18 (2): 331–61.
Hefner, Robert
1994. Of Faith and Commitment: Christian Conversion in Muslim Java. In *Conversion to Christianity*, ed. R. Hefner. Berkeley: University of California Press.
Hicks, David
1989. *A Maternal Religion: The Role of Women in Tetum Myth and Ritual.* DeKalb: Northern Illinois University, Center for Southeast Asian Studies.

Hollan, Douglas W., and Jane C. Wellencamp
1994. *Contentment and Suffering: Culture and Experience in Toraja*. New York: Columbia University Press.
1996. *The Thread of Life: Toraja Reflections on the Life Cycle*. Honolulu: University of Hawaii Press.
Hoskins, Janet
1985. A Life History from Both Sides: The Changing Poetics of Personal Experience. *Journal of Anthropological Research* 41 (2): 147–69.
1986. So My Name Shall Live: Stone-Dragging and Grave-Building in Kodi, West Sumba. *Bijdragen tot de taal-, land-, en volkenkunde* 142: 31–51.
1987a. The Headhunter as Hero: Local Traditions and Their Reinterpretation as National History. *American Ethnologist* 14 (4): 605–22.
1987b. Complementarity in This World and the Next: Gender and Agency in Kodi Mortuary Ceremonies. In *Dealing with Inequality: Analysing Gender Relations in Melanesia and Beyond*, ed. M. Strathern. Cambridge: Cambridge University Press.
1988. The Drum Is the Shaman, The Spear Guides His Voice. *Social Science and Medicine* 27 (2): 819–28.
1989a. On Losing and Getting a Head: Warfare, Alliance and Exchange in a Changing Sumba 1888–1988. *American Ethnologist* 16 (3): 419–40.
1989b. Why Do Ladies Sing the Blues? Indigo, Cloth Production and Gender Symbolism in Kodi. In *Cloth and Human Experience*, ed. A. Weiner and J. Scheider. Washington, DC: Smithsonian Institution Press.
1990. Doubling Deities, Descent and Personhood: An Exploration of Kodi Gender Categories. In *Power and Difference: Gender in Island Southeast Asia*, ed. J. Atkinson and S. Errington. Stanford, CA: Stanford University Press.
1991. Snakes, Smells and Dismembered Brides: Men's and Women's Textiles in Kodi, West Sumba. In *Weaving Patterns of Life. Indonesian Textile Symposium 1991*, ed. M. Nabholz-Kartaschoff, R. Barnes, and D. Stuart-Fox. Basel: Museum of Ethnography.
1993a. *The Play of Time: Kodi Perspectives on Calendars, History and Exchange*. Berkeley: University of California Press.
1993b. Violence, Sacrifice and Divination: Giving and Taking Life in Eastern Indonesia. *American Ethnologist* 20 (1): 159–78.
1996a. Sacrifice and Sexuality: The Triumph of the Buffalo's Daughter. In *For the Sake of Our Future: Sacrificing in Eastern Indonesia*, ed. S. Howell. Leiden: Centre of Non-Western Studies.
1996b. The Heritage of Headhunting: Ritual, Ideology, and History on Sumba, 1890–1990. In *Headhunting and the Social Imagination in Southeast Asia*, ed. J. Hoskins. Stanford, CA: Stanford University Press.
1996c. From Diagnosis to Performance: Medical Practice and the Politics of Exchange in Kodi, West Sumba. In *The Performance of Healing*, ed. C. Laderman and M. Roseman. New York: Routledge.
1996d. Introduction: Headhunting as Practice and as Trope. In *Headhunting and the Social Imagination in Southeast Asia*, ed. J. Hoskins. Stanford, CA: Stanford University Press.
Howell, Signe
1989. Of Persons and Things: Exchange and Valuables Among the Lio of Eastern Indonesia. *Man* (n.s.) 24: 419–38.

1995. Rethinking the Mother's Brother: Gendered Aspects of Kinship and Marriage Among the Norther Lio, Indonesia. *Indonesia Circle* 67: 293–317.

1996a. Many Contexts, Many Meanings? Some Aspects of Gendered Values Among the Northern Lio of Flores, Indonesia. *Journal of the Royal Anthropological Institute (incorporating Man)* (n.s) 2: 253–69.

1996b. The Value of Androgyny. Paper presented at the IIAS Conference in Hierarchization, Leiden, The Netherlands.

Jameson, Fredric

1983. Postmodernism and Consumer Society. In *The Anti-Aesthetic: Essays on Postmodern Culture*, ed. H. Foster. Port Townsend, WA: Bay Press.

1989. Nostalgia for the Present. *South Atlantic Quarterly* 88 (2, Spring): 517–37.

1990. Reification and Utopia in Mass Culture. In *Signatures of the Visible*. New York and London: Routledge.

Jessup, Helen

1990. *Court Arts of Indonesia*. New York: The Asia Gallery in association with Harry N. Abrams. Catalog for a traveling exhibit.

Kaplan, Caren

1992. Resisting Autobiography: Outlaw Genres and Transnational Feminist Subjects. In *De/colonizing the Subject: Politics and Gender in Women's Autobiographical Practice*, ed. J. Watson and S. Smith. Minneapolis: University of Minnesota Press.

Keane, E. Webb

1988. Shadows of Men, Shadows of Spirits: The Mamuli of Sumba. *Tribal Art*. Geneva: Barbier-Mueller Museum.

1997. *Signs of Recognition: Powers and Hazards of Representation in an Indonesian Society*. Berkeley: University of California Press.

Keeler, Ward

1987. *Javanese Shadow Plays, Javanese Selves*. Princeton, NJ: Princeton University Press.

Keesing, Roger

1985. Kwaio Women Speak: The Micropolitics of Autobiography in a Solomon Island Society. *American Anthropologist* 87: 27–39.

1987. *Ni Gini*: Women's Perspectives on Kwaio Society. In *Dealing with Inequality: Analysing Gender Relations in Melanesia and Beyond*, ed. M. Strathern. Cambridge: Cambridge University Press.

Keller, Edgar

1993. Barkcloth Production and Dress in Laboya, West Sumba. In *Weaving Patterns of Life. Indonesian Textile Symposium 1991*, ed. M. Nabholz-Kartaschoff, R. Barnes, and D. Stuart-Fox. Basel: Museum of Ethnography.

Kermode, Frank

1995. Autobiography and Memory. *Raritan Review*: 35–51.

Kipp, Rita

1995. Conversion by Affiliation: The History of the Karo Batak Protestant Church. *American Ethnologist* 22 (4): 868–82.

Kondo, Dorinne

1990. *Crafting Selves: Power, Gender amd Discourses of Identity in a Japanese Workplace*. Chicago: University of Chicago Press.

1996. *About Face: Performing Race in Fashion and Theater*. New York and London: Routledge.

Kopytoff, Igor
1986. The Cultural Biography of Things: Commoditization as Process. In *The Social Life of Things: Commodities in Cultural Perspective*. Cambridge: Cambridge University Press.

Krupat, Arnold
1985. *For Those Who Came After: A Study of Native American Autobiography*. Berkeley: University of California Press.

Kuipers, Joel
1990. *Power in Performance: The Creation of Textual Authority in Weyewa Ritual Speech*. Philadelphia: University of Pennsylvania Press.
1998. *The Inner State: Self, Nation and Linguistic Marginality on an Indonesian Island 1860–1994*. Cambridge: Cambridge University Press.

Langness, L. L., and Gelya Frank
1985. *Lives: An Anthropological Approach to Biography*. Novato, CA: Chandler and Sharpe.

Lavie, Smadar
1990. *The Poetics of Military Occupation: Mzeina Allegories of Bedouin Identity Under Israeli and Egyptian Rule*. Berkeley: University of California Press.

Lejeune, Philippe
1975. *Le pacte autobiographique*. Paris: Editions de Seuil.
1988. *On Autobiography*. Minneapolis: University of Minnesota Press.

Lepowsky, Maria
1993. *Fruit of the Motherland: Gender in an Egalitarian Society*. New York: Columbia University Press.

Levy, Robert
1994. Person-Centered Ethnography. In *Assessing Cultural Anthropology*, ed. Robert Borofsky. New York: McGraw-Hill.

Lewis, E. Douglas
1988. *People of the Source: The Social and Ceremonial Order of Tana Wai Brama on Flores*. Dordecht and Providence: Foris Publications.

Linde, Charlotte
1993. What Is a Life Story? In *Life Stories: The Creation of Coherence*. Oxford: Oxford University Press.

Lutkehaus, Nancy, and Paul B. Roscoe, eds.
1995. *Gender Rituals: Female Initiation in Melanesia*. New York: Routledge.

Lutkehaus, Nancy
1995. *Zaria's Fire: Engendered Moments in Manam Ethnography*. Durham, NC: Carolina Academic Press.

MacCormack, Carol, and Marilyn Strathern, eds.
1980. *Nature, Culture and Gender*. Cambridge: Cambridge University Press.

MacKenzie, Maureen
1991. *Androgynous Objects: String Bags and Gender in Central New Guinea*. London and Chur: Harwood Academic Publishers.

Mauss, Marcel
1985 [1938]. A Category of the Human Mind: The Notion of Person; The Notion of Self, translated by W. D. Halls. In *The Category of the Person: Anthropology, Philosophy, History*, ed. Michael Carrithers, Steven Collins, and Steven Lukes. Cambridge: Cambridge University Press.

Maybury-Lewis, David, and Uri Almagor, eds.
  1989. *The Attraction of Opposites: Thought and Society in the Dualistic Mode.* Ann
  Arbor: University of Michigan Press.
McCracken, Grant D.
  1988. *Culture and Consumption: New Approaches to the Symbolic Character of
  Consumer Goods and Activities.* Bloomington: Indiana University Press.
McKinnon, Susan
  1991. *From a Shattered Sun: Hierarchy, Gender and Alliance in the Tanimbar Islands.*
  Madison: University of Wisconsin Press.
Miller, Daniel
  1987. *Material Culture and Mass Consumption.* London: Basil Blackwell.
  1988. Appropriating the State on the Council Estate. *Man* (n.s.) 23: 353–72.
  1995a. Consumption and Commodities. *Annual Review of Anthropology* 24:
  141–61.
  1995b. *Acknowledging Consumption.* London and New York: Routledge.
Mills, Margaret
  1982. A Cinderella Variant in the Context of a Muslim Women's Ritual. In
  Cinderella: A Casebook, ed. A. Dundes. Madison: University of Wisconsin Press.
Mohanty, Chandra Talpade
  1991. Under Western Eyes: Feminist Scholarship and Colonial Discourses. In
  Third World Women and the Politics of Feminism, ed. C. Mohanty, A. Russo, and
  L. Torres. Bloomington: Indiana University Press.
Morin, Violette
  1969. L'objet biographique. *Communications* 13: 131–39. Ecole Pratique des
  Hautes Etudes, Centre d'Etudes des Communications de Masse.
Munn, Nancy
  1986. *The Fame of Gawa.* Cambridge: Cambridge University Press.
Needham, Rodney
  1957. Kodi Fables. *Bijdragen tot de taal-, land en volkenkunde* 113: 361–79.
  1960. Jataka, Pancatantra and Kodi Fables. *Bijdragen tot de taal-, land en
  volkenkunde* 116: 232–62.
  1980. Principles and Variations in the Structure of Sumbanese Society. In *The
  Flow of Life: Essays on Eastern Indonesia*, ed. J. J. Fox. Cambridge: Harvard
  University Press.
Okley, Judith
  1992. Anthropology and Autobiography: Participatory Experience and Embodied
  Knowledge. In *Anthropology and Autobiography*, ed. Judith Okley and Helen
  Callaway. ASA monographs 29. London and New York: Routledge.
Olney, James
  1972. A Theory of Autobiography. In *Metaphors of Self: The Meaning of
  Autobiography.* Princeton: Princeton University Press.
Ong, Aihwa, and Michael G. Peletz, eds.
  1995. *Bewitching Women, Pious Men: Gender and Body Politics in Southeast Asia.*
  Berkeley: University of California Press.
Onvlee, L.
  1929. Palatalisie in eenige Soembaneesche dialecten. *Batavisch Genootschap von
  Kunsten en Wetenschappen.* Weltvreden: Kolff & Co.
  1938. Over de weergave van 'heilig' in het Soembaasch. *Tijdschrift voor indische
  taal-, land en volkenkunde* 78: 124–36.

[1933] 1973. Na huri hapa. In *Cultuur also antwoord.* Verhadelingen van het KTLV, 66. The Hague: Martinus Nijhoff.

[1949] 1977. The Construction of the Mangili Dam: Notes on the Social Organization of Eastern Sumba. In *Structural Anthropology in the Netherlands*, ed. P. E. de Josselin de Jong. The Hague: Martinus Nijhoff.

[1952] 1980. The Significance of Livestock on Sumba, trans. J. J. Fox and Henny Fokker-Baker. In *The Flow of Life: Essays on Eastern Indonesia*, ed. J. J. Fox. Cambridge: Harvard University Press.

Ortner, Sherry B.
1974. Is Female to Male as Nature is to Culture? In *Woman, Culture and Society*, ed. M. Rosaldo and M. Lamphere. Stanford, CA: Stanford University Press.

1981. Gender and Sexuality in Hierarchical Socieites: The Case of Polynesia and Some Comparative Implications. In *Sexual Meanings*, ed. S. Ornter and H. Whitehead. Cambridge: Cambridge University Press.

1984. Theory in Anthropology since the Sixties. *Comparative Studies in Society and History* 26 (1): 126–66.

1996. *Making Gender: The Politics and Erotics of Culture*. Boston: Beacon Press.

Pemberton, John
1994. *On the Subject of "Java."* Ithaca, NY: Cornell University Press.

Personal Narratives Group, ed.
1989. *Interpreting Women's Lives: Feminist Theory and Personal Narratives.* Bloomington and Indianapolis: Indiana University Press.

Polkinghorne, D. E.
1988. *Narrative Knowing and the Human Sciences.* Albany, NY: SUNY Press.

Postel-Coster, Els
1977. The Indonesian Novel as a Source of Anthropological Data. In *Text and Context: The Social Anthropology of Tradition*, ed. Ravindra Jain. Philadelphia: Institute for the Study of Human Issues.

Raheja, Gloria, and Anne G. Gold
1994. *Listen to the Heron's Words: Reimagining Gender and Kinship in North India.* Berkeley: University of California Press.

Ralston, WRS.
1982. Cinderella (originally published in 1879 in *The Nineteenth Century* 6: 832–53.) Reprinted in *Cinderella: A Casebook*, ed. A. Dundes. Madison: University of Wisconsin Press.

Ricklefs, M. C.
1993. *A History of Modern Indonesia since c. 1300.* 2d ed. Stanford, CA: Stanford University Press.

Rodgers, Susan
1979. A Modern Batak Horja: Innovation in Sipirok Adat Ceremonial. *Indonesia* 27: 102–108.

1995. *Telling Lives, Telling History: Autobiography and Historical Imagination in Modern Indonesia.* Berkeley: University of California Press.

Rooth, Anna Birgitta
1951. *The Cinderella Cycle.* Lund, Sweden: CWK. Gleerup, Skanska Centraltryckeriet.

Rosaldo, Michelle Z.
1980. The Uses and Abuses of Anthropology: Reflections on Feminism and Cross Cultural Understanding. *Signs* 5 (3): 389–417.

Rosaldo, Michelle Z., and Louise Lamphere, eds.
  1974. *Woman, Culture and Society*. Stanford, CA: Stanford University Press.
Rosaldo, Renato
  1976. The Story of Tukbaw: "They Listen As He Orates." In *The Biographical Process: Studies in the History and Psychology of Religion*, ed. F. Reynolds and D. Capps. The Hague: Mouton and Co.
  1989. Grief and the Headhunter's Revenge. *Culture and Truth: The Remaking of Social Analysis*. Boston: Beacon Press.
Rosenwald, George C., and Richard L. Ochberg
  1992. Introduction: Life Stories, Cultural Politics and Self-Understanding. In *Storied Lives: The Cultural Politics of Self-Understanding*. New Haven, CT: Yale University Press.
Schudson, M.
  1984. *Advertising, the Uneasy Persuasion*. New York: Basic Books.
Schwarz, J. A.
  1907. *Tontemboansche teksten, uitgiven 1–3*. Leiden: KTLV.
Scott, Joan
  1988. Gender as a Useful Category of Analysis. In *Gender and the Politics of History*. New York: Columbia University Press.
  1991. The Evidence of Experience. *Critical Inquiry* (Summer) 17 (4): 777.
Shapiro, Judith
  1988. Gender Totemism. In *The Dialectics of Gender*, ed. Richard Randolph and David M. Schneider. Boulder, CO: Westview Press.
Sears, Laurie, ed.
  1996. *Fantasizing the Feminine in Indonesia*. Durham, NC: Duke University Press.
Smith, S.
  1987. *A Poetics of Women's Autobiography*. Bloomington: University of Indiana Press.
Sommer, Doris
  1988. "Not Just a Personal Story": Women's Testimonios and the Plural Self. In *Life/Lines*, ed. B. Bordzi and C. Schenk. Ithaca, NY: Cornell University Press.
Steedly, Mary Margaret
  1993. *Hanging Without a Rope: Narrative Experience in Colonial and Postcolonial Karoland*. Princeton: Princeton University Press.
  1996. The Importance of Proper Names: Language and "National" Identity in Colonial Karoland. *American Ethnologist* 23 (3): 447–75.
Strathern, Marilyn
  1980a. Culture in a Netbag: The Making of a Subdiscipline in Anthropology. *Man* (n.s.) 16: 665–88.
  1980b. No Nature, No Culture: The Hagen Case. In *Nature, Culture and Gender*, ed. C. MacCormack and M. Strathern. Cambridge: Cambridge University Press.
  1987a. An Awkward Relationbship: The Case of Feminism and Anthropology. *Signs* 12 (2): 276–92.
  1987b. Introduction. *Dealing with Inequality: Analysing Gender Relations in Melanesia and Beyond*. Cambridge: Cambridge University Press.
  1988. *The Gender of the Gift: Problems with Women and Problems with Society in Melanesia*. Berkeley: University of California Press.
  1993. Entangled Objects: Detached Metaphors. In *Social Analysis*, no. 34: 88–101.

Sugishima, Takashi
    1994. Double Descent, Alliance and Botanical Metaphors Among the Lionese of Central Flores. *Bijdragen tot de Taal-, Land-en Volkenkunde* 150: 146–70.
Taylor, Paul Michael
    1994. *Fragile Traditions: Indonesian Art in Jeopardy*. Honolulu: University of Hawaii Press.
Thomas, Nicholas
    1991. *Entangled Objects: Exchange, Material Culture and Colonialism in the Pacific*. Cambridge: Harvard University Press.
    1993. Related Things. *Social Analysis* 34: 132–41.
Thomson, Alan
    1993. The Churches of Java in the Aftermath of the 30th September Movement. In *The Journal of Southeast Asian Theology* 9: 7–20.
Torgovnick, Marianna
    1990. *Gone Primitive: Savage Intellects, Modern Lives*. Chicago: University of Chicago Press.
Traube, Elizabeth
    1986. *Cosmology and Social Life: Ritual Exchange Among the Mambai of East Timor*. Chicago: University of Chicago Press.
Tsing, Anna Lowenhaupt
    1993. *In the Realm of the Diamond Queen: Marginality in an Out-of-the-Way Place*. Princeton: Princeton University Press.
Valeri, Valerio
    1980. Notes on the Meanings of Marriage Prestations among the Huaulu of Seram. In *The Flow of Life: Essays on Eastern Indonesia*, ed. J. J. Fox. Cambridge: Harvard University Press.
    1990. Both Nature and Culture: Reflections on Menstrual and Parturitional Taboos in Huaulu (Seram). In *Power and Difference: Gender in Island Southeast Asia*, ed. J. Atkinson and S. Errington. Stanford, CA: Stanford University Press.
    1994. Buying Women But Not Selling Them: Gift and Commodity Exchange in Huaulu Alliance. *Man* (n.s.) 29 (1): 1–26.
    1998. *Fragments from Forests and Libraries*. Durham, NC: Carolina Academic Press.
Van Wouden, FAE.
    [1935] 1968. Types of Social Structure in Eastern Indonesia. The Hague: Martinus Nijhoff.
    [1956] 1977. Local Groups and Double Descent in Kodi, West Sumba. In *Structural Anthropology in the Netherlands*, ed. P. E. de Josselin de Jong. The Hague: Martinus Nijhoff.
Veldhuisen-Djajasoebrata, Alit
    1991. Snakeskin Motifs on some Javanese Textiles: Awe, Love, and Fear for Progenitrix Naga. In *Indonesian Textiles. Symposium 1985*, ed. G. Volger and K. v. Welck. Ethnologica. Band 14. Cologne: Rautenstrauch-Joest Museum.
Visweswaran, Kamala
    1994. *Fictions of Feminist Ethnography*. Minneapolis: University of Minnesota Press.
Wagner, Roy
    1995. If You Have the Advertisement You Don't Need the Product. In *Rhetorics of Self-Making*, ed. D. Battaglia. Berkeley: University of California Press.

Watson, J., and S. Smith, eds.
  1992. *De/colonizing the Subject: Politics and Gender in Women's Autobiographical Practice.* Minneapolis: University of Minnesota Press.
Weiner, Annette
  1976. *Women of Value, Men of Renown: New Perspectives in Trobriand Exchange.* Austin: University of Texas Press.
  1985. Inalienable Wealth. *American Ethnologist* 12 (2): 210–27.
  1989. Why Cloth? Wealth, Gender and Power in Oceania. In *Cloth and Human Experience*, ed. A. Weiner and J. Schneider. Washington, DC: Smithsonian Institution Press.
  1992. *Inalienable Possessions: The Paradox of Keeping-while-Giving.* Berkeley: University of California Press.
Weiner, A., and J. Schneider, eds.
  1989. *Cloth and Human Experience.* Washington, DC: Smithsonian Institution Press.
Wiener, Margaret J.
  1995. *Visible and Invisible Realms: Power, Magic and Colonial Conquest in Bali.* Chicago: University of Chicago Press.
White, Geoffrey M., and John Kirkpatrick
  1985. *Person, Self and Experience: Exploring Pacific Ethnopsychologies.* Berkeley: University of California Press.
Wilken, P. N.
  1863. Bijdragen de kennis van de zeden en gewooten der Alfoeren in de Minahassa. *Mededeelingen van wege het Nederlandsche Zendelinggenootschap.* Rotterdam 7: 117–59, 289–332, 371–91.
Willis, Susan
  1991. *A Primer for Daily Life: Is There More to Life Than Shopping?* London and New York: Routledge.
Yolen, Jane
  1982. America's Cinderella. In *Cinderella: A Casebook*, ed. A. Dundes. Madison: University of Wisconsin Press.
Young, Michael
  1983a. "Our Name is Women; We Are Bought with Limesticks and Limepots": An Analysis of the Autobiographical Narrative of a Kalauna Woman. *Man* (n.s.) 18: 478–501.
  1983b. *Magicians of Manumanua.* Berkeley: University of California Press.

INDEX

A
SNAKE
IS
TOTALLY
TAIL.

By Judi Barrett

Drawings by L. S. Johnson

Atheneum
New York

Maxwell Macmillan Canada
Toronto

Maxwell Macmillan International
New York   Oxford   Singapore   Sydney

Library of Congress Cataloging in Publication Data

Barrett, Judi.

   A snake is totally tail.

   Summary: Brief text suggests essential characteristics
of various animals, including the snake as well as the
porcupine, skunk, bear, and others.

   1. Animals—Pictorial works—Juvenile literature.
[1. Animals] I. Johnson, Lonni Sue, ill.
II. Title.

QL49.B26   1983   591   83-2657

ISBN 0-689-30979-1

Atheneum
Macmillan Publishing Company
866 Third Avenue, New York, NY 10022
Collier Macmillan Canada, Inc.

Composition by Dix Typesetters, Syracuse, NY
Published 1983 by Sing Tao Newspapers Ltd.
Designed by Judi Barrett
Printed in the United States of America

First American Edition 1983

    5   7   9   11   13   15   17   19

20 18 16 14 12 10 8 6 4

A snake is totally tail.

A porcupine is piles of prickles.

A skunk is oodles of odor.

A bear is generally Grrrrrrrrr.

A bee is blatantly Bzzzzzzzzz.

A kangaroo is partially pocket.

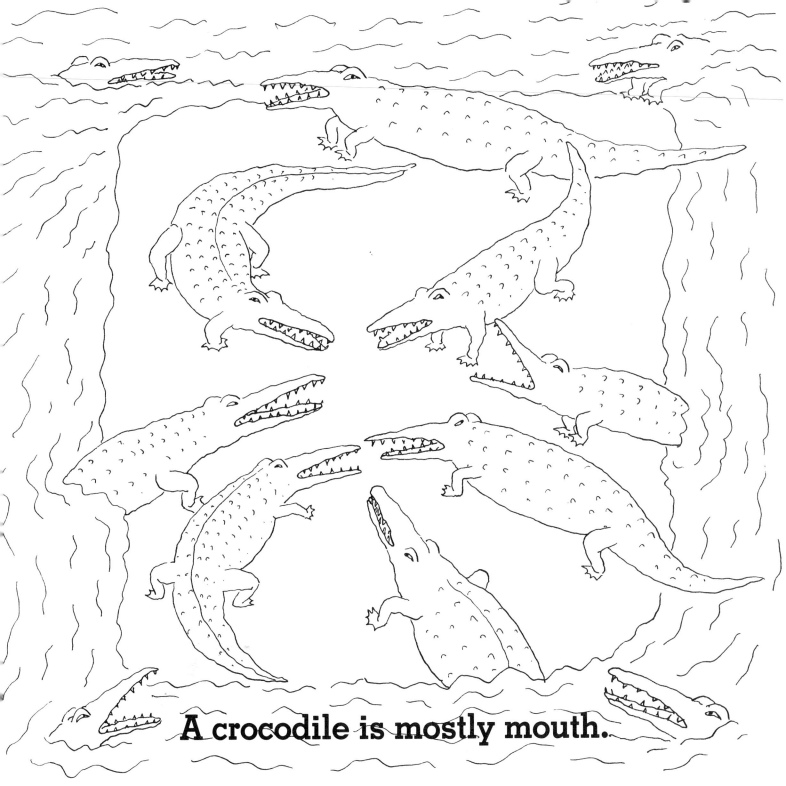

A crocodile is mostly mouth.

A fish is slews of scales (and a few fins).

A leopard is scores of spots.

A seal is seemingly slippery.

A snail is solidly shell.

A toucan is basically beak.

A giraffe is noticeably neck.

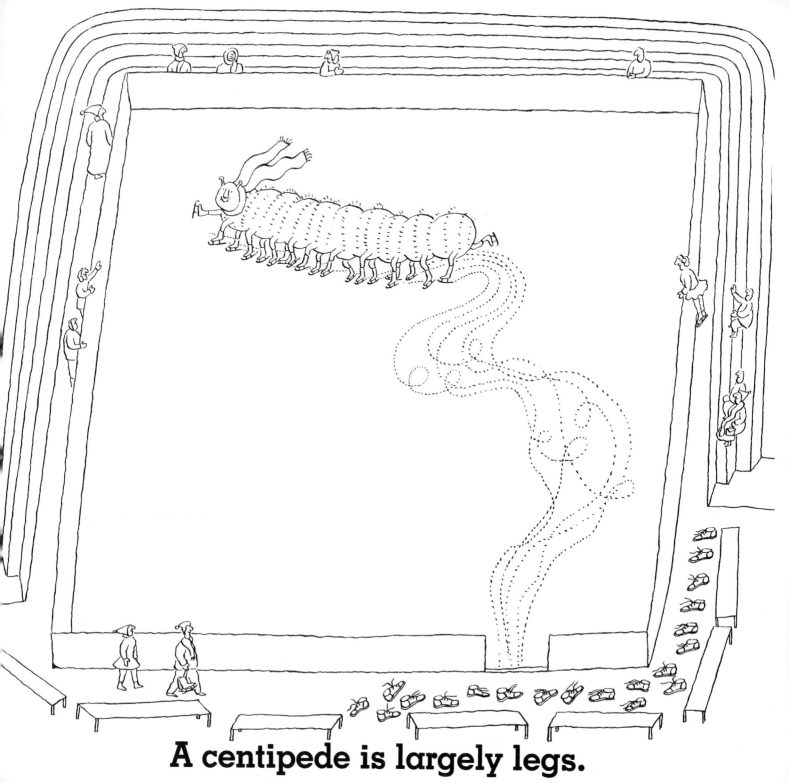

A centipede is largely legs.

An elephant is essentially ears.

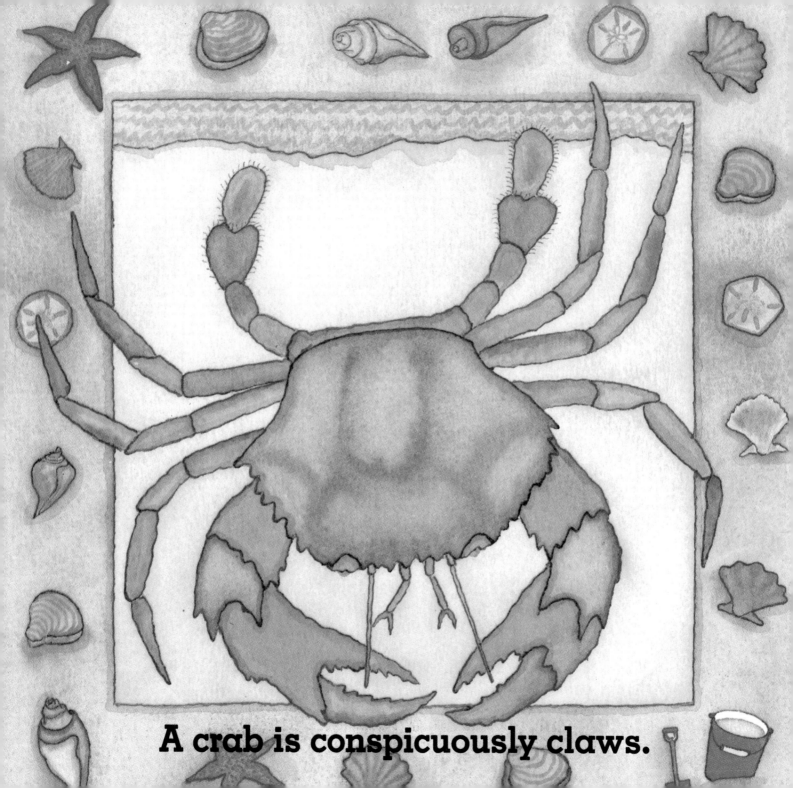

A crab is conspicuously claws.

A bird is fundamentally feathers.

An anteater is somewhat snout.

A grasshopper is just jumps.

hoot hooooot hoooot hoo

An owl is heaps of hoots.

A duck is quantities of quacks.

A moose is appreciably antlers.

A zebra is specifically stripes.

A camel is half humps.

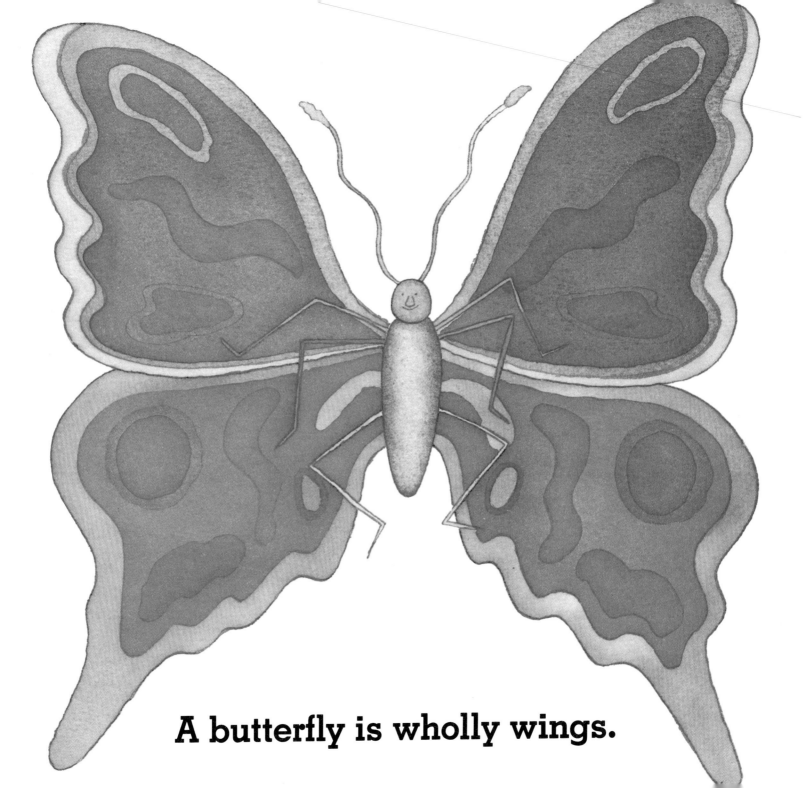

A butterfly is wholly wings.

A shark is tons of teeth.

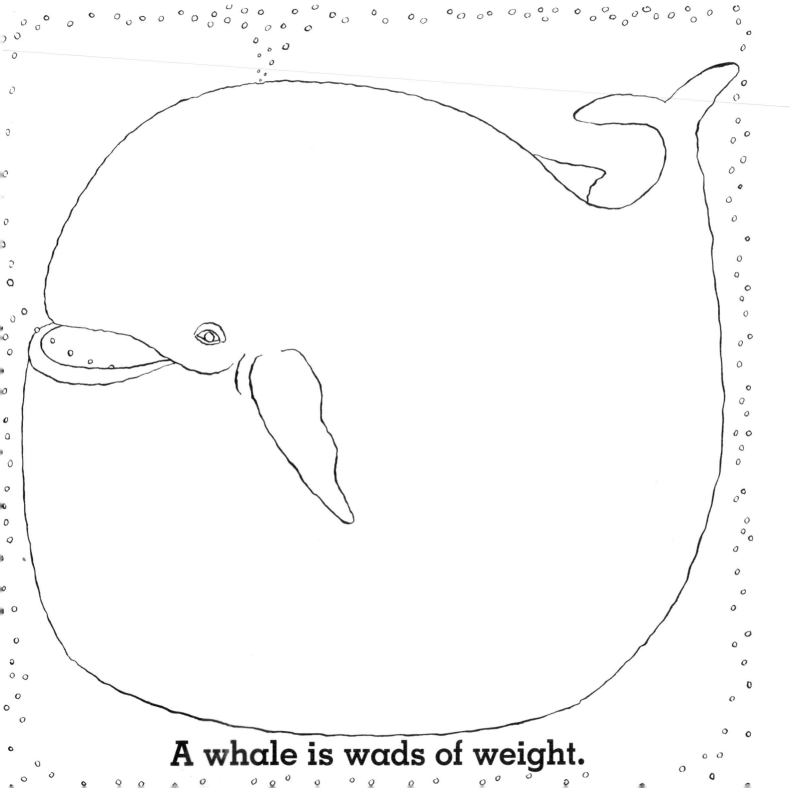

A whale is wads of weight.

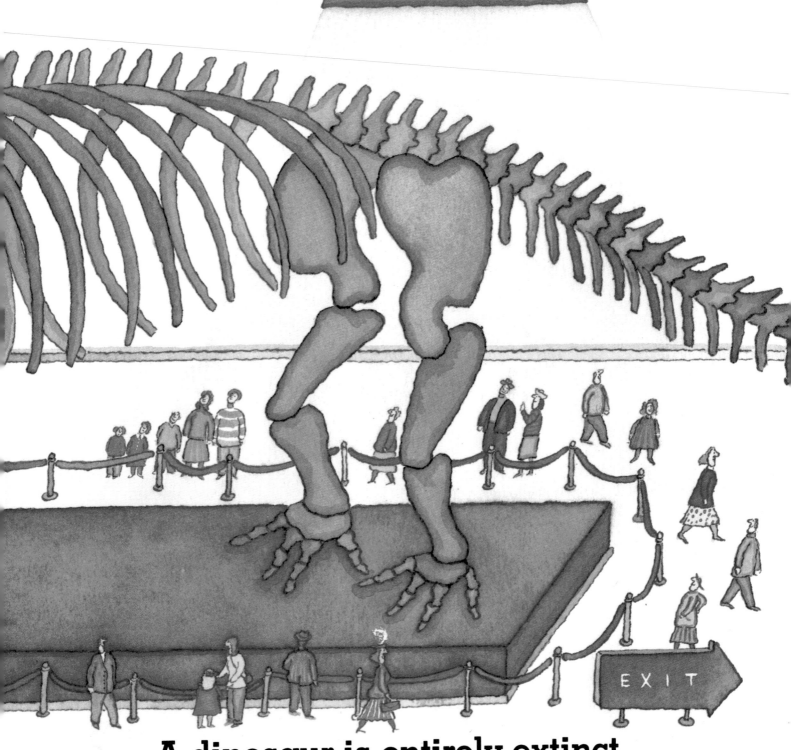

A dinosaur is entirely extinct.

This book is finally finished.